WORD FOR TODAY

WORD FOR TODAY

Sally Garwood

WORD FOR TODAY

ISBN: 9781494878443

Printed in the United States of America

Dedica

I dedicate this book of devotions to children. First I dedicate my children, Becca, Jamie, Rachel and Kyle. Next I dedicate it to all children, not just the young ones but children of all ages. We are all children of God and I pray these words encourage you daily for as long as it is called Today.

Blessings and love in Christ,
Sally Garwood

Acknowledgements

I want to express my thanks to many people who have encouraged and challenged me during the writing of these devotions.

Thank you to my family who gave me the time I needed to write and compile the writings into a book.

Thank you to Michelle and Colleen, my daily editors. Michelle, another thank you for your final proof reading, it is a priceless gift and words cannot express my gratitude.

Thank you to Linda for regular encouraging words and questions to make me think. We have all benefited from this.

Thank you to those who receive my daily devotion writings and occasionally write back, you keep me inspired.

The biggest thanks are to my God. He moved me to write and continues to move me to write. He gives me what I need to share these devotions with others and I could not do this without him.

INTRODUCTION

Hebrews 3:12-13 "Take care, brothers and sisters, that none of you may have an evil, unbelieving heart that turns away from the living God. But exhort one another every day, as long as it is called 'today,' so that none of you may be hardened by the deceitfulness of sin."

I know God uses people in spite of their downfalls but, me? When I began writing daily devotions I never thought it would become a published book. I started out sending an email to my sisters to encourage them and myself and to help us each be in the Word of God each day. God uses us in amazing ways when we allow him to. My small daily email devotion has grown by the grace of God and through his guidance and the encouragement of many, I humbly submit these devotions. I hope these daily Scriptures, musings and prayers bring blessings to your days. If they do, please share them with others. As I said, my sole purpose in writing these is to share the gracious Word of God with other people every day.

Jan 1 - *Psalm 57:10-11 "For your steadfast love is as high as the heavens; your faithfulness extends to the clouds. Be exalted, O God, above the heavens. Let your glory be over all the earth."*

Let the New Year begin!
Last night reverie began to celebrate the New Year commencing. Today the celebration continues with parades and family gatherings. Releasing the old and embracing the new is cause for celebration.
As we continue our celebration today I encourage us to remember that each new day, each New Year is a time to praise the Lord. He rules the nations and his steadfast love is as high as the heavens. His faithfulness extends beyond the stratosphere; beyond the clouds.
Eat your feasts, set off your fireworks, and watch your football games.
Whatever it is that you do to ring in the New Year, do it with praise and thanksgiving to our God. He is to be exalted above the nations and above the heavens; above all things! As we lift his name we spread his glory, let it be spread over all the earth so everyone can live in hope and peace.

Lord,
Your name is above all names; your kingdom is above all kingdoms. As we turn the calendar to the next year let us turn our hearts to you even more. It is because of your love and faithfulness that we can celebrate new days. Help us bring glory to you so that it fills the earth and all come to know you as the King of kings. Amen.

Jan 2 - *Proverbs 3:5-6 "Trust in the Lord with all your heart, and do not rely on your own insight. In all your ways acknowledge him, and he will make straight your paths."*

It is about all I can do to try and watch the news anymore right now. The leadership of our country seems unable to move forward with anything.

There are battles about taxes and money and there are battles about gun control. These issues are only a scratch on the surface of things they talk about but do very little about. It is kind of like watching little kids bickering about who is smarter, bigger, or stronger.

When I watch kids arguing about these kinds of things I can only shake my head at the lack of insight they seem to have. Can't they see that they are all created in their own unique way, each one with their own strengths and struggles?

As I gaze upon that picture in my mind, I can clearly see God doing the same thing to me. Why do I compare myself to anyone else? Why do I forget that I have been created in my own unique way with strengths and struggles to serve a purpose in his kingdom?

As I step into a new phase of growth and healing this year, I need to remember to trust in the Lord with all my heart, not in my (lack of) understanding. Keep focused on him through every step and his guidance and mercy will be clear to me.

Lord,
Keep me close to you, I need you every step. Guide each of us clearly in the path you have chosen and help our hearts give you the glory for everything good. Amen.

Jan 3 - *Galatians 4:4-5 "...God sent his son, born of a woman, born under the law, in order to redeem those who were under the law, so that we might receive adoption as children."*

I know a few adopted people.

Two families I know have adopted kids and countless others I knew growing up. The thing is that maybe there were more but I never knew it. Parents of adopted kids do not treat those kids any different than they treat blood related kids. When someone decides to adopt a child, they open their hearts and bring that child in as their own flesh and blood. I remember one of my friends growing up telling me they were even more special because they had been chosen and not just given.

God has chosen each of us as his adopted child. He opened his heart and brought each of us to his arms as his own flesh and blood. It amazes me to think about that. He sent Jesus to erase the barrier between all of us and him. Now we can run into the arms of our Father anytime. We can come in joy, sorrow, anger, frustration; anytime.

Let's go out into this day with love in our hearts because we are special. We have not only been created by God, but we are chosen, adopted children of the Almighty. Praise God from whom all blessings flow!

Lord,
As we prepare for the day, infuse us with your love. Whisper in our ears and our hearts to remind us that we are your children; chosen and special. Guide our steps in obedience and in celebration of your love. Amen.

Jan 4 -*Obadiah vs. 12 "But you should not have gloated over your brother on the day of his misfortune; you should not have rejoiced over the people of Judah on the day of their ruin; you should not have boasted on the day of distress."*

When someone does wrong to us it is a natural response to wish bad on them or to even the score. It is written all over history; people, nations, and governments rejoicing in their enemies' downfall.

When people are downtrodden or suffering, there are many who say they deserve it. Look how they live, look how they treat others, this is justice. They are getting what they deserve.

This verse, along with so many others in the Bible, encourages us to have mercy on others. Turn the other cheek, feed the poor, and love your neighbor. We are called by God to be more than "natural" humans.

Our fallen nature has been redeemed by Christ, so we are called to be merciful as Christ is merciful to us.

Lord,
Erase my pride, stop my judging heart, and close my mouth from bragging. Focus my being on you and what you give to me so I may live. Without your mercy and love, I would have no ground to stand on, nothing to be proud and bragging of. I have only walked in my shoes. Open my eyes to see that other people, those that I would judge, have walked a much different journey, one I do not know. Forgive me for being closed minded and hard- hearted. Bring my soul into unison with you so I may be who you called me to be. Amen.

Jan 5 - *John 15:8 "My Father is glorified by this, that you bear much fruit and become my disciples."*

In this passage of John, Jesus talks about the vine and the branches. He is the true vine and we are his branches. God the Father prunes branches so they bear more fruit and he cuts off branches that are not bearing any fruit.

I remember seeing a tree that had been planted or grown very close to barbed wire fence. As the tree grew, the fence and its barbs were enveloped into the very meat of the tree. The branch simply swallowed up the part of the fence that was in its way. That can't be healthy for the branch or the tree.

If I am that branch, and I easily could be, I need God to remove the barbs that I have swallowed up so that I can grow without hindrances or disease. As he painstakingly and lovingly removes the disease and damage from me, I know he brings healing to me so that I can bear more fruit for his kingdom.

I will follow him to the ends of the earth and beyond. His word speaks to my heart and his Spirit guides my path. I am a disciple of the Lord and I strive to be a healthy and strong branch on his vine.

Lord,
I am precious to you, we all are. As we step into a new day, give us the strength to be your disciples. Use your word and your Spirit to guide each of us and I ask you to bring healing and wholeness to me and all of your children, my brothers and sisters in Christ. I ask all this for your glory and praise. Amen.

Jan 6 - *Matthew 2:1-2,12 "In the time of King Herod, after Jesus was born in Bethlehem of Judea, wise men from the East came to Jerusalem, asking, 'where is the child who has been born king of the Jews? For we observed his star at its rising, and have come to pay him homage.' And having been warned in a dream not to return to Herod, they left for their country by another road."*

Today we celebrate Epiphany. We remember the wise men coming to worship the baby Jesus.
Do you think they packed their bags and loaded up their camels in a hurry or were they thoughtful and deliberate? I imagine they wanted to hurry but realized deep inside of them that they needed to take time and be prepared. Matthew says they brought gold, frankincense, and myrrh. These are not gifts of haste.
I also imagine when they arrived they were ready to rest for a while. They would pay homage and then take their time resting and preparing for the long journey home. A dream warns them and they leave then by a different road. They had an epiphany, an awakening, when they saw the star and when they received this warning.
What epiphany will we receive if we are open and listening? What road are we being led to take? Just as he guided the wise men long ago, he guides us so we too can come and worship the Christ.

Lord,
Thank you for the promise of steadfast guidance and mercy through Jesus. Help us accept these gifts and then turn to worship Christ the King in adoration and praise. Amen.

Jan 7 - *Ecclesiastes 3:1 "For everything there is a season, and a time for every matter under heaven."*

This passage is familiar to so many people. I would write the whole thing, verses 1-8 but I would run out of room to write and it would take away the urge for you to read it for yourself.
Two things came to me during the reading and meditation of this passage. The first is this: How can we measure time when we live in eternity? There is no end and so what is the purpose in measuring something eternal? Measuring time is like measuring a circle. We can decide to begin at a specific point and measure from there but we simply continue around and around with no end. My second thought is that in the midst of eternity there are truly times or seasons. We watch the seasons on earth change, we see the seasons of human life from infancy all the way to old age. What is it time for? What season is it now? As the verses lead us is it time to be born or time to die; time to plant or time to reap? Even in this passage the circle is evident. As we plant we already begin to think of harvest. As we break down we have already begun the process to rebuild.
This passage brings hope and peace to me today and I pray that it does for you as well.

Lord,
Thank you for these verses. Thank you for the bigger picture. As winter continues on outside, moving closer to spring, so the seasons in my heart continue to move forward. Help me release the old in order to receive the new. Amen.

Jan 8 - *Isaiah 41:4 "Who has performed and done this, calling the generations from the beginning? I, the Lord, am first, and will be with the last."*

The Alpha and the Omega, the beginning and the end...
In the beginning God created the heavens and the earth and at the end, God brings the New Jerusalem into fruition. In between those times, God carries through, watching his creation move forward in time. He carries through, guiding and orchestrating his plan.
I suspect there are many times he feels great sadness, anger, and even joy with his human creation. We are the only part that causes him so much grief and yet, we are the ones that can bring him so much joy.
He continues to call forth the generations. He calls them forth from the first to the last. He is the One, the everlasting God, creator of all.

Lord,
Forgive me for taking your creations for granted. You are
master of your creation and there is balance in all you do.
Remind me that I am here because you created me and likewise,
each person, every living thing is also here because you created
them. Everything, flower, tree, beetle, bird, child, everything is
here because you called it into being. Help me to honor your
creations today. Help me to see you in them. Amen.

Jan 9 - *Mark 4:39-40 "He woke up and rebuked the wind, and said to the sea, 'Peace! Be still!' Then the wind ceased and there was a dead calm. He said to them, 'Why are you afraid? Have you still no faith?'"*

I was looking back in my prayer journal over the last few days and seeing the blessings of prayers answered. There has been healing from sickness and change of heart to reconciliation. There have been other prayers answered in ways I could not have imagined.

There are times in each of our lives where we feel like we are on the boat in this passage. The storm is raging and the boat is quickly filling up to the point of sinking. Fear takes hold of us and we cry out to our Lord for rescue. We feel like he left us in this storm without realizing our plight. We call out to "wake" the Lord and make him aware of what we are going through, as if he did not already know.

I can just see my Lord calming the storms I have ridden through. He comes and in his infinite mercy, he stills the winds and calms the waves. He looks at me in love and says something similar to what he said to the disciples then. "Why are you afraid? Have you still no faith?" After all he has brought me through, everything he has protected and guided me away from, how can I doubt?

Lord,
You continue to amaze me to the depths of my soul. In mercy, forgive my doubt and unbelief. In grace, take my hand and lead me once more through sunny days and stormy nights. I walk in trust, with you by my side. Amen.

Jan 10 - *Habakkuk 3:18-19 "yet I will rejoice in the Lord; I will exult in the God of my salvation. God, the Lord, is my strength; he makes my feet like the feet of a deer, and makes me tread upon the heights."*

Even though this passage starts mid-sentence as I read I thought starting here made sense. After all is said and done, no matter what happens, all the trials and tribulations we go through- "yet I will rejoice." Simply put, this is what we are called to do.
God is always there, always. He is walking with us, he is carrying us, nurturing us, and teaching us. He is our strength and our shield. Without him we would all be certain to fail, to fall. He is the one who makes our feet sure and stable, like the feet of a deer. He keeps me in balance, even on the edge of the precipice. Only with him can I reach the heights he has in mind for me. Whether I am in a valley or at the highest heights he wants us to be joyful in him.
Everything we do, we do because he gives us the strength to do it so I rejoice and I am grateful for his faithfulness in being my God and my Savior.

Lord,
You are creator of all; you are creator of me. You watch over each of us and love all of your creations. The earth sings your praises every day and every night. Let my heart join in the songs of praise and guide my soul to leap in joy for you, my Savior. Please let me feel your strong arms guiding me through the day so I know that I am with you in all that I do and say. Amen.

Jan 11 - *Psalm 103:1 "Bless the Lord, O my soul, and all that is within me, bless his holy name."*

He has done great things so I bless his holy name.
I lift my voice in prayer and praise. I fold my hands and bend my knee in worship and adoration of his greatness. There is healing in the midst of sickness, restoration in the midst of brokenness, love in the midst of hate, and light in the midst of darkness. Wherever I look I see struggles, hardship, and evil lurking. Wherever I look I also see strength, endurance, and goodness overcoming it all.
We recently lay to rest one of our elder church members. It is always so hard to say good bye to someone we know and love and tears of sadness freely flow as we grieve. This day marks the anniversary of my Mom passing away and the shadow of sadness is there. Even in those sorrows and sadness I see blessing and love from God. He brings compassion and mercy to us through his Spirit and through others. He gives us his word to guide and to comfort us.
I could write for days about how much he has blessed me. Can I do the same for how I have blessed him? I want to bless his holy name with all that is within me.

Lord,
I lift you up this morning. Help me serve and bless you today. Use my hands, my words, and every part of me to bless you and serve your kingdom. Thank you for all the many blessings you give each of us every moment, every day. Help us live in gratitude and thanksgiving. Amen.

Jan 12 - *Proverbs 23:26 "My child, give me your heart, and let your eyes observe my ways."*

Last night was a Mom's night out with my homeschooling group. The topic of discussion was building character in our children. There were many helpful ideas shared and loads of resources referred to but when it comes right down to it, I walked away with two things.

The first was to teach by example. How I treat my children and how I treat others teaches my children character traits. They learn what they see. One of the ladies told how she grew up in a house of door slamming. When her Mom was upset or angry she would slam doors. As a girl she was not "taught" to slam doors but when she grew up, she says she could slam doors with the best of them. Children learn what they see. The word of the Lord is our guide. As we learn to be children of God, giving him our hearts and observing his ways, we are able to live according to those ways.

This is the second thing I walked away with: I need to learn from the Word and I need to teach my children the Word. As we both learn to walk a little closer to God's ways, good character grows. In the meantime, I need to remember grace.

Lord,
As you allow each day to be a new start for me, help me allow that for all your children as well. As I realize character building is a lifelong task, open my eyes to observe your ways this day and every day. Father, my heart is yours. Amen.

Jan 13 - *Job 13:5 "If you would only keep silent, that would be your wisdom!"*

We live in a world of noise.

Oftentimes there is a television on in the background of homes, a radio or music on in the cars and talking, playing, or banter of some sort going on all day long. Even when it is quiet, there is the hum of a computer, the ticking of the clock, or the barking of a dog.

Silence is a discipline I thought I could handle pretty well. I am, by nature, a quiet person. It is harder than I thought. I am certainly fine with no TV and no radio. I enjoy the time when everyone is sleeping and the house is quiet. Getting my mind and heart to be silent in the presence of God is another matter entirely.

As I sat this morning trying to be silent, little thoughts and prayers slipped out. My mind wandered off on a tangent or something came to mind that I needed to do or pray about. Maybe God brought those prayers to my heart. As they came I quickly lifted them to the Lord and tried to silence myself again. I like the idea of sitting, silently, in the presence of the Lord. I want to just be with him. He knows my every thought so no words are necessary. It may be true that silence is golden.

Lord,

Thank you for the gift of quietness. In this busy, chaotic, always on the go world, it is a blessing to sit in silence with you. Your presence is renewing and healing, soothing and refreshing. Help us all take time to receive this blessing of silence with you. Help us listen, only listen. Amen.

Jan 14 - *Colossians 2:6-7 "As you therefore have received Christ Jesus the Lord, continue to live your lives in him, rooted and built up in him and established in the faith, just as you were taught, abounding in thanksgiving..."*

I think about a sapling tree.

When it is first planted, the roots are small and it is fragile. As it gets the nutrients it needs, it grows and flourishes and over the years is able to provide for others. We can sit in the shade of the tree and birds build their homes in the branches.

Trees that are full of leaves and blossoms seem to lift their branches to the sky, praising and thanking the Lord for all he provides for them, yet they are firmly rooted and built from the ground up.

That is how I see faith. We receive Christ and we are the sapling. As we study his word and live as he calls us, we grow in strength, rooted firmly in his word. Then we are able to serve others and properly lift our hands, eyes, and hearts to God in praise and thanksgiving.

Lord,
I am humbled by your word today. Thank you for reminding me to stay grounded. It is with my feet planted firmly on the ground, the food of your word in my heart and soul, that I am able to serve those around me. Keep this word written on my heart this day. Amen.

Jan 15 - *Acts 5:32 "And we are witnesses to these things, and so is the Holy Spirit whom God has given to those who obey him."*

Have you ever been a witness to something happening and then just kept quiet? Maybe you weren't sure what you saw or you didn't want to get involved so you tucked it away in your mind and did not share that story.

Occasionally I hear stories in the news about witnesses coming forward years later to tell their story bringing justice or healing to another person.

What led that person to come forward? Did that story lurk and simmer in their hearts the whole time or did they ignore it for a long time and then it popped up again somehow until they were convicted and had to share it?

The disciples had every reason to hide the story they had witnessed. They knew they would be persecuted, jailed, beaten, and possibly killed for spreading this story that they had witnessed. That did not stop them. The Holy Spirit gave them the courage and the strength to go forth and spread the gospel story.

The Holy Spirit gives us the courage and strength to share the love of God with each other and to love one another as he loves us. Let us go out and love!

Lord,
You promise to give us what we need to serve you as you call us to. Open our hearts to receive the guidance your Spirit gives so freely. Help us move in love and light each moment of today so that all we are and all we do will bring glory to your holy name. I thank you and praise you. Amen.

Jan 16 - *Hebrews 1:3 "He is the reflection of God's glory and the exact imprint of God's very being, and he sustains all things by his powerful word..."*

This is the side of Jesus we don't really learn about as children. We first learn of him as a tiny baby in Bethlehem and some people never move beyond that image. Almost immediately the stories show him at a young age in Jerusalem for a festival. He stays at the temple teaching while his Mom and Dad frantically look all over the city for him.

We flash forward to the baptism of a 30 year old man who is starting his life ministry. There are many stories and teachings to read from his ministry and it takes a lifetime or more to truly learn and understand them. How do we see Jesus in those stories? Do you picture him blending into the crowd or is there something different that makes him stand out?

The verse from Hebrews tells me he must have stood apart from the crowd because "He is the reflection of God's glory." He is a gentle shepherd, a friend and leader, a teacher, and healer. He also "sustains all things with his powerful word."

He is no longer a baby in the manger; he reigns with power and majesty!

Lord,
Thank you for coming down to teach us from the very basic to a depth we cannot yet grasp. Thank you for the promise that you will sustain us. Your word is our guide, help us hear you and have ears to listen. Amen.

Jan 17 - *Psalm 111:2 "Great are the works of the Lord; studied by all who delight in them."*

This morning I was watching the moon set. That is actually more my speed since I am more of a night person.
It was almost full, just beginning to wane from full yesterday, softly glowing behind the stark branches of the winter trees in my back window. It paints a beautiful winter picture in my mind.
As I read this verse it brings to mind other works, the intricacy of each snowflake, of each spring leaf on a tree blossoming. I ponder the miracle of the flight of the bee, which based on science, should not be able to fly. I am amazed at the balance in nature, the insects that are necessary to feed other creatures, the birds and spiders who help keep insects in balance, the creatures above those and then above those. These are the great works of God.
I can barely balance my checkbook, so when I ponder all of these, I do delight in his works. If he can defy science and make the bee fly, what can he do with me?

Lord,
Allow my heart to ponder your works and wonders all day today.
Open my eyes that I may see the works that I overlook so many
days. You are the Creator, the Almighty and I want to delight in
you. Thank you for your creation and the care you give to all
you have created. My heart is joyful as I ponder your works.
Great are you, my God. Amen.

Jan 18 - *Psalm 139:7-8 "Where can I go from your spirit? Or where can I flee from your presence? If I ascend to heaven, you are there; if I make my bed in Sheol, you are there."*

I hate to admit it but there is a part of me that wants to run away sometimes.

I have run away in different ways many times in life and only by the grace of God have I come to him on my wandering path. As I meditated on this passage a couple of sayings came to mind: "you can run but you cannot hide" and "when the going gets tough, the tough get going." I am guessing that second one didn't really mean running away, what do you think?

When I was just a child, I ran away from home. I took my bike and with the help of my best friend I ran away to her house. I was astonished and discouraged when we got there because as soon as we arrived, my bike and I were promptly placed in a car and driven back home. That child, the one that wants to run from difficulty, still lurks in me.

I thank the Lord that I hear his voice louder than the little one telling me to escape. I know wherever I am and whatever I do the spirit of God is there. He is always with me, he lives in my heart.

Whatever you are going through, whatever you are doing, take heart, God is with you.

Lord,
We either honor you or dishonor you with our thoughts and actions. Please forgive any dishonor I have brought on your name and guide my thoughts, desires, and actions so that if I run, it is only into your holy arms of love. Amen.

Jan 19 - *Isaiah 35:5-6 "Then the eyes of the blind shall be opened, and the ears of the deaf unstopped; then the lame shall leap like a deer, and the tongue of the speechless sing for joy..."*

When I look over my prayer list at a glance, it is filled with requests for healing of some sort. I have several friends suffering diseases of some kind. There are petitions for guidance and relief of worry. Laced in among the requests I see joys. A rejoicing for healing given and praise for reconciliation lay entwined between the petitions.

A few days ago we remembered my Mom's passing. Last night I was informed that a dear friend's Mom just passed away and I know one of the people I pray for daily is waiting for the call that their sister has passed on as well. In the midst of sorrow and grief, it is hard to see the blessing of God.

As I look back at the time of my Mom's illness and since then, there has been an abundance of grace and healing given to my family by God. I look to the day of redemption for all with hope and rejoicing; these verses speak to that day. There will be a day when we all join together and in wholeness and love, sing for joy to the Lord, our God.

I sing in hope and joy on this day.

Lord,
You are God of healing and grace; You are God of love and light. Please open our eyes and unstop our ears, heal our brokenness so we can see, hear, and leap for you. Lift our hearts and voices in songs of hope and praise to you, the God of all. Amen.

Jan 20 - *1 Peter 3:8 "Finally, all of you, have unity of spirit, sympathy, love for one another, a tender heart, and a humble mind."*

One of my children is likely a born leader.
Unfortunately as children with this gift are growing up, they tend to be bossy and arrogant. It has become very clear to me that it is partially my task as a mother and teacher to guide and teach how to use this gift of leadership as well as humility and compassion. I have no idea how to teach those things other than live them and show by example.
I trust in the Lord to guide my teaching, hope in the Lord that he will plant the good seeds and throw away the bad ones. When my children are grown, I pray they live in harmony, be sympathetic, and love as brothers, being compassionate and humble.
It will be only by the grace of God that they learn these things and live them to the glory of our Lord.

Lord,
Fill me with the peace that passes understanding this day. Use me to teach my children in your paths. Open my eyes to see the gifts they bring and allow them to teach me in your paths. Bring us all to your Holy feet; embrace us in your love and mercy. Bring harmony to our souls this day. Amen.

Jan 21 - *Luke 15:20 "So he set off and went to his father. But while he was still far off, his father saw him and was filled with compassion; he ran and put his arms around him and kissed him."*

This verse comes out of the parable of the prodigal son. We all know the story even if we haven't read it in the Bible because there are many of these stories in real life.

One of the kids takes his money and runs. He lives in style, spending like there is no tomorrow, and then the bottom drops out. After trying to figure it out on his own, the boy comes home with his tail between his legs. He hopes to be brought in as a slave, even to have a warm place to sleep and a bite of food or two. He comes home grungy and smelly. He comes downtrodden and ashamed.

His father was filled with compassion. He was not concerned with how clean he was or what monies he brought back. He did not require him to shower and present himself properly. The father ran out to him and wrapped his arms around him and kissed him. He welcomed him in love and grace.

This is the picture of God Jesus was painting. This is the God we run to and the God we abide in.

Lord,
Thank you for loving us just as we are; however we come, you embrace us with love and grace. We cannot be presentable to you except through the redeeming blood of Jesus. Your love knows no bounds. Help us share your love with others so they may come home too. Amen.

Jan 22 - *Mark 8:15 "And he cautioned them, saying, 'Watch out – beware of the yeast of the Pharisees and the yeast of Herod.'"*

At first glance when I read this passage I shook my head at the disciples.

Of course I have the benefit of knowing the whole story before hearing these words so it is easier to decipher their meaning. Then I realize that deciphering the meaning is the least of the battles. In the moment I shook my head the yeast of the Pharisee threatened. When I think of the stories I know about the Pharisees, it seems to me that their yeast might be pride. Would the yeast of Herod be selfishness or self-righteousness? These human characteristics draw us away from God.

When I am busy looking down on someone I am not looking at them in the love of Christ and when I am busy working on my plans I am not furthering the kingdom of God, I am furthering the kingdom of Sally. When these grains of yeast begin to grow, it is a recipe for failure.

I come to the Lord today, in humility, asking for cleansing of this bad yeast from my life.

Lord,
Just yesterday I sought to live in love and grace. Through your guidance there were moments I may have blessed others with those gifts but I know there were moments I did not. Each day is a new day filled with promise. Help me take the clean slate, given through forgiveness, and serve you well today. Remove any yeast of destruction in me. I ask this through Jesus, who lives and reigns forever and ever. Amen.

Jan 23 - *Jeremiah 29:11-12 "'For I know the plans I have for you', declares the Lord, 'plans to give you hope and not to harm you. Then you will call upon me and come and pray to me, and I will listen to you.'"*

It is easy for me to look at my children and know that God has great plans for them. They are precious, intelligent people placed on this earth to make a difference in whatever way God has planned. I can see it easily.

When I look in the mirror, knowing the good and the bad, the beauty and the ugliness in me, it is much harder for me to see that God would have a plan for me. Yet, I know God guides me. When I close off the noise in my mind and in my world, when I focus on his voice, when I ask for his help, I see it and I hear him. All of the ugliness I see, God has already forgiven; all of the bad has been healed.

When I look through the eyes of God, the scars from my wounds only give me experience, compassion, and mercy to share with others who struggle. God has not harmed me, but he uses me in spite of my weakness, for with him, I can serve him.

What a blessing to know God does listen when we call upon him and pray!

Lord,
Let us feel your presence without doubt today when we are in prayer to you. Your presence brings peace beyond all understanding and in the present darkness, we need your peace. Speak to us, give us hope, and help us to trust in your divine plan. I ask all this in the name of Jesus Christ, my Savior. Amen.

Jan 24 - *Acts 11:20-21 "But among them were some men of Cyprus and Cyrene who, on coming to Antioch, spoke to the Hellenists also, proclaiming the Lord Jesus. The hand of the Lord was with them, and a great number became believers and turned to the Lord."*

This morning my son and I watched the sky for a moment, and the color in the sunrise was magnificent.

When I see a sunrise or sunset, I can "feel" a heavenly symphony, the majesty and wonder, beauty beyond words that can only be matched with the music I "hear" along with it.

Music ... it is a most precious language in my world.

I sing hymns in church, praises in the car, songs in my dreams; words put to music that speak of or to the Lord are like nothing else to me. The fire, the excitement, and the awe I feel during those moments are, I imagine, like what these disciples must have felt when telling others about the Lord Jesus. They must have been practically bursting with the news!

I want to feel that full of the Lord, so full I can barely contain myself, and, in fact, do not even try to contain myself.

Lord,
We are called to share your good news to all. I know music is one way that your message can speak to many, thank you so much for that. Help me to see, move me to do more. When the moment is right, call me to be ready, willing and able to share your love and your good news. Amen.

Jan 25 - *Psalm 23:1 "The Lord is my shepherd, I shall not want."*

The first verse of this Psalm says it all.
It is not a command, rather a statement of trust. As the good shepherd that he is, he provides everything I need; I will not be left without anything.
My Bible suggests rewriting this passage in today's terminology. Try to find a different metaphor than shepherd to use. I did not do a very good job with that. I cannot think of any really good metaphor, only truth.
The Lord is my Divine Parent; he provides everything I could ever need. He gives me rest, he sustains me and refreshes me; he restores the very essence of my being. He guides my path for his glory. Even though I am surrounded by darkness and evil, I am not afraid because the Lord is with me. His guidance and correction bring me comfort in the midst of strife. He brings me blessings and love, nourishment and renewal in the midst of battle. He always brings more than enough, he gives in abundance. I have no doubt that his goodness and mercy will always be with me and I will dwell in his love and light forever.
For what it is worth, I like David's version better...

Lord,
Thank you for your love and guidance. Thank you for the words of the psalmist that bring blessings to our souls. Your word is our path and your Spirit is our guide. Help us step out in faith, knowing you are there in all things. Amen.

Jan 26 - *2 Corinthians 4:7-9 "But we have this treasure in clay jars, so that it may be made clear that this extraordinary power belongs to God and does not come from us. We are afflicted in every way, but not crushed; perplexed, but not driven to despair; persecuted, but not forsaken; struck down but not destroyed;"*

When I picture jars of clay I see brown earth colored pots that crumble and break so easily.

Once the potter has put them in the kiln and fired them they are stronger and much sturdier. Sometimes they are glazed or painted to look more beautiful to the eye and then they are fired in the kiln again. Regardless of the decoration on the outside of the pot, it is as useful as it was before it was decorated.

We are jars of clay made by the potter. It is only through the Spirit of God that we can serve well in his kingdom. It is through his grace and mercy that we provide grace and mercy to others. It is through his words that we are able to proclaim his message to others. The struggles and weaknesses we endure serve to remind us that it is not us, but he who works through us. He does not allow us to be crushed, brought to despair, forsaken, or destroyed. He renews us and we persevere so that his glory shines on.

There is joy in this passage, let us all be vessels of Light and Love and spread that joy to others.

Lord,
Take this vessel and use it to your glory. I am yours and you are mine. Help all that I do and say, all that I think and pray, glorify your holy name. Amen.

Jan 27 - Acts 4:32 *"Now the whole group of those who believed were of one heart and soul, and no one claimed private ownership of any possessions, but everything they owned was held in common."*

Sharing is a hard lesson to learn.

From the time we are small we struggle with the idea of sharing our things with others. You can just sit in any home or preschool to watch the battle ensue. "That is mine" or "I had it first" are daily reminders that we do not like to share. Sometimes even as adults we are living as though we are still children. We may not say those same things out loud but we shout them in our minds.

I am not feeling the call to sell all of my possessions and take my family to live in a commune. I am saying this: if, as Christians, we are of one heart and soul, how can we not share with one another? Just as when we were children we had to learn, step by step, how to share, as adults we may need to remember step by step how to share.

I encourage you to take one step further than you have in the past to share with others. Share by offering money or food. Share by offering time or talents. Share by offering prayer for one another.

As our hearts move closer to being one in the Christ, let us share.

Lord,
Help these words move from this page into my heart and soul.
You are the tie that binds and yet we often see each other as so different and separate. Open our hearts and our hands to give and receive in blessing. Amen.

Jan 28 - *Genesis 45:5 "And now do not be distressed, or angry with yourselves, because you sold me here; for God sent me before you to preserve life."*

Do you remember the story of Joseph and the beautiful coat that his father gave him?

Joseph had dreams that he proudly shared with his older brothers because those dreams told how he would be more powerful than they were. God really did have big plans for Joseph. First, God needed to give Joseph a heart of humility and servitude.

It took years from the time the brothers sold him into slavery (instead of killing him outright) until he was finally placed in the position of power that he held in this passage. It took years for him to gain the perspective that maybe there was more to his story than being the favorite son and being hated by his brothers. What plans does God have for you and me? What wandering journey are we on to shed unwanted characteristics we have and step into our role to further his kingdom? As I look back on my life so far, I can clearly see the hand of God guiding and correcting me. I can see his grace and mercy protecting me. Look back and see for yourself. God has plans for you too.

Lord,
Forgive my grumbling. How often do I lose sight of your hand? Help me remember the different experiences in my life are molding me into the person you created me to be. You are amazing God, truly amazing. I pray we all bring honor and glory to you this day. Amen.

Jan 29 - *Psalm 37:31 "The law of their God is in their hearts; their steps do not slip."*

My daughter recently started attending a Christian kids club once a week. I put her in this program as part of school and to give her another social outlet.

Each week they start the program time with pledges. Along with the pledge of allegiance to the American flag, they pledge allegiance to the Bible, God's word. They promise to hide the word in their hearts that they might not sin against God.

The first time I heard this I almost choked. Are they really teaching kids that living a sinless life is possible? I know I jumped to conclusions on that one but I had to stop and consider it carefully. I have talked with my daughter about human nature and sin to the degree I believe she needs to hear and understand it. I also know that as I study and learn more scripture, it changes my heart and my life.

I hope the law of God will be written deeply in the hearts of my children as well as my spouse and me. The deeper that law of love is embedded the easier it is to get back on track. Tuck a new verse into your pocket or purse.

Tuck a new verse into the depths of your heart.

Lord,
The words you place in my heart are truly precious to me. They guide my words and my deeds much of the time. Forgive me when I forget them or ignore them, falling out of step. Thank you for your Spirit who guides me back. Amen.

Jan 30 - *2 Chronicles 5:13 "It was the duty of the trumpeters and singers to make themselves heard in unison in praise and thanksgiving to the Lord, and when the song was raised, with trumpets and cymbals and other musical instruments, in praise to the Lord, 'For he is good, for his steadfast love endures forever,' the house, the house of the Lord, was filled with a cloud."*

In my church the only time we would have trumpets would be on Easter morning. I cannot recall cymbals at any service and the other instruments are generally much quieter, like flute, violin, or cello.

I know there are churches that use a lot of instruments like drums, cymbals, guitars, banjos, brass...When there is raucous praise the presence of the Lord seems stronger. When we allow our hearts and souls to break free and sing with all we have, our temple is filled with the presence of God.

In Chronicles, the temple was a building, but since Christ came and died for us, we are the temple.

How amazing!

Lord,
*Fill this temple with your presence today. Make my being quiet for a moment this day so that I can acknowledge, embrace and celebrate your presence in my life. Let me feel your energy, your love, you, filling me up so that I overflow with your light and love, spilling all of your goodness on everything around me. Lord, you are good and your love endures **forever**! Praise be to you always! Amen.*

Jan 31 - *Hebrews 12:11 "Now, discipline always seems painful rather than pleasant at the time, but later it yields the peaceful fruit of righteousness to those who have been trained by it."*

When I read this passage I had to pause for a moment and consider the word discipline here.

Growing up I always thought of discipline as punishment but they are not necessarily the same thing. There are two sides to the word discipline in my mind.

There is the discipline a parent gives to a child or God gives to us as his children. Rather than thinking of it as punishment I think of the verse 4 in Psalm 23 that says "your rod and your staff – they comfort me."

The rod and staff are tools to guide and nudge, not a stick to beat with. God uses them to pull us out of the brambles and back onto the path. He uses them to keep us from falling into the brambles in the first place.

There is also discipline such as study or discipleship. I am learning to pray, study, meditate and more. These are disciplines I take on as a disciple of Christ. With his word and Spirit as guides, I move forward in my disciplines and in my discipleship. His rod and his staff, they still comfort me.

Lord,
Help me be as gentle as you are when I discipline my children. I pray that my discipline will encourage them to seek yours in earnest. Help me train them in grace. I pray they also find comfort and joy in your discipline and in becoming your disciples. Amen.

Feb 1 - *2 Kings 2:9 "When they had crossed, Elijah said to Elisha, 'Tell me what I may do for you, before I am taken from you.' Elisha said, 'Please let me inherit a double share of your spirit.'"*

Elisha seems very brave when I read this verse.
Elijah was a very powerful prophet in his time, one of two visitors that were seen by the disciples in the Garden of Gethsemane.
When I think about the spiritual powerhouses in our time, one that comes to mind is Billy Graham. Would I even desire to ask for double the portion of his spirit? I need to realize the spirit moves us all in different ways.
I am not called to be an evangelist (thank you Lord!) but the Spirit does call me to share the Word each day with whoever will listen. The call helps me get back into the Word of God and while I am at it, bring others with me. Life is so busy that we easily put our Bible up on the shelf and forget about it.
May these verses fill our hearts each day so that we are blessed by them. Then the portion of Spirit we have will be strengthened to do work in our lives.

Lord,
Move me out of the way so the Spirit may use me in the way you ordain. I have my ideas, my desires, and my agenda for each day and much more but I am not in charge. Help me release control to you, you do so much more and so much better than I can even imagine. Thank you for leading me and for using me, broken and tarnished, just as I am. You are amazing! Amen.

Feb 2 - *Numbers 11:4 "The rabble among them had a strong craving; and the Israelites also wept again, and said, 'If only we had meat to eat!'"*

The stories of the Israelites and their relationship with God are a mirror for our own relationships with God.

From the beginning God sought to love and be loved by his chosen people. He blessed them and he cursed them. He did everything to get their attention and devotion.

He rescued them from slavery and bondage. Then during the journey to freedom, the Israelites became ungrateful again. God was providing manna; giving them daily rations of food to maintain their health. He gave them water to satisfy their thirst but these things were not enough. They wanted more.

God guided them by a cloud during the day and a pillar of fire by night. The Israelites wanted more.

How often do we close our eyes to the many blessings we have been given by God only to come to him asking for even more? We live in a country where abundance is the norm and instant gratification is expected.

It would be good for us to remember that God has chosen us. He rescued each of us and during our journey to the Promised Land he provides for our every need. Take time this morning to simply say thank you to God.

Lord,
Forgive my ungrateful heart. Open my eyes to see the blessings you give so freely to me and open my hands to share those blessings with others. Thank you Lord. Amen.

Feb 3 - *1 John 4:10-11 "In this is love, not that we loved God but that he loved us and sent his Son to be the atoning sacrifice for our sins. Beloved, since God loved us so much, we also ought to love one another."*

This sounds so easy on the surface, doesn't it?

We have received love beyond our comprehension from the Divine and he calls us to share that love with others. The spirits in this world that John writes about just before this passage whisper lies to us. They do not want us to feel loved or to love others.

I have heard and have known for almost all my life that God loves me. He has given more than I could ever begin to give back in love.

With these verses fresh on my heart, how can I deign to ask him for anything? How do I have the audacity to whine or complain or petition for anything? He has already given everything; he gave it all in love.

As I go forth into this day I am humbled once more. I have been at the foot of his throne and I am made clean once again. As we all go into this day, let us encourage each other, lift one another up and let us love one another.

Listen to the Spirit of Truth and live in the love of God.

Lord,
Thank you for your unending grace and mercy. Thank you for your unending love for me and all of your children. Protect us from the spirits that lie, and open our ears only to your Spirit of Truth so that we live in your love and share it with all people. It is only because of you that I live and breathe. Thank you for this day to love. Amen.

Feb 4 - *Revelation 1:3 "Blessed is the one who reads aloud the words of the prophecy, and blessed are those who hear and who keep what is written in it; for the time is near."*

All of my life, and for many generations before mine, we have heard the time is near. These days I hear a lot of people discounting or just disregarding the prophecies in Revelation as well as the other prophecies in the Bible.

No one knows the time or day when these things will come to fruition; will it be in my lifetime? Maybe in my children's lifetime? I cannot know.

What I know is that I feel compelled, more now than ever, to put scripture in my heart so that I can be ready for anything that may try to derail my faith.

Without the Word, I have no sword to fight the battle that Paul talks about in Ephesians. I have tried, over the years, to fight with a plastic shield and a butter knife and it is only by the grace of God that I have survived to tell about it.

I read the prophecies and most of what they say are beyond my understanding. Part of what I know they say is that I am blessed and that if I study these words and take them to heart, I will continue to be blessed.

May these words bless you too!

Lord,
I have tried to live in accordance with your plan and fallen on my face more times than I can count. Thank you for always being there to pick me up and get me going once more. Help me study and grant me understanding so that I may be blessed and bless those around me because of it. Amen.

Feb 5 - *Acts 5:19-20 "But during the night an angel of the Lord opened the prison doors, brought them out, and said, 'Go, stand in the temple and tell the people the whole message about this life.'"*

What an amazing experience!
Imagine being locked up in prison and then, right in front of the prison guards the doors open and you are set free. As you walk out in amazement you are told to go out and tell the story...
This passage in the book of Acts tells about Peter and the apostles being arrested and imprisoned for sharing the gospel story of Jesus. The Sadducees were jealous of the healing the apostles were providing through God and the people they were converting with their story.
The thing is if you believe the gospel truth, you have shared this amazing experience. God frees each of us from our prison of sin when we confess to him and turn away. Often times we are released from our prison only to sit there in the darkness unwilling to go out as we have been directed.
Just as God sent Jesus to lead us into abiding love, he sends his Spirit to guide us out of the prison we are in and into the break of day to share our story of freedom. Wherever you are and whatever chains bind you, call on the Lord, accept and revel in the freedom he provides.
Celebrate and tell the message of this amazing experience!

Lord,
You have set us all free; I sing praises and songs of thanksgiving to you for that blessed truth! Help us step out in courage and faith, sharing your freedom with all! Amen.

Feb 6 - *Psalm 89:17-18 "For you are the glory of their strength; by your favor our horn is exalted. For our shield belongs to the Lord..."*

I am nothing without God.
I am a speck of dust; a withering leaf blowing in the wind and then gone.
As I sat in mediation I acknowledged to God that all I accomplish, anything I say or do that is right, belongs to him. It is his protection and guidance that allow me to honor him instead of disgracing him. Without his Spirit, I would be lost beyond recognition.
I am a vessel to be filled and used for his kingdom. He lovingly created me knowing each and every part of me. I am his creation, his child, and because of this I seek to please him. I can step forward in hope because I know that he is faithful; he is my strength and my shield.
I take hold of the hand of God and he pulls me to my feet. I lift my hands and heart in praise and adoration of the Almighty, my Rock and my Redeemer.
He created each of us in love and he gives us what we need to serve him. Call on his name and step into your day with the comfort of his Spirit leading the way.

Lord,
Pour your grace into every crevice of my soul. As it seeps in and brings healing and restoration, strengthen my spirit with yours. Thank you for your continued guidance and love through every moment. Thank you for protecting me from so many unknown attacks. I lift your name on high and praise you on this glorious new day. Amen.

Feb 7 - *1 Corinthians 13:4-7 "Love is patient; love is kind; love is not envious or boastful or arrogant or rude. It does not insist on its own way; it is not irritable or resentful; it does not rejoice in wrongdoing, but rejoices in the truth. It bears all things, believes all things, hopes all things, endures all things."*

Our society has botched the meaning of the word love so badly it is almost unrecognized in its true meaning. Love is not a feeling. Really, love is *not* a feeling!

Love is action. We love something or someone. Love is not joy, happiness or infatuation. It is not excitement, racing hearts or head over heels. When we love, we do something. We act in ways that are patient, kind, forgiving, trusting and protecting. There are times we may not feel like loving someone. If we choose to love in spite of our feelings, we begin to feel like loving once more; then it becomes easier.

We are called to love one another as ourselves. This is just a different way of saying the golden rule - do unto others as you would have them do unto you. I need to try harder to follow this simple command in my home and in my day.

Lord,
Feelings get in the way of love so often. Help me to honor my feelings, and love anyway. You are the supreme giver of love and this passage reminds me that you embody love. Soften my heart so that I may love as you have shown me. Erase the negative energy flowing from me and allow me to radiate your love to all those in my world. Amen.

Feb 8 - *2 Chronicles 15:1-2 "The Spirit of God came upon Azariah son of Oded. He went out to meet Asa and said to him, 'Hear me, Asa, and all Judah and Benjamin: The Lord is with you, while you are with him. If you seek him, he will be found by you, but if you abandon him, he will abandon you.'"*

This message from Azariah reminds me of a saying about feeling the presence of God. If the Lord feels far away, check to see who moved?

During this season in my life, when I have been blessed to attend a Bible study on a regular basis, along with the call to get into the Word each day it has proven beyond a shadow of a doubt; if I seek the Lord, I will find him.

He is always right there waiting to be sought, longing for our company. He does not force himself upon us and if we turn our back and reject him, until we come back he may not make his presence known.

Seek with me so we may find him together and rejoice in him.

Lord,
Compel me to always search for you, always see you, and stay with you in all circumstances. I never want to be abandoned by you; I cannot imagine my life without your love and grace. Thank you for your Word that guides my day, teaches me, comforts me and challenges me. May this word bless my day and may my day glorify you! Amen.

Feb 9 - *Luke 22:61-62 "The Lord turned and looked at Peter. Then Peter remembered the word of the Lord, how he had said to him 'Before the cock crows today, you will deny me three times.' And he went out and wept bitterly."*

I guess Peter was probably scared.
He had just been with Jesus in the garden praying after supper and now Jesus was under arrest and being questioned. At supper Jesus told Peter he would deny him and Peter didn't believe him. Now during the questioning, three different people gave Peter the opportunity to fess up that he was a follower of Jesus.
All it took was one look from his Lord at the sound of the crowing and Peter woke to the realization that he had denied the Lord; he denied three times that he was with him.
There are all kinds of justification I can come up with for Peter. He didn't see any reason to be arrested. Someone needed to stay outside of the circle to observe and tell others what happened. How often do we try to justify our action or inaction? How often, without really trying, do we deny Jesus in our daily lives? When we wake up and realize the Lord is looking at us, we are blessed to know he looks with love and forgiveness.

Lord,
When bitter tears of condemnation fall, wipe them away with your forgiveness and mercy. When we fall away and turn our backs, call to us and open our ears to hear you. Cleanse our souls with your precious blood so we are able to go forward again, new creations abiding in your love. Amen.

Feb 10 - *John 9:33 "If this man were not from God, he could do nothing."*

This verse comes from a passage where the Pharisees are investigating a healing that Jesus gave.
The man had been blind from birth and Jesus gave him sight on the Sabbath day. This got the Pharisees all upset. Jesus did not follow their rules and procedures. He broke the mold on so many levels and that made some of the people very uncomfortable. Sometimes we get so wrapped up in keeping things as we think they should be that we lose sight of the truth. We cling to our rules, our precepts, and our laws as if our very lives depend on it. Jesus did not conform to human laws and neither does God.
If we trust in that truth, we are able to let go of our man-made rules and be free in his truth. God enables us to accomplish whatever he calls us to do.
His holy power healed the blind man and his power will guide you in the tasks he has planned for you when the time is right. We are all called to live in love, to love God and love each other as he loves us.
Whatever else we do, this is the law of God. Living under this law allows us to do whatever we do to the glory of God.

Lord,
Give us sight to see your truth. Help us set down our chains that bind us, whatever they may be. Guide our steps into freedom granted through your unending love and help us to live under the law of your love this day and all days so we can do what you call us to do. Amen.

Feb 11 - *Psalm 90:17 " Let the favor of the Lord our God be upon us, and prosper for us the work of our hands – O prosper the work of our hands!"*

Each of us is given gifts, talents, things we are really good at and none of us is the same.

We are made to serve the purpose that only we can meet in God's kingdom, it is our task to find that purpose and fulfill it to the glory of God. This verse begs a question in my mind: If we have the favor of God resting on us, do our talents and gifts show themselves more readily? Are we more attuned to his divine presence and so then also more to where we fit into the grand scheme of things?

I spent so much of my youth floundering around, not really understanding any of this. It has only been in the last few years that my walk has brought me closer, where I started trying to listen instead of always talking to God. When I stopped to listen, to observe, my call became very clear to me.

God has established the work of my hands and now I must do what I can, with his help, to serve his kingdom in the way he has created me to.

Lord,
Thank you for continuing to call my name until I finally came to hear you. Quiet our souls, minds, and busy lives so that we may hear you, so that your favor rests upon us. Fill us with urgency to use the gifts you have given us, so we may fulfill your purpose with our hands and our lives. Amen.

Feb 12 - *Matthew 19:26 "But Jesus looked at them and said, 'For mortals it is impossible, but for God all things are possible.'"*

I had a picture in my mind as I meditated on this verse. I was a record, an LP.

If you don't remember those, ask someone a generation older than you to explain them. The needle started playing and as it moved in, there was a scratch on the vinyl. The needle would jump back and start again only to find the scratch again and again. The needle was not able to go past the scratch until it was manually picked up and guided to a new spot on the record.

When I was young, we had a record player and records. If there was a scratch too deep, we simply had to throw out the record.

When I look at me as a record, I am filled with scratches. If I were left to my own resources I know I would be no good and would need to be thrown away.

This verse gives me hope. Humans cannot repair a scratch too deep on the vinyl but with God, all things are possible. He can pick up the needle and move it but he can also repair and mend the scratches on the vinyl until they are made new.

Let our days be filled with music and trust in the Lord that if there is a skip, he will be faithful to us in repairing it so the music goes on uninterrupted.

Lord,
You know our hearts beyond what we know of our hearts. Thank you for stepping in and not leaving us to our own devices. Give us the courage to call on you for help and to trust in you to keep the music going as you designed. Amen.

Feb 13 - *Philippians 4:8 "Finally, beloved, whatever is true, whatever is honorable, whatever is just, whatever is pure, whatever is pleasing, whatever is commendable, if there is any excellence and if there is anything worthy of praise, think about these things."*

As I write there is a very light blanket of snow lying on the ground outside and snow is still falling. The flakes are powdery light and so gentle.

The forecast is a blizzard with several inches of snow. Schools are cancelled; lots of people will stay home from work or end up coming home early. This puts a wrinkle in my schedule and if you know anything about me you know I like a schedule. All day yesterday and some this morning I am praying for the snow to be less than predicted, I want... I want... I want.

This verse and passage came to me as I was lifting others in prayer and it hit me like a gentle snowflake on the head. Oh, how I need to gain perspective. I can begrudgingly accept the changes in my day or I can embrace them. We need this snow so badly and my children, most children, love to play in it.

Soup will be cooking on the stove later today and blessings abound.

Lord,
Thank you for perspective. Help me release my agenda and embrace yours. Open my eyes to see what is honorable, just, and pure. Open my mouth to acknowledge what is pleasing, commendable, and excellent. I lift my heart to praise you, for you are worthy of praise forever. Amen.

Feb 14 - *2 Thessalonians 3:16 "Now may the Lord of peace himself give you peace at all times in all ways. The Lord be with all of you."*

In my prayer time this morning it seems that peace was my overriding request above all other things.

There are people battling sickness and disease, others seeking protection or guidance for certain things in their lives.

Sometimes I am so busy telling God what I think he needs to do for someone I forget for a moment that he knows what needs to be done, not me.

At the end of each of Paul's letters, he has a closing or a benediction. It is easy for me to just gloss over those verses and move on to the next thing but today I paused.

No matter what else Paul has said in his letters, when all is said and done, he wishes grace and peace on the church people he writes to. How would that change our days if our exchanges with others ended with a benediction of grace and peace? If there is a person you are not looking forward to conversing with, would it help if you see them in this light of bestowing God's peace on them in all times and in all ways?

This is my prayer for each of you this morning. I pray that God fills you with his peace and that you feel the presence of his grace abiding in you today.

Lord,
Thank you for opening my eyes to see this little verse tucked in at the end. There is nothing this world needs more than your peace. Be with each of us today and let your peace flow through us and out into the world around us. Amen.

Feb 15 - *Psalm 107:20-21 "He sent out his word and healed them, and delivered them from destruction. Let them thank the Lord for his steadfast love, for his wonderful works to humankind."*

When I was a kid, I used to say that sticks and stones could break my bones but words would never hurt me.

People's words are powerful. They can build you up or tear you down. They can bring forth feelings of love or feelings of hatred. Our words are something to be used with care but they are nothing compared to the Word of God. We can speak of our hopes and desires, our plans and thoughts but when God speaks it is so.

From the beginning of time, when God spoke it happened. He created everything from the stars in the sky and all the planets to the smallest flower petal with his words. Since the time I began studying his word, I have seen transformation in my life beyond explanation. He has guided, corrected, comforted, and blessed me with his word. He has brought healing and kept me from destruction.

I have seen this in so many lives and so today, I give thanks to the Lord for his steadfast love and his wonderful works to humankind.

Lord,
There is much sickness and destruction in this world. When we suffer, often times we forget or do not realize we should call out to you. Lift the voices of our souls to cry out to you for healing and restoration. Thank you for the healing you bring through your steadfast love and grace. Amen.

Feb 16 - *Isaiah 40:28, 31 "Have you not known? Have you not heard? The Lord is the everlasting God, the Creator of the ends of the earth. He does not faint or grow weary; his understanding is unsearchable... but those who wait for the Lord shall renew their strength, they shall mount up with wings like eagles, they shall run and not be weary, they shall walk and not faint."*

Yesterday there was a big debate on my local news channel's Facebook page.
Atheists are posting some billboards and the news channel asked for feedback on how their fans felt about that. While reading some of the banter on both sides, I was surprised how many people don't have knowledge of the words of God.
This verse is balm for the souls who hear it. We cannot understand his ways but we can trust that he never tires and he renews our strength.
As tired and worn down as I have been, when I called on the Lord, he gave me the strength to carry on and he always will.

Lord,
I am humbled once more at your words for me today. Yesterday the stress of the unknown was heavy on my shoulders yet again. You are the everlasting. You walk with me, you carry me; you lift me up. Thank you for reminding me to let go and trust in you and your holy ways. Thank you for a new day every day. Help me see each new day as joyfully as my toddler who cheers because the sun is waking up again. Alleluia, I praise you for a brand new day of your creation. Amen.

Feb 17 - *John 5:16 "Therefore the Jews started persecuting Jesus, because he was doing such things on the Sabbath."*

The Sabbath has been a day of rest since God created the world. In Genesis the Bible tells us that he blessed the seventh day and hallowed it. Jesus healed a man on the blessed Sabbath day and the Pharisees considered that forbidden. If the Jewish leaders had believed Jesus was from God they would not have questioned his behavior but why are they questioning what Jesus is doing anyway?

Are they trying to keep the peace or are they trying to maintain control over their people? Are they pointing out an infraction of the law or are they getting puffed up in their own rule following? Rules are a good thing and they serve a purpose but rule keepers can cross a line pretty quickly when they follow the rules simply for the sake of the rule. Do we drive the speed limit because it is the rule or because it is a safe speed to drive?

God gave us the Sabbath as a day of hallowed rest. In today's society I suspect we would be persecuted for observing the Sabbath rather than what Jesus was experiencing here.

Take time in the next day to find some rest in the Lord. Start with a tiny Sabbath hour and see what blessings you receive for it.

Lord,
You call us to rest in you, to rest in honor of you, and we never stop running. We go from dawn to dark every day and wonder why we feel so worn down sometimes. Help us take time to rest in your presence and to thank you for the rest you so lovingly provide to us. Amen.

Feb 18 - *Psalm 51:12 "Restore to me the joy of your salvation, and sustain in me a willing spirit."*

I just want to say that when I read this Psalm, I thought I should memorize the whole thing. The heading in my Bible right above the first verse says "Prayer for Cleansing and Pardon."
Who of us could not use a beautifully written confession? David wrote this after he had been confronted by Nathan about the sin he committed with Bathsheba. I lift a quick prayer that none of us reading this are in the throes of that particular sin, but sin is sin and we all fall short of the glory of God.
There is not one of us reading this or even any that aren't that could not use a prayer for cleansing and pardon. It was easy for me to find sins of pride and selfishness, sins of thoughtlessness and hard-heartedness. I encourage you to open your Bible to this chapter, or if you don't have one handy, you can look it up on the internet (thank you God!). Find a quiet space and ask the Lord to show you what needs cleansing.
He is faithful and merciful. He shows you and then in your petition for forgiveness he forgives! This is the joy of our salvation!

Lord,
Bend my will to yours. Sustain in me a willing spirit that calls on you and receive your everlasting love and forgiveness. Give my voice courage to sing out your praises to all the earth. Joy is mine, thanks to you! Amen.

Feb 19 - *2 Thessalonians 3:2-3 "and that we may be rescued from wicked and evil people; for not all have faith. But the Lord is faithful; he will strengthen you and guard you from the evil one."*

Have you ever felt or heard the Lord protecting you from evil? There have been times in my life when temptation is knocking on my door, times where the voices of despair are whispering lies that are easy to believe, but the power of God, when I call upon him, is true.

I read a book about a man who lived a life denying the Lord but in his darkest moment, he fell back on the songs of his childhood and called upon the Lord to save him. If I ever had doubt in God, that story erased it.

Trust his word; call upon him to deliver you, to deliver those you love. Evil is real and strong.

God is real and is infinitely stronger. Praise God!

Lord,
You delivered us all from sin with the life of Jesus the Christ. When we are tempted, when we fall away, when we are troubled by evil or wickedness, remind us to pray for your strength and protection. I ask for your strength and protection this day on me, my family, and those who read this message today. Place your divine light around each of us as a shield so that nothing can penetrate it but your love. Strengthen each of us to fight well when the evil one comes to taunt us. I praise you and thank you for being faithful to us and giving us what we need to win each battle. Amen.

Feb 20 - *Amos 7:14-15 "Then Amos answered Amaziah, 'I am no prophet, nor a prophet's son; but I am a herdsman, and a dresser of sycamore trees,' and the Lord took me from following the flock, and the Lord said to me, 'Go, prophesy to my people Israel.'"*

I am quietly thanking the Lord this morning that he has never called me to be a prophet and I hope and pray that he will not. God uses unlikely characters to bring his message to the people. He calls Samuel as a small boy, raises a small shepherd boy to destroy a giant and become King. He makes Esther a queen and brings salvation to the world through a small town carpenter and his betrothed.

The list of unlikely characters continues through his disciples and apostles and even on to today. I still wonder at the call I follow to send his word to others; why me?

He uses the most unlikely of characters. Amos was a faithful servant of the Lord as well. He hears the word of the Lord as he is sitting watching his flocks of sheep and he obeys. Are we listening to hear the word of the Lord to us?

Will we hear and obey?

Lord,
We are, by nature, a willful people. So often we go through our days thinking we have it all under control and all it is going according to plan. We forget to seek your plan and we forget whose plan is true. Encourage us to lift our prayers to you, O God. Open our hearts and our ears to hear and follow your word for us. Amen.

Feb 21 - *1 John 3:23 "And this is his commandment, that we should believe in the name of his Son Jesus Christ and love one another, just as he has commanded us."*

I woke up with a start this morning.

I am an hour later than usual. I thought I set my alarm, I checked it before I went to bed but somehow I was wrong. It was hard to quiet my mind and soul to sit in the presence of the Lord and listen this morning. When I was led to this passage my first thought was that we have already been there. This message is written throughout the books of the New Testament. I know I have written about this before.

Then it struck me. If this message is written over and over again in the Bible, it bears repeating. People are forgetful. We hear the messages and try to live according to the word but before we even blink we start to slide back into our human ways.

I need to let go of the hands on the clock and hold the hand of my Savior, Jesus Christ.

I need to release control of my day and allow the grace and love of Christ to be my guide for today. I thank the Lord for that extra sleep and the blessing of still giving me quiet time. I thank the Lord for my husband who let me sleep in out of kindness and consideration. I thank the Lord for my kids who are still sleeping as I write this, by the grace of God.

Now I go forward in my day and do my best, with the guidance of the Spirit, to love as he commanded us to love.

Lord,
Thank you for all you do, for your grace and love. Help us live showing your grace and love to others so we honor you with our lives each day. Amen.

Feb 22 - *Psalm 57:7-8 "My heart is steadfast, O God, my heart is steadfast. I will sing and make melody. Awake, my soul! Awake, O harp and lyre! I will awake the dawn."*

Music is a language.

It does not use words to communicate, but with notes strung together in a melody or harmony a message is shared with everyone who hears it. Music can bring a message of love, strife, or healing. It can share a message of hope or despair; brokenness or wholeness.

When I struggle to find peace in my heart I know I can sing to the Lord and peace will come. The songs in church are so beautiful to me because they put prayers and praise to music that resonates within my soul so deeply. Music takes the message out of my head and moves it into my soul.

Whether you sing songs in your heart or with your voice lift a song to the Lord! Find songs on the radio or on a CD that draw you into the presence of the Lord. Listen to the music of nature as it awakens and moves to the rhythm of the day. Join me in songs of adoration and praise to the God of gods, the Lord of lords.

He is steadfast and merciful so I lift songs to awaken the dawn and my soul will sing through the day.

Lord,
May the music in my heart and voice bring you glory and honor. Help the thoughts and meditations of my heart be music to your ears. Open my ears to hear the music of others so we may join together in one voice singing praises to you and your Holy name. Amen.

Feb 23 - *Matthew 5:16 "In the same way, let your light shine before others, so that they may see your good works and give glory to your Father in heaven."*

Light has not yet begun to peek over the horizon. Soon there will be a gentle glow as daylight begins and darkness fades in the morning.

Can we bring a glow of light in this world of darkness? How can we bring forth the daylight of Christ? When we infuse our daily tasks, our morning routine, whatever we do with the love of God we shine his light into the world. When we seek to serve the Lord with our thoughts and our actions we shine the light of God in our day.

This passage talks about setting your light up on a hill for all to see. Jesus reminds us that no one lights a lamp and then hides it so no one can see the light. We turn on the lights in our homes so that we can see better and bring a sense of warmth.

When I take time to sense the light of Christ in my heart, I see more clearly and there is a sense of warmth coming from him in the midst of whatever I am doing. He calls us to share this light; to let it shine for others so we might bring glory to God.

I end with this ... "This little light of mine, I'm gonna let it shine..."

Lord,
Disperse any darkness that lurks and let your light fill my heart and soul. As I move forward in this day, help me to share your light so that darkness flees from others as well. I ask this in the name of my Savior, Jesus. Amen.

Feb 24 - *Romans 8:15-16 "For you did not receive a spirit of slavery to fall back into fear, but you have received a spirit of adoption. When we cry, 'Abba! Father!' it is that very Spirit bearing witness with our spirit that we are children of God."*

I remember back when my kids were just tiny babies. Their eyes were open and they gazed around at things but it took a few weeks before they could focus on my face. It brought a sweet moment of love the first time I saw them really looking at me. Then they started babbling and making sounds. I still feel the joy I felt when they finally connected the sound "Mama" to me. It took no time at all for them to call Mama and Dada when they wanted something.

This is how children are. They need us for everything at first and even as they grow in their independence we hope they continue a deep relationship with us.

We are children of God. When we first begin to recognize him as our Father, I imagine he feels joy and love too. As we grow into independence, he longs for us to continue a relationship with him, just as we do with our children.

Seek the arms of your heavenly Father. Call on him and grow a deeper relationship with him.

His Spirit calls to us.

Lord,
Just as our earthly parents always remain our parents so you always remain our heavenly Father. Pull us into your arms of love during this season of preparing to receive your ultimate gift of love. Guide our hearts into relationship with you in our everyday lives. Speak, Spirit, and let us hear. Amen.

Feb 25 - *Galatians 1:10 "Am I now seeking human approval, or God's approval? Or am I trying to please people? If I were still pleasing people, I would not be a servant of Christ."*

Why do we do the things we do?

When I used to work outside the home, I would receive reviews from my boss on how I was doing. Before that, in school, I received grades on the work I produced and its quality. When we were small children we would seek the approval of our parents or our friends. From the time we are little, we learn to seek the approval of those around us.

As we walk the paths of our spiritual journeys we are awakened to a new purpose, a new reason to do what we do. As Christians, we are servants of Christ, not servants of the world. We may still be subject to human approval for tasks and jobs we have to do, but if we seek the approval of Christ in our jobs, we work to bring glory to him in whatever we do. We quickly realize what things do not bring him glory and it is easy to lay those aside if we are living in him.

It is when we lose sight of him that we begin to serve humans and ourselves again. As we go into another day of service, let's keep Jesus in our sights.

Look for his nod of approval or a smile on his face and we will feel joy in what we are doing. To God be the glory!

Lord,

We have things we must do and things we enjoy doing. Help us find joy in all things as we seek to bring glory to your kingdom. Help me teach my children to serve you above all else so they may find the true joy of being your servants. Amen.

Feb 26 - *Ephesians 2:8-9 "For by grace you have been saved through faith, and this is not your own doing; it is the gift of God – not the result of works, so that no one may boast."*

Just yesterday I was writing about motive. Why do we do what we do?

These verses move to the same rhythm. When we are working in service to the Lord, we can still have impure motives. There is a fine line between serving in thanksgiving and serving for approval. I know there is no way I can ever work hard enough or well enough to earn God's love or grace.

I have seen myself fall and fail too many times to think that I could succeed in pleasing God with *my* work. It feels different when I am doing his work; seeking to serve the Lord in thanksgiving for the grace he has given to me. I am not seeking approval or redemption through my hands, I am simply giving my work and my life in thanksgiving and praise to God who already gave all to me. I have heard many people say that when they get to heaven they want to hear God say "well done good and faithful servant."

I hope to hear that too but even more I long to hear the voice of God and see his face as he says to me "Welcome home my beloved child, welcome home!"

Lord,
Thank you for all you give, fill our hearts so we can sing in joy and thanksgiving. Help us live in your grace each day and compel us to share your grace with others so that this world can live in love. Let your light shine through us as a beacon so all the world can find the way home to you. Amen.

Feb 27 - *Obadiah verse 15 "For the day of the Lord is near against all the nations. As you have done, it shall be done to you; your deeds shall return on your own head."*

Is it just me or does it seem like our nation is in some kind of a tail spin?

If I watch the news or read articles on the internet, the stories tell me our nation is headed for financial ruin. There are battles brewing about everything from gun control to immigration, gay rights to national defense. Not only do battles wage on the national level, there are battles fought even on the individual level.

When I am making music do I seek reward from others; am I proud of what I do or am I seeking to bring hearts to God?

When I am teaching my children am I seeking power or seeking to bring hearts to God? I cannot win the battles of the nation but what I can do is work to do the will of the Lord in my own heart and life. Just as nations fail, we all fail.

The blessing we have is the unending grace of God through Jesus. He continues to seek the hearts of Israel; he continues to seek our hearts. Take time to pray for your own heart, the hearts of those you love, and the hearts of nations.

May God's love and peace fill them all.

Lord,

I pray for peace on earth and good will toward men but even as I utter the words, I know those things must come from me. We are the people to share what you sent through Jesus. We are the ones to spread your peace and good will. Help us live as Jesus lived and help us be the people you created each of us to be, all for your glory. Amen.

Feb 28 - *Deuteronomy 6:4-5 "Hear, O Israel: The Lord is our God, the Lord alone. You shall love the Lord your God with all your heart, and with all your soul, and with all your might."*

The Shema.

I learned this verse several years ago while taking a meditation class in my church. I used this as a breath prayer for a while and for some reason this morning the Shema came back to me.

Shema means an affirmation of Judaism and a declaration of faith in one God.

I have fallen out of habit of breath prayers although, some days, I say a lot of prayers under my breath!

Today I encourage you to join me in finding a verse, one I have sent or one of your own, and make it a breath prayer. Write it on your heart and then say it in your mind or whisper it out loud while breathing in and out, making the prayer a part of your normal breathing.

How could this change my day if I say these verses as a breath prayer while I am driving to the store, while standing in line, while cooking dinner?

Lord,
Let these verses complete my day. Let them seep into my very being. Let my breath remind me that you are my God, and I love you with all my heart, soul, and strength. Thank you for the Shema and all your teachings we have from the Bible. Open us today to your Word. Amen.

Feb 29 - *Genesis 3:9-10 "But the Lord God called to the man, and said to him, 'Where are you?' He said, 'I heard the sound of you in the garden, and I was afraid, because I was naked; and I hid myself.'"*

My kids love to play hide and seek and as they get older they get much better at hiding and keeping quiet while the person who is "it" searches for them. Isn't it interesting how we never stop hiding, even as adults?

We become masters at hiding what we do not want to be seen or even acknowledge ourselves. Just as I often know where my kids are hiding, God knew then and he knows now. He knows where we are hiding and what we hide.

He knows that we need to be the ones to come out on our own. We need to be able to show what we are hiding before we can release it. He does not snatch it or pry open our hands to force it away. He does not come and yank us from our hiding places. He calls "Ollie, Ollie, oxen free" and waits for us to come in when we are ready.

I heard him calling and I am coming out of hiding. He greets me with love and grace. He receives my hidden secrets with love and grace. As I release them to him, the empty spots where those secrets were hidden are filled up with his love and grace. Will you join me in the free space?

Lord,
Forgive me for holding on so long. I run to you now taking full advantage of the freedom you offer. Take all my hurts, all my secrets and replace them with your healing love so I can go out and draw others in to your freedom too. Amen.

Mar 1 - *Hebrews 12:14 "Pursue peace with everyone, and the holiness without which no one will see the Lord."*

It feels like life is on a pendulum.

The rocking back and forth can be soothing and peaceful or it can feel extreme and fearful. Babies like to be rocked and when they get a little bigger they move on to swings. Children love to swing, some of them swing gently and others like to go fast and high.

As I think back to the times I would swing, it felt like freedom. There is a breeze that blows on your face as you rush forward on the swing and then as you swing back, it gently flows forward. There is freshness, a peace the flows in that back and forth motion. Even as high as you go, you know that you will come to settle back into gentle peace in the end. I hope that I can pursue the gently calming peace in the midst of chaos.

As we move into this day, I pray you feel the gentle breeze of peace and freedom flowing in your soul. Let it refresh you and bring you a new sense of calm that you can share with others. Peace to each of you today.

Lord,
You are the Prince of Peace. Take the chaos of our days from us and help us be filled with your peace. Allow your peace to flow from us out into the world so that all people would be drawn to it, coming closer to your holiness and closer to you. Allow them to see you in us this day. Amen.

Mar 2 - *Psalm 150: 3-4 "Praise him with trumpet sound; praise him with lute and harp! Praise him with tambourine and dance; praise him with strings and pipe!"*

Sometimes I feel a lot like Cinderella.

I have worked so hard, struggling in the trenches to get things done and when I finally clean myself up and get ready to present myself to the Prince, my finery gets torn to bits by the harsh desires of the world around me.

I wish I had a fairy godmother to spin me the finery that Cinderella had in the story. The thing I begin to remember as I see this unfold in my mind is that God sees me in all my finery through the eyes of Jesus. I may think I am dressed in dirty rags from being dragged through the muck and mud but to him, I shine like the sun because I have been washed in the blood and cleansed by the healing love of the Christ!

Let the ball commence! Let the music play on and in thankfulness and with a grateful heart, I step forth and move to the beautiful music. He is the Lord of the Dance, and even when I step on toes or if my hem gets torn a bit, I dance on to honor and celebrate all he has done for me; for each of us. We all have rags to riches stories.

Take the hand of the Lord of the Dance; celebrate all he has given us!

Lord,

Thank you for the beauty you created in me and in all your children. Open our ears to hear the music and move our souls to dance in praise and honor of you. You take our hands and lead us to the floor and the dance goes on! Hallelujah! Amen.

Mar 3 - *Psalm 23:4 "Even though I walk through the darkest valley, I fear no evil; for you are with me; your rod and your staff – they comfort me."*

We move into a time of reflection and preparation again as the remembrance of Jesus death draws near.

Thousands of years ago he walked the earth and was teaching, healing, and showing us how to abide in God. Only he could foresee what was to come and he willingly continued on the path given to him.

Over the last few years I have chosen to sacrifice something during the season of Lent. I choose something that distracts me from abiding in God or something that holds that potential. I choose something that I desire or a frivolity that I often take for granted. As those desires or distractions peek into my days, I take that moment to lift a prayer to the Lord, asking him to search the darkness in my heart and cleanse me of whatever sin I may have within me. There is nothing darker than the darkness of sin. Through the sacrifice Jesus gave so long ago, I am able to call on the Lord to walk with me through the darkness.

My tiny 40-day sacrifice is simply a token; a reminder to me of the sacrifice that he gave for me; for us all.

Lord,
As we remember the journey to the cross and the reason you went there, guide our hearts in a journey of cleansing and healing so when that triumphant day of Easter is here, we can truly be filled with joy. Help us prepare so we can sing Hallelujah with every ounce of our being. Amen.

Mar 4 - *Galatians 6:9 "So let us not grow weary in doing what is right, for we will reap at harvest time, if we do not give up."*

This calls to mind my pepper plant from last summer.
I planted my garden from seed except the tomato plants. Almost everything sprouted and grew as we watered and weeded, nurtured and cared for the plants.
We were doing well and did not become weary. The little section where I planted my peppers, nothing grew. There were no sprouts, no weeds; nothing. All summer I watered that area along with everything else, what harm could come from that?
In August, a pepper plant sprouted! Because it was so late in the season I knew it would not have time to produce any peppers so when it got big enough I transplanted it into a pot and brought it inside.
We got one good pepper off of that plant before we gave up on it. I often wonder if I had continued to care for it and not become weary, would we still be harvesting peppers?
How much more should we care for each other, calling on strength from the Lord when we tire?

Lord,
When I grow weary, when I want to give up, remind me of this pepper plant. Only you know when the proper time for harvest is, you call us to continue doing good until the harvest is ripe. Infuse your light and energy into us this day so we can go out and do good with renewed spirits, trusting fully in your timing. Amen.

Mar 5 - *Mark 1:12-13 "And the Spirit immediately drove him out into the wilderness. He was in the wilderness forty days, tempted by Satan; and he was with the wild beasts; and the angels waited on him."*

I have had times in my life where I felt I was in the desert. The number forty holds mystery: It rained forty days and nights for Noah, Moses led his people in the desert for forty years and Jesus was sent to the desert for forty days. We spend forty days before Easter in the season of Lent.

Noah saw rain for forty days and nights and then waited a year before he could set feet on dry land and open the doors of the ark to let the animals out. The Israelites wandered for forty years then they blew it and had to wander even more before they were led to their promised land. Jesus was transformed after his forty days in the desert.

In all of these stories of wandering, temptations, darkness, and doom, God was always there. It says, "Angels attended him." God guided the Israelites with a pillar of fire and a cloud. God sent wind for Noah to dry the waters. He never leaves us.

If you are in a time of wandering, darkness, desert, or flood, may these words give you hope. We have trials and temptations but God is with us. Look for your angels, search, for God is here!

Lord,
Thank you for your word today. It is a good reminder that whether forty days or forty years, we are attended and cared for. Open our eyes and help us see our angels. Use us to be your servants to those who are in need of your love and assistance. Amen.

Mar 6 - *Psalm 130:5-6 "I wait for the Lord, my soul waits, and in his word I put my hope; my soul waits for the Lord more than those who watch for the morning, more than those who watch for the morning."*

The Bible study I am participating in is about discerning the voice of God.

The overwhelming message I am getting from the Lord and the Holy Spirit is this - wait. I am not the most patient person when it comes to waiting. When things are started I am all about efficiency, and most of the time I have so much on my agenda I have little patience. I want my daughter to hurry up and get her shoes on, hurry up and brush her hair, hurry up and do the workbook page for school, etc. I want traffic to hurry up and move; I want the Lord to hurry up and send me my verse of the day.

I am working on slowing down, taking deep breaths and actually scheduling time to sit and listen, sit and wait for God. He will speak, he gives me what I need; he will come. My soul waits and I have hope. I know without a doubt he is here in spirit and he will come again.

Until then, I wait.

Lord,
I get so very tired. I run myself ragged, put too much on my plate and cannot find enough rest. Remind me that waiting begs for time of quiet. Help me find time to be quiet and just sit in your presence. During the times I am "doing" let my soul continue to search for and feel your presence. Let my being be ever watchful for you in this day and for the day when you come again. Amen.

Mar 7 - *Galatians 5:13-14 "For you were called to freedom, brothers and sisters; only do not use your freedom as an opportunity for self-indulgence, but through love become slaves to one another."*

Freedom. This is something that is so easy to take for granted, especially in our country.

It is also easy to run away with freedom, to forget who we are and lose our inhibitions. This is when we run the risk of indulging in the sinful nature. I have heard people say things like "it is okay, God will forgive me". This attitude has, unfortunately, been mine in the past on occasion. Indulgence in sin has come back to bite me every time.

I know that if I am not diligent, it will consume me; devour me. The second part of this passage is twofold for me. "Love your neighbor"- that part is easier for me, thank God. My challenge comes with the second part: "as yourself."

If I indulge in sinful nature, I do not love myself. I am called to love everyone as I love myself so I must treat myself as I would treat others and then, also, treat others as I would like to be treated.

As I see it, this is a circle of love for all.

Lord,
You are love. Thank you for showering your love on me this morning. Help me to love all, myself and others, as you have loved me. In this way, I can serve in love and be truly free. Alleluia and Amen.

Mar 8 - *Isaiah 48:21 "They did not thirst when he led them through the deserts; he made water flow for them from the rock, he split open the rock and the water gushed out."*

God is a God of miracles.

Throughout history he has provided and rescued. He has brought wrath, instructed and guided, and so many times by the use of miracles.

We cannot explain or understand how water could come from a rock or how water can create a wall in a river bed. We cannot explain how a baby can be born of a virgin or how death on a cross can bring forgiveness for all.

There are also daily miracles: the growth of a child, our body healing from sickness, a caterpillar turning into a butterfly.

These are harder to notice for sure, yet, no less a miracle. We are tarnished, battered, and sometimes broken but we can hold hope in our hearts in spite of that with messages like this one.

They did not thirst... water gushed out.

What miracle will you witness today?

Lord,
Thank you for your abundant love and thank you for all of the miracles you create to speak to us and to give your love and life to us. Open our eyes this day to see the miracles we would have missed. Help us to drink your gushing water so we may no longer be thirsty. All glory and honor are yours, forever. Amen.

Mar 9 - *Isaiah 46:9-10 "remember the former things of old, for I am God, and there is no other; I am God, and there is no one like me, declaring the end from the beginning and from ancient times things not yet done, saying 'My purpose shall stand, and I will fulfill my intention,'"*

This passage in Isaiah deals with the worship of idols.
The people had fallen away from God and were praying to gods created by people. These verses call to remind them that there is no other God before Yahweh, he is the Almighty. He is the One, Alpha and Omega. He spoke and it happened; he speaks and it happens.
What idols do I put before God? What things or people keep me from praying to and serving the one true God? Is it that one TV show I can't miss? Is it that instant connection to the happenings in my world via the internet? Is it the jealousy of what others have that I do not or is it the judgment of others that "worship" these idols?
Today I search my heart again, uprooting anything that pulls me away from the one true God and serving his purpose. I seek to serve the Lord in word and deed, working to assist in fulfilling his intention.

Lord,
Show me where I err. Bring to me the things that I have set before you so that I can banish them from me and focus on your presence and your purpose. Forgive me for losing sight of you and your kingdom. You are my God. I lift your name on High and I worship you and serve you with all that I am and all that you are creating me to be. Amen.

Mar 10 - *Acts 11:18 "When they heard this, they were silenced. And they praised God, saying, 'Then God has given even to the Gentiles the repentance that leads to life.'"*

From the beginning of the Bible, people searched for a greater power.

People fell into idolatry searching for someone greater than themselves. There are organizations that are exclusive in today's world just like Judaism would have been before Christ. You had to be Jewish to worship their God, to be one of his chosen people. It was a birth right rather than a depth of faith.

When God opened this up to all who would hear, everyone became the chosen. I sit here looking out at twenty inches of snow; the world is asleep and quiet. Even on this sleepy winter day, trees and animals in hibernation, I know life waits to come again.

This season of dormancy is a cycle of life and when the earth warms again, trees and flowers will bloom; creatures will stretch in the new life given again.

Rest, ponder, and heal. When you are ready, move into the life we have been given. Then you will dance and sing in joy, for his love endures forever!

Lord,
Thank you for rest. Let us use these times to receive healing. When the time is right, pull us from slumber; wake our spirits to do your work in joy. Like the caterpillar in the cocoon, soon we will be butterflies, spreading your beauty, inspiring others to find you and become one of your chosen with us. Amen.

Mar 11 - *Isaiah 6:8 "Then I heard the voice of the Lord saying, 'Whom shall I send, and who will go for us?' and I said, 'Here am I; send me!'"*

We have a hymn song, "Here I am Lord", we sing in church when new officers are being ordained. I have often pondered the words of this song and this morning I was led to this verse.
I believe we are all called to serve the Lord in some way but, being the body of Christ, I know we do not all have the same job just as our eyes do not hear and our tongue does not walk. As I walk the journey of finding my service task, I encourage you to do the same with me.
What is God calling you to do? He created you for a specific purpose in his kingdom; do you know what that purpose is?
The dream I remember from last night confirmed to me that I need to remove the distractions in my day, even if they are "Christian", stop doing what I deem important and truly listen for what I should be doing. This is a struggle for me, for sure.
I will succeed at this, with God's help.

Lord,
Please help me. I am really struggling with distractions. I love doing Word for Today, I love homeschooling, I love music, I love my family, and I love you. How do I organize my life so that you are my first priority all of the time? When can I truly focus and have quiet time for you? Thank you for dreams, thank you for your word; thank you for being willing to use broken souls like mine. Amen.

Mar 12 - *James 1:22 "But be doers of the word, and not merely hearers who deceive themselves."*

I have a saying from my Mom rattling in my memory about hearing and not doing. She used to say she could talk 'til she was blue in the face and nothing would get done.

I remember times she would give us children a direction, we would acknowledge her and then continue on with whatever we were doing. We heard her, really we did. We heard the garage door opening with my Dad coming home from work better though.

Invariably, if we had not done what was expected yet, we would jump up and rush to do it before Daddy would walk in the door.

I don't think we felt disobedient but we did deceive ourselves. These actions and inactions were disobedient. When we hear the word of the Lord and simply continue on the path of our choice without change that too, is disobedient. God gives clear guidance for us to love as he loves; to abide in him, to serve one another.

I look at my own heart and know I do not always do this. Of course I am not infallible but I do not always strive to do. When we act and do follow the word, James tells us we are blessed in our doing.

Listen to the word and then go out and do so you will be blessed.

Lord,
Forgive my inaction and my disobedience in "forgetting" the direction you have given. Move my heart into action so I may be blessed in acting for your kingdom and so that others may be blessed by my following and doing of your word. Amen.

Mar 13- *Deuteronomy 8:3 "He humbled you by letting you hunger, then by feeding you with manna, with which neither you nor your ancestors were acquainted, in order to make you understand that one does not live by bread alone, but by every word that comes from the mouth of the Lord."*

A few years ago you would not see gluten-free anything on the shelves at the store and now it is everywhere.

I know people who are gluten intolerant, people who are allergic to wheat, and people who choose not to eat wheat for other reasons. They still find food to eat.

This verse reminds me of the story of Jesus' temptation in the book of Luke. He was led into the desert, fasted for forty days, and was tempted by Satan. Jesus quoted this verse in response to Satan's call for Jesus to turn stone into bread.

As you eat your meals (whether or not you eat bread), I encourage you to take time to remember this fast of the Lord. Just as we nourish our bodies with food that he provides, we must nourish our souls with the words of his mouth.

Celebrate and give praise; the word of the Lord will truly feed us for eternity!

Lord,
Thank you for your word and thank you for your Spirit that guides us in it. You provide our nourishment; help us to gather what we need just as the Israelites gathered manna in the desert. Then, as we partake, help us give thanks and praise to you, our provider! Amen.

Mar 14 - *Psalm 71:14 "But I will hope continually, and will praise you yet more and more."*

So often, when I am sitting in prayer or study of scripture, time flies by. I gaze at the clock and cannot fathom where the time went! One hour seems like five minutes. Then there are days where the clock never seems to move.

I remember days when I used to work outside of the home, many of us were watching the clock, waiting for it to reach the blessed time to leave for lunch or leave for the day. It seemed to take forever!

When we are enjoying ourselves, having a good time and feeling happy, time moves more quickly and when we are weighed down and struggling through the moment at hand it seems it will never end.

As I begin another day in the season of Lent, I am reminded to pray. 1 Thessalonians 5:17 tells us to pray without ceasing. This Psalm reminds us to live in hope and praise God more and more. Today I serve the Lord in whatever I do, I pray in hope and give thanks and praise for all the blessings he has already given us.

Will you join me?

Lord,
Guide my heart and my hands so that my thoughts and my deeds may be a good prayer to you. Let the meditations of my heart and the words of my mouth lift praises to your name. Open my eyes to see the many blessings you give and the work of your hand in this world. Thank you Lord! Thank you for your grace and mercy, thank you for everything. Amen.

Mar 15 - *2 Corinthians 5:6-7 "So we are always confident; even though we know that while we are at home in the body we are away from the Lord – for we walk by faith, not by sight."*

Have you ever played the game where one person is blindfolded and another leads them? It is a trust building game I have seen played in church youth groups.

Sometimes it feels like we wander through our days blindfolded with no one guiding us. We stumble and bump into things.

There are times we have someone guiding our steps but unbeknownst to us, they are blindfolded too. It is the case of the blind leading the blind.

While we are here on earth the body gets in the way of seeing the truth in full. There is hope.

The Holy Spirit lives within us and is our guide. He guides us more readily and safely than our best friend holding our arm and whispering directions in our ear. He *is* our best friend and he is holding us, guiding us; whispering direction in our ear. With him as our guide, we do not need our eyes. Trust in the Lord; walk with him in faith and in confidence. One day we will see all his glory. Until then, he guides us in truth.

Lord,
Thank you for your Spirit and your Word to guide us each day. Help us listen to our hearts and your voice more than trusting our eyes which are easily deceived. Help us place our trust in you, allowing you to lead us in truth and light today and all days. I ask this through the name of Jesus my Redeemer, Savior, and best friend. Amen.

Mar 16 - *Numbers 6:24-26 "The Lord bless you and keep you; the Lord make his face to shine upon you, and be gracious to you; the Lord lift up his countenance upon you, and give you peace."*

Last night when I was putting my daughter to bed, I sang a song with these words in it.

I wasn't sure I remembered all of them correctly so when I was done tucking her in I came to look it up on the computer. It is always such a nice surprise when I find that a song I sing in my heart is based on a scripture. The passage right before this blessing talks about the Nazirites setting themselves apart for the Lord; to be holy unto him.

As I read all the things they did to be holy in the sight of the Lord I asked myself this: How do I set myself apart to be holy unto him?

Through the sacrifice of Jesus, the Lamb of God, we have been given the gift of forgiveness. It is because of this that we can be holy in the sight of the Lord. Do I blend in to the world around me or am I different? Do people who don't know me ever wonder what is different about me?

Take time this morning to soak your soul in this blessing of old. When we are filled with his grace and blessings, we are different.

Lord,
Thank you, thank you, thank you! Help me make a difference in the world around me by sharing the grace and the peace you have poured out on me. Remind me that I am made holy in your sight. Guide me to live in that holiness and cleanse me once more when I falter. Thank you Lord. Amen.

Mar 17 - *Romans 3:23-24 "since all have sinned and fall short of the glory of God; they are now justified by his grace as a gift, through the redemption that is in Christ Jesus,"*

All night long this verse was with me; not the words, but the reference. I knew it sounded familiar and then when I looked it up I remembered it. This is a favorite verse of a lot of Christians for good reason.

This is not a verse I ever memorized but the message is certainly one worth writing on my heart and in my mind. How much more clearly could the good news have been stated?

We are all broken and tarnished with sin, but because of Christ coming to cleanse us, to redeem us, we are now justified! This is the good news!

May your day be a little more joyful, a little more peaceful, with this knowledge tucked away in your heart. In Luke we are told if we do not praise God, the stones will cry out in praise. Take a few moments today sitting in the late winter light.

See if you can hear the stones, the trees, the snow, nature, and all, crying out in praise to God and let's join in! Praise God and glory in the Highest! You reign now and forever, Hallelujah!

Lord,

Once again I come to you with a blessed humble heart. I cannot imagine what compels you to keep giving us humans more and more grace. I can only see the small comparison in how I love my children. Thank you for your unending love and thank you for the gift of life in you. You have given us amazing grace. Praise to you, this day and all days! Amen.

Mar 18 - *James 1:12 "Blessed is anyone who endures temptation. Such a one has stood the test and will receive the crown of life that the Lord has promised to those who love him."*

As I read this verse there are a few people I know that come to mind immediately. The trials they are facing are daunting to say the least.

I have faced trials myself and know my life is not free of them yet. What I see when I step back from the "fire" is this: God gives us the assistance, guidance, and mercy to get through them. They are not easy, we may come out with scars, but we will persevere if we call on him. He uses friends, family, doctors, therapists, teachers, children, nature... There are endless methods of assistance God uses to sustain us in our trials.

I lift you in prayer today, that you may feel his presence and his love as you face whatever trial you are going through. In his grace, persevere, and then we can praise him and thank him together!

Lord,
Watch over your flock this day. You know our struggles and our trials that we are forging through or running away from. Call us to you and support each of us so we may stand firm and be blessed as we persevere with your help. Thank you for your promises and your constant assistance to reach the goal of being with you in glory. Surround us in your love and peace this day so that we feel strong enough to face the test and finally pass it. Thank you for your message this day. Amen.

Mar 19 - *Psalm 91:1-2 "You who live in the shelter of the Most High, who abide in the shadow of the Almighty, will say to the Lord, 'My refuge and my fortress; my God, in whom I trust.'"*

There are days I feel like my mind never stops whirling. If I were a cartoon, there would be so many conversation bubbles that nothing else would be in the frame.

This morning when I came to my quiet time, it was a challenge to pull myself in and simply be in the presence of the Most High. It is so easy for me to get caught up in the troubles of the world around me and when I do, they threaten to overwhelm me. In his mercy, God led me to this today.

I live in the shelter of the Most High. I can breathe deeply and find deep peace in his shadow. Like sitting under the shade of a beautiful and strong tree, he refreshes me.

The world around me can threaten to drag me down but he is my fortress, and he shelters me, keeping me safe in his presence. I lift the people I love, the sorrows of my heart, and the brokenness of the world to the Lord. I rejoice because he is the Almighty.

All are welcome in the fortress of the Lord, come abide in his loving and gracious shadow. Release your worries and troubles and trust in him.

Lord,
I am humbled by your mercy over and over. I thank you for this passage to remind me that you are, in fact, the Most High. Regardless of all else, you are my Lord, my protection; my shelter in the storms of life. I abide in You. Amen.

Mar 20 - *Hebrews 4:16 "Let us therefore approach the throne of grace with boldness, so that we may receive mercy and find grace to help in time of need."*

The verses before this talk about Jesus being tempted; he does sympathize with us in our weakness.

I picture myself in front of the throne. When I come to confess my sin I come in humility, with sorrow in my heart. When I see myself I am on my knees with my face down, tears streaming down my cheeks unable to face the King of kings, knowing I failed once again.

In my brokenness, in my humility, in my remorse, I do have the confidence to come without hesitation, without delay. I know beyond a shadow of doubt that when I come, he gives me mercy and grace in abundance that I cannot fathom. He bathes me in his love and forgiveness until I shine like the sun.

I am often left speechless in these times and this morning as I picture this scene, I have no words to describe how I feel in God's amazing grace.

Lord,
You overwhelm my senses. No matter how I try to embrace and accept without question all that you give me, I am consistently astounded. Thank you seems so small a gesture to give back so I give you my life in return for all you give me. I am yours; use me as you will. Help me to remember that you are always there, at the throne of grace to accept me, to heal me, to cleanse me and help me start anew. Wow. You are amazing... Amen.

Mar 21 - *Philippians 2:4-5 "Let each of you look not to your own interests, but to the interests of others. Let the same mind be in you that was in Christ Jesus."*

This morning we are getting ready to head up to the mountains for a day of play in the snow.

I have not skied in several years and I am looking forward to it. There is a part of me that would rather stay home, not deal with the traffic and the chaos of checking my daughter in at ski school. Since my son is too young to ski at the area we are going to, he and my husband will go tubing in the morning and then I will switch with my husband in the afternoon. The grump in me says this is all such a hassle. I don't even get to ski with my husband or my kids today. Poor me.

I choose this day to be a blessing rather than sit in the darkness and gloom of pouting. As we drive I pray for those on the road with us. As I ski down the slopes I give thanks for the beauty and the stillness that surround me. As I spend time with my family this afternoon, I share in the joy of their experiences this day.

Today my heart is filled with the joy and peace that only he can give. I will share this heart of joy and peace with my family so they find joy and peace in this day as well. I love as he loves. In this way, I strive to be of the same mind as Christ.

Lord,
I lift my heart into your hands. Fill me with love, peace, kindness, self-control, patience, goodness, generosity, faithfulness, and gentleness. I want to be like you. Amen.

Mar 22 - *Psalm 113:2-3 "Blessed be the name of the Lord from this time on and forevermore. From the rising of the sun to its setting the name of the Lord is to be praised."*

The seasons change from winter to spring and life is ready to spring forth.

There are blessings in all moments of life and because the God of the Universe sends these I praise his name from morning until night. The trees bud and flowers bloom. The grass grows green and animals birth their young. All these things are because of the creator and I praise him.

Of course, I am human and there are times it is much harder to sing praises but if I can step back, open my heart and my eyes to him, the praises come without ceasing no matter what chaos may be happening in my world.

This is the day the Lord has made. He makes each day and searches for us, listens for us to respond to him in praise. Join me today in singing songs of praise and thanksgiving for all the good God has done and will do!

Lord,
Thank you for the sunrise, thank you for my growing children, thank you for spring and a new season of life coming forth.
Above all that, I know you are the one orchestrating it all. You are the maestro, directing all things to glorify your kingdom. Thank you for letting me be part of it.
Open my ears, my eyes, and my heart today so that I hear, see and feel you in all I do. I lift my voice in praise and thanksgiving to you, my Almighty Lord, Sovereign King: Abba. I love you! Amen.

Mar 23 - *Isaiah 30:21 "And when you turn to the right or when you turn to the left, your ears shall hear a word behind you, saying, 'This is the way; walk in it.'"*

Have you ever been going somewhere, had a map and yet you got completely lost?

I really like to use maps and directions when I am going somewhere new but as good as the internet map sites are they are not perfect and not always up to date.

There have been a couple of times when I followed the map and eventually realized I could not find the place I was looking for so I called for help. They graciously "walked" me the rest of the way to my destination. Step by step they told me what to look for and which way to go.

As I think about how the Spirit works it is much like this. There are times I think I have a good map and good directions in life and all of a sudden I am lost. God is gracious. When we call out to him for guidance, he is faithful. If we quietly listen, staying focused on his guidance, he will not let us down. He guides us step by step, until we reach our destination.

We don't need a cell phone or Wi-Fi for his guidance...prayer works just great!

Lord,

Words escape me when I come to you this morning but you know my heart and your Spirit intercedes for me. Open our ears and close our mouths so that we may hear the guidance you so lovingly give to us. Thank you gentle Shepherd. Amen.

Mar 24 - *Mark 6:31-32 "He said to them, 'Come away to a deserted place all by yourselves and rest a while.' For many were coming and going, and they had no leisure even to eat."*

Wow, how I needed to read this passage.

I have written many times about how much I appreciate my quiet time in the morning. Spending time alone with the Lord is invaluable to me.

This morning my young son walked into my room just moments before my alarm went off and has been awake ever since. When he came in, I gently guided him back to bed and then a few minutes later he startled me while I was praying. I put him back again and turned on his music to give him something to listen to and hopefully lull him back to sleep; it was only 5:20! Now 30 minutes later I sit at the computer and hear him playing in his room.

My husband is up early because we have a lot of snow on the ground so getting to work takes longer. From this point on, there is no quiet or rest.

With the sermon on Sunday encouraging me to pursue spiritual disciplines and this scripture this morning, I am encouraged to press on. Will you choose one to pursue? Will it be meditation, prayer, or fasting? Do you feel called to study, worship, or celebrate? I long for a bit of solitude... maybe tomorrow.

Lord,
Thank you for the blessings of family and children. Thank you for the moisture in the snow we received. Thank you for the much needed rest. Help me see the love and joy in this day and in all days. Amen.

Mar 25 - *John 6:33 "For the bread of God is that which comes down from heaven and gives life to the world."*

Life giving food... I need more of that.
Just yesterday, I read another article in a magazine about how fast food clogs up parts of our brains and bodies creating blockages that cause long term damage. The more of that food we eat, the more our bodies cannot manage and we become diseased over time.
I struggle to eat healthy food. I try to buy vegetables and fruit, I research and shop for the best grains and the least processed foods. There is so much information out there I do not know what is really true sometimes.
The bread that feeds our souls is just like this. There is junk food, fast food, and healthy food for our souls. It is tempting and easy to take in the fast food and the junk food and sometimes it is hard to decipher what is really healthy. This verse brings clarity to the mystery.
The bread of God gives life. Any other bread we take in might taste good but over time it brings disease to our souls. His Spirit guides us if we listen so that we can be sure to partake of life giving bread and leave the other options alone. Let us pray!

Lord,
I cannot stop thanking and praising you for you are awesome. Thank you for life, thank you for life giving food. Through your Son and your Spirit, you continue to offer life, health, and well-being. Help us pass up the fast food and come straight to you for life giving bread. It is only in you that we find it and find true life. Amen.

Mar 26 - *John 6:27 "Do not work for food that perishes, but for the food that endures for eternal life, which the Son of Man will give you. For it is on him that God the Father has set his seal."*

I don't know how many times I end up throwing leftovers away. We do our best to eat them at this house and sometimes we succeed but there are too many occasions where I am putting food down the disposal because it is spoiled. Bananas get made into banana bread frequently too so that I can use up the blackening ones without wasting those. The list goes on and on. This verse is a reminder to me today and hopefully going forward every time I am cooking, eating, or cleaning out the fridge. Things of this earth are all perishable.

I need to make the Word of God, my daily spiritual food, my number one priority. That is the only food that stays with me, feeds me, nourishes me, and protects me from disease in the eternal realms.

May these words of Jesus bring you the spiritual food that you need.

Lord,
Thank you for putting things in the proper perspective once again. I see all your creation and all you do. I know there is more than just this planet I live on for now. Keep my eyes on the eternal prize so that I may not worry about the perishable, temporary things in this life. Help me be focused on my eternal existence and living in that glory, bringing as many loved ones as I can with me. Amen.

Mar 27 - *Proverbs 3:6 "In all your ways acknowledge him, and he will make straight your paths."*

There are several people I know that are searching for the path God has set before them. They are in my prayers because I know how hard it can be to find the path.

At times it seems like the path has not been traveled in a long time. It is grown over with grasses and bushes, almost completely hidden by trees and undergrowth.

This morning I hear something new in this verse. If we acknowledge him in everything we do, everything we say, and all we are, our view of him becomes so much clearer. As we seek to serve him the path begins to open up without so many brambles in the way. If we acknowledge him when we nourish our bodies at meals, while we sit in traffic driving to work, running busy errands, and shopping for groceries his presence is clear to us. As we seek to live in him and focus on him, the distractions and barriers that were so insurmountable become less and less until the path before us is unmistakable.

It sounds so easy, doesn't it? It is by the grace of God that we get to try over and over again. Start today.

Start again tomorrow and then again the next day to acknowledge him in all your ways, he will guide you.

Lord,
You are my heart's desire but the world distracts me. I pray that you strengthen me and all those reading this so that we do acknowledge you in all our ways. I know it is the only way. Today I ask you to show me your way again. Amen.

Mar 28 - *1 Peter 5:8-9 "Discipline yourselves, keep alert. Like a roaring lion your adversary the devil prowls around, looking for someone to devour. Resist him, steadfast in your faith, for you know that your brothers and sisters in all the world are undergoing the same kinds of suffering."*

If I were to go on safari I would learn all I could about the area to be visited and how to protect myself and those I love against the predators that live there. The lion has no regard for its victim; it only wants to feed its seemingly insatiable appetite.
The devil is just like this - he has no regard for us and he will devour us if given the chance.
Our defense is simple. Gain knowledge in the word; grow in faith through this knowledge and be diligent in prayer. Learn all we can to defend against the predator in this world. Stay alert as if there were a lion prowling in your home, in your neighborhood, because there is. Praise God for his love and protection. Through him we can protect ourselves and then in the end defeat the lion.

Lord,
Without your word and Spirit to guide us we would be lost for sure. You give us what we need to fight and win. Thank you. Help us pick up our weapons and be ready. We pray for your protection and guidance for ourselves and all those suffering throughout this world on this day. Amen.

Mar 29 - *Revelation 3:19-20 "I reprove and discipline those whom I love. Be earnest, therefore, and repent. Listen! I am standing at the door, knocking; if you hear my voice and open the door, I will come in to you and eat with you, and you with me."*

Discipline is not an easy thing for the parent or the child. Children feel like you are being mean and sometimes, as a parent, when discipline is handed down it makes the parent suffer as well. Parents discipline their children because they love them and they want their children to be the best they can be. This is just what God wants for us. It is tiring to discipline for the same behaviors over and over again. Can you imagine how God feels with us and our lack of discipline as his children? It must be exasperating!

Even with all that, he knocks and waits to be invited in to dine and feast with us. Let him in. Dine with him and receive his love and discipline so that we may become better, stronger, and more like him to serve this world until he comes again.

Lord,

Thank you for freedom. We often choose the wrong path and you guide us back to yours in spite of us. The phrase "thy rod and thy staff, they comfort me" comes to mind as that is sometimes how you discipline and guide. Thank you for your merciful guidance and everlasting love. Let us learn from your rebuke, let us change from your discipline. Come, Lord Jesus, come. Amen.

Mar 30 - *Matthew 5:6 "Blessed are those who hunger and thirst for righteousness, for they will be filled."*

I cannot imagine what true physical hunger or thirst must be like, nor would I like to.

We are so very blessed in the abundance of our society to be able to turn on a faucet and be granted a drink of clean water. We open the pantry or run to the nearby store and our hunger is satisfied.

Yesterday I had some dental work done and for a little while afterwards, I could not successfully drink or eat anything due to the numbness in my mouth. The smell of popcorn wafting through my house made my stomach growl but I needed to wait. Spiritual hunger and thirst are just as real and there are no barriers as to who can receive nourishment.

There is such great promise in this verse and the other verses of the Sermon on the Mount. God promises that if we seek righteousness, we receive it. We don't even have to go to the pantry or the grocery store.

When I sit in the quietness of the Lord, I am filled with his presence and his love. I am filled and renewed by his Spirit.

I rejoice in the day I will be filled and never be emptied again. Until then, I continue to hunger and thirst and to be thankful for the filling up that only he can provide.

Lord,
Thank you for the promises in your word. Your word is truth and truth does set us free. Turn our hearts to you as we realize our hunger can only be satisfied through your love and mercy. Fill us up once again Lord. Thank you! Amen.

Mar 31 - *Ezekiel 37:3-4 "He said to me, 'Mortal, can these bones live?' I answered, 'O Lord God, you know.' Then he said to me, 'Prophesy to these bones, and say to them: O dry bones, hear the word of the Lord.'"*

This passage has been lurking in my mind for weeks now and today it has come to the front.

The story of the valley of dry bones is an allegory about Israel and their lost hope. This is so true for our world today.

As I look back over my life so far, I have definitely been these dry bones with no spirit and no hope. When the breath of God, the Spirit, is in them once more, they come to life.

I am speechless once more at how deeply this speaks to me. When I had shut out the Spirit, closed out God, my life was like dry bones lying in a desert. Once I allowed the Spirit to move in me again, I had green pastures, a running stream, deep clean air in my lungs, I was alive!

Join me in this life; ask the Spirit to move in you once more! Let's dance!

Lord of the dance,
Bring our dry bones out of the desert, bring us to life so we can dance in your light, praise your holy name, sing and make a joyful noise to glorify your name forever! Make us radiant with your love and joy so that those around us are compelled to search for that love and joy in their lives too. Draw your Spirit to life in us so that we can no longer sleep away our lives but live fully in you, I ask this through our Redeemer, Jesus Christ. Amen.

Apr 1 - *Hebrews 12:28 "Therefore, since we are receiving a kingdom that cannot be shaken, let us give thanks, by which we offer to God an acceptable worship with reverence and awe"*

When I am being shaken, it is not easy to be filled with reverence and awe. It is much easier for me to call out to him asking for the shaking to stop. His shaking is a purifying process and without it, I would not be made into the new creation.

Picture an archaeologist with a sifter. He gently pours the dirt and artifacts into the sifter and sifts the waste to reveal treasure. This is how we are shaken.

It can feel like our whole world is rocking but in reality the gentleness of the Lord keeps us safe and we are cleansed, allowing the treasure he created us to be to break forth. As we come through this process, his kingdom is revealed in new ways and though we are shaken, his kingdom will remain forever. Because we have been shaken, cleansed and redeemed, we can bound forth into his holy kingdom, thanks be to God!

Lord,
Sometimes it feels like a wild ride but I know you have me in your gentle hands. Thank you for loving us enough to shake the waste and dirt away and allowing us to come into your kingdom renewed and shining as you created us to shine. I lift your name in praise even as the shaking continues here; there is no shaking in your holy kingdom. You and your kingdom remain constant forever and ever. Amen.

Apr 2 - *Matthew 16:18 "And I tell you, you are Peter, and on this rock I will build my church, and the gates of Hades will not prevail against it."*

The hymn "Rock of Ages" is going through my head this morning and it brought to mind this Bible passage.
Peter, the disciple who denies the Lord three times before his crucifixion, is the rock the church is built on. The Bible is full of stories of fallible people stepping up, listening to the Lord, starting again after falling down, and keeping the faith. No one, not one, is without sin.
Come to the seat of the Lord with me this morning. I confess my downfalls and ask to start fresh again. I am certainly not Peter, but Peter was human, just as I am. Just as Peter was forgiven so am I; so are you.
Praise to our Redeemer!

Lord,
Thank you for the words of a beautiful hymn in my heart this morning. I know you are the Rock of ages and you have given all so that I can come to you this morning, confess my sins, cleanse my soul, and begin fresh in building your kingdom. Hades will not overcome it, thank you Jesus! We humans taint and tarnish everything we touch; it is only through you that things can shine like the sun. Bless all I do this day and use it to your glory. Amen.

Apr 3 - *Philippians 3:1 "Finally, my brothers and sisters, rejoice in the Lord. To write the same things to you is not troublesome to me, and for you it is a safeguard."*

Most of us require hearing something more than once to instill it into our brains. I have heard it said (a few times) that people need to hear things or read things four times to lock it into their memory banks.

The Bible is written to help us remember the important things. There are things that are mentioned countless times like pray, rejoice, worship. Here Paul reminds the Philippians to rejoice in the Lord.

Finally... after everything is said and done, rejoice in the Lord. Finally, no matter what else has happened, rejoice in the Lord. The call to rejoice is written so many times in the Bible and Paul is one that reminds us of it several times in his letters. God knows how important this is so he reminds us often to do it. When I came to this verse this morning I realized if I needed to hear it again it was likely some of you did too.

Let me remind us all to rejoice in the Lord. In all things rejoice in the Lord. Sing songs of praise and play music, lift your hearts and voices in shouts of praise to the Lord!

Lord,
As the sun peeks over the horizon my soul sings a song of praise to you. You create every breath in my lungs, the stars and the moon, the birds that sing morning songs, and you create the joy in my heart that causes me to sing. Help me make this day a day of rejoicing, for this is a day you have made and we are called to rejoice! Amen.

Apr 4 - *Psalm 136:1-3 "O give thanks to the Lord, for he is good, for his steadfast love endures forever. O give thanks to the God of gods, for his steadfast love endures forever. O give thanks to the Lord of lords, for his steadfast love endures forever."*

As I was tucking my little boy back into bed at 4:58 this morning wishing I was still asleep, hoping I would go back to sleep, I thought how blessed I am to have children.
I am blessed that they feel comfortable enough to wake me whenever they need me. Okay, I wish they wouldn't need to wake me up... ever. I treasure my sleep. It is precious to me. That said - my children are more precious to me. I will always love my children through thick and through thin, no matter what. There is nothing I wouldn't do for them.
How much more does God love his children? Bask in the knowledge and the treasure that God loves us and his love endures *forever*! Hallelujah!

Lord,
You are my all and all. You are the God of all gods, Lord of all lords. It is easy to be distracted by other gods and lords but you have told us to worship no other god. Keep my eyes focused on you, the one true God, and let my heart, my actions, my soul praise and thank you this day! Amen.

Apr 5 - *Psalm 150:6 "Let everything that breathes praise the Lord! Praise the Lord!"*

I love watching the sun come up over the horizon. Even as I type that I am astonished at my own words.
I used to relish sleeping in and it would take me a couple of hours to really wake up and be present to the day and there are still moments I can see the luxury of sleeping in. However, there is something about the freshness of the morning that cannot be replaced.
The birds start singing their songs; the sun brings gentle light to the sky and gradually brightens to gleaming gold pouring out over the landscape. The air is crisp and cool after a soothing night of rest. I can almost hear the grass and trees stretching their voices of praise to God for another day of life. As spring continues to unfold its wings the buds of the flowers and the buds on the trees unfold their petals and leaves in glory, singing songs of praise and honor to their Creator.
On this glorious spring day, I encourage us to stretch and unfold our hearts to our Creator as well. Listen to the earth singing and join in your own song of praise for God is great and with our breath we are called to lift praises to him!

Lord,
When I look at all of your creation I cannot help but lift my voice in praise to you. Your world, the universe and all things beyond are so glorious. Thank you for the gift of life and the gift of your love. I praise your name this day for all you have done and all you will do. Amen.

Apr 6 - *Genesis 6:6-7 "The Lord was sorry that he had made humankind on the earth, and it grieved him to his heart. So the Lord said, 'I will blot out from the earth the human beings I have created – people together with animals and creeping things and birds of the air, for I am sorry that I have made them.'"*

Yesterday in home school we were studying Noah's ark.
We went outside to measure how long the ark was and even though it was HUGE, it seems amazing that all those animals and the family of Noah would be on that ark for a year.
As I thought more about this story I wonder how grieved God is now at man on earth. Surely there have been many times since the flood that God wishes he had not made that promise to Noah.
We are a fallen race and we fill his heart with pain still.
I am so humbled and grateful that we have the gift of Jesus to mend the brokenness in our relationship with God. We can all go into today filled with peace and joy because of the love of God, his grace and his forgiveness.

Lord,
Forgive me for the grief and sadness I cause you. Thank you for sparing the earth those many years ago and allowing mankind and all your creatures to thrive once again; to have another chance. You are the God of second chances, the God of grace. Move me to treat your creation with the respect and awe that it deserves. Make this earth and the beings living here draw closer to you and your love so we may live in harmony together once more. Amen.

Apr 7 - *Psalm 43: 3-4 "O send out your light and your truth; let them lead me; let them bring me to your holy hill and to your dwelling. Then I will go to the altar of God, to God my exceeding joy; and I will praise you with the harp, Oh God, my God."*

There is something comforting about a light in the distance when you are traveling in darkness.

I remember when I was a child, when we would drive into the mountains in the dusk and then darkness. I would search the mountainside for lights.

There were little dots of light that indicated a home here and there so I knew we were not alone. I knew we could go toward that light for help if we needed it.

Finally I would see the one light that grew bigger as we came closer and then we had arrived at Grandma and Grandpa's house!

David is calling for God to send his light and rescue him from the darkness of his enemies.

David knew that he could call out and God would come. He would rescue him with light and truth. God still listens for us to call out to him. His light and truth are his guides for us. When we follow the guide to his altar, we are in the presence of our soul's greatest joy!

Celebrate and rejoice for the Lord, our God is our refuge and our help in all times.

Lord,
Thank you for this passage to calm my spirit and remind me one more time to rest in the comfort of your light and truth. I come to you with praise and thanksgiving because you have given all for me. Thank you for never giving up on us. Amen.

Apr 8 - *John 1:14, 16 "And the Word became flesh and lived among us, and we have seen his glory, the glory as of a father's only son, full of grace and truth. From his fullness we have all received, grace upon grace."*

This morning when I read this passage I was struck by these verses. The Word, the very thing I seek each morning, lives within me.
His Spirit, My Lord and Redeemer, is the Word.
The words in this beautiful book I read each day lead to the true Word. They all point to the God of Moses and Abraham and they all point to the Messiah, Jesus Christ. I asked myself why I need this book if I have Jesus in my heart. I know the message but I am human and I need daily reminders to keep me from falling away from his love.
So here is a story of love and grace.
I heard of a man who chooses homelessness so he is not subjected to his wife's drug addiction. He works full time so he can provide a home and nourishment for her but does not live there and cannot afford to live anywhere else. He sacrifices out of love and grace. We do not know anyone else's story, what we know is that everyone has a story. God loves them despite and because of it. So should we.
Reach out in grace and mercy today. Receive the grace and mercy offered to you today. This will change our world.

Lord,
May your truth and grace fill us to overflowing. As we are filled inspire us to share with others so that all people receive this grace upon grace. You are God of abundance. Thank you for all you have given and keep giving. Amen.

Apr 9 - *Matthew 14:29-30 "He said, 'Come.' So Peter got out of the boat, started walking on the water, and came toward Jesus. But when he noticed the strong wind, he became frightened, and began to sink, he cried out, 'Lord, save me!'"*

The saying "Keep your eye on the prize" is running through my head.

This story came to me last night as I was doing some prep work for homeschooling. When I read this passage I could not help but come back to these verses.

Peter calls to Jesus and then on Jesus' command he climbs out of the boat and starts walking. I imagine his eyes intently focused on Jesus and for a moment all trust and faith are in him. Then the wind and the storm around him distract him and he loses his step. He looks around and remembers the waves and wind that had tossed him around all night and he begins to sink. He calls out and Jesus rescues him.

How often does this happen to us? We struggle to keep distractions at bay and keep our eyes focused on God. He is there to rescue us whenever we call out to him. We simply turn our focus toward him again and he takes our hand.

Do not turn back, turn toward the Lord.

Lord,
Thank you for always being there ready to grasp our hand when we call out to you. Help us keep our focus on you, walking toward you in faith, trusting in you. When we are distracted, help us turn toward you again so we continue to walk a little closer to you each day. Amen.

Apr 10 - *Hebrews 11:6 "And without faith it is impossible to please God, for whoever would approach him must believe that he exists and that he rewards those who seek him."*

This brings me back to my childhood and a song I sang not realizing it was a Bible verse.

When I read the verse this morning the word earnestly jumped out at me. The song I know does not use the word earnestly in it. Do I truly seek him in earnest?

As I sat trying to do my devotion this morning, I found myself much more into my head than my heart and as much as I tried to get out of my head it stayed in the way. I only take satisfaction in the fact that I stayed with it. It is tempting for me to say "this isn't working, I will just go back to bed" but I know that even when I struggle through my quiet time, I receive blessings. It is in those times I must earnestly seek him.

He is always there, easy to believe in. He desires to be sought with our whole heart, in earnest. Go into your day and earnestly seek him, I know you will find him and be rewarded.

Lord,

Thank you for perseverance. You never give up on me and I never give up on you. I seek you with all my heart, all my soul, and all my being until I am blessed to see your face and stand in your glory. Strengthen my heart on days that my head, my busy world, and my distractions get in the way of my heart searching for you. You are my all and all. In all things I find you when I seek. Amen.

Apr 11 - *1 Corinthians 13:3 "If I give away all my possessions, and if I hand over my body so that I may boast, but do not have love, I gain nothing."*

I like to think I am not a materialistic person.
I do not cling to items and having things does not make me feel happier. It is easy for me to say that because I have so much. There are two cars in my two car garage and a pantry full of food in my kitchen. I have a beautiful home and a big yard for the kids to play in. There is a great garden for growing produce in the summer and toys are never ending. Our closets are full as are the chests of drawers. Water and electricity flow without fail.
If I were asked to give up all my possessions in the name of love, would I hesitate and give reasons beyond reasons why I shouldn't?
My kids need a ... We can't be healthy without... In Colorado you need... I am not feeling called to give away all my possessions and I don't believe most people are. I do think we need to look at things with a different view.
Our possessions do not give us love; they do not give us the ability to love. Love transcends the tangible world. Let go of things, even yourself, and turn them all over to the Lord so that he may in turn fill you with a love beyond anything you can imagine. When we let go, we gain much.

Lord,
As I sort through things and give away stuff, remind me to make room for more love. Clear away the clutter and possessions that I cling to so that I may hold on to you more deeply and then share your love more fully. Amen.

Apr 12 - *Philippians 4:6-7 "Do not worry about anything, but in everything by prayer and supplication with thanksgiving let your requests be made known to God. And the peace of God, which surpasses all understanding, will guard your hearts and your minds in Christ Jesus."*

Oh, if I had only taken the time to read this passage this morning, maybe my morning would have been much calmer and smoother. This is a day where everything that could weigh on my shoulders, real and imagined, has been weighing heavily.
I know we all have days like this and a passage like this is, indeed, a balm to soothe the sin-sick soul. Take a moment with me today and turn over your worries and anxieties, take all those things that cause stress and lay them at the feet of Jesus.
Feel the peace of God, promised to guard our hearts and minds, consume all the negative energy in us and replace it with restful positive relaxing peace.

Lord,
You know the tension that consumes me this day. You know the worries and troubles of my heart. I lay all these things at your feet and commit them to your care. Release them from me so I may go through the rest of this day in peace and enabled to serve you to the betterment of your kingdom. Thank you, Jesus, for your peace and love forever. Amen.

Apr 13 - *Psalm 34:22 "The Lord redeems the life of his servants; none of those who take refuge in him will be condemned."*

Yesterday morning the sky was gray and a fog was looming in the air.
I was looking forward to sunshine and warmth but trying to find the joy in the moisture that the fog and coolness was bringing our grass. Fog enveloped the trees and the houses. It closed around us like a blanket.
I resigned myself to the fact that we would have another gray and cold day. I don't know when it happened because I was busy and not paying attention but the clouds lifted and the sun came out. The kids were playing outside with water and sand by the end of the day.
Spring arrived! This is how I feel when I revel in the refuge and redemption of the Lord. I take refuge in him and I am enveloped in his arms of love, grace, and forgiveness. When I have been restored I go out into the world filled with light and life through him. As spring comes out in all of its glory, let us each take hold of the newness of life that is granted to us. Let spring flowers like crocuses and tulips be reminders to us.
Let the singing birds and the budding trees call to our hearts...
Life is new again!

Lord,
Thank you for your sacrifice and your grace. I praise you today for all the blessings you give us. Through your death and resurrection we have all been given new life. Guide me today as I seek to honor the life you have given me in everything I do.
Amen.

Apr 14 - *Isaiah 55:7 "Let the wicked forsake their way, and the unrighteous their thoughts; let them return to the Lord, that he may have mercy on them, and to our God, for he will abundantly pardon"*

When I was a child I was hesitant of revolving doors. I had little experience with them and it made me nervous to jump in before it was too late.

Escalators had a similar effect. I had to jump on at just the right time or wait and try again. If I didn't do it just right I could get hurt! Once I got the hang of it, I had fun riding up and down, over and over again. The purpose of revolving doors and escalators is to assist people in getting where they are going, not a fun ride to repeat continuously.

Sometimes it feels like repentance, turning away from sin and toward God, is a revolving door. I go through it into the blessed presence and grace of God only to continue around and end up back outside in the darkness of the world. Each day, I jump into the roundabout again, turn toward the Lord and then before I know it, I have turned away to my own ways once more.

The Lord is gracious and he has mercy unending. He abundantly pardons when we turn to him.

Take my hand, we can go in together!

Lord,
Each time I turn to you, I come a little closer and stay a little longer. Thank you for receiving us all, over and over again. Cleanse our sins this morning so we can start this new day fresh and renewed through your mercy, I pray in Jesus name, my Redeemer and my friend. Amen.

Apr 15 - *Hebrews 3:12-13 "Take care, brothers and sisters, that none of you may have an evil, unbelieving heart that turns away from the living God. But exhort one another every day, as long as it is called 'today' so that none of you may be hardened by the deceitfulness of sin."*

I wake up this morning surprised again.
The forecast was for wind and a trace of snow. We had the wind alright but we have a couple of inches of snow. The other surprise was this Scripture.
Every day God surprises me with his word. I ask for a verse or two and every day I get something so appropriate. I am amazed. If you feel blocked from God, like he has stepped away, I tell you he has not moved. God is always there, ***always***.
He waits, he calls, and then when you turn and soften your heart to him he embraces you with love and grace. Cast away the demons and sludge that pull you away from God. Call on the name of the Lord. Sin is deceitful. Do not listen to the lies, they will destroy you.
God is faithful; he saves you if you only ask.

Lord,
Let these words bring encouragement to someone today. You are sovereign and I trust you will use me as you need to. Spread your word through me in any way, I want to do your will every moment, every day. Keep us safe from the deceit of sin, it is powerful, but you are all powerful. I praise you and thank you, this day, for all you do and for the surprises of love you show me so often. Amen.

Apr 16 - *John 6:12-13 "When they were satisfied, he told his disciples, 'Gather up the fragments left over, so that nothing may be lost.' So they gathered them up, and from the fragments of the five barley loaves, left by those who had eaten, they filled twelve baskets."*

Leftovers...

I know people who refuse to eat leftovers at all and I know I am not alone in finding something hidden in the back of the fridge that needs to be thrown out. Sometimes there is just a little bit left, a few bites not worth saving.

I find Jesus' words interesting. Gather the fragments so nothing may be lost. It makes me wonder what else we toss aside as worthless that he would want us to gather. What talent or skill do we have that we discount never even considering it of value? Who do we toss aside when in reality they are precious creations of God?

What situations do we sweep under the rug or into the trash that Jesus would have us work on?

As we sit and gaze out into nature that he so lovingly created, let us search our hearts for leftovers that we need to gather up. Search for the fragments that we had tossed away and gather them so that they may not be lost.

Lord,
What beautiful words these are to my soul. As the sun comes up on this day, open my eyes so I may see clearly what I need to gather. Soften my heart so that the fragments you treasure, I also treasure. Guide my gathering, Lord. I don't want to have anything or anyone be lost. Amen.

Apr 17 - *Mark 16:7-8 "But go, tell his disciples and Peter that he is going ahead of you to Galilee; there you will see him, just as he told you. So they went out and fled from the tomb, for terror and amazement had seized them; and they said nothing to anyone, for they were afraid."*

How often have I been like these women?
I receive a clear message, a directive, and because I do not trust myself or the message I run and hide. God wants to use us all to spread his love and his message. Like me, so many turn and quietly slip into the shadows.
The good news in this passage is that the women were not the only people that were given this message. Part of the problem was that women held no status in this time and place. If they had bravely gone to the men and passed along the message would they have been laughed at or scolded for being silly?
The bigger question of the day is: Should we not be willing to be laughed at or scolded in the name of our Savior?
Be brave, brush the fear away from yourself, and trust in the Lord to use you well.

Lord,
Thank you for not letting the story end here and thank you for reminding us that fear will always pull us away from you and your love and guidance. You are all knowing and almighty. Help us to trust in your path for us, to trust that we will feel your love more and more each day as you use us to spread your love to the world. Amen.

Apr 18 - *Ecclesiastes 3:11 "He has made everything suitable for its time; moreover he has put a sense of past and future into their minds, yet they cannot find out what God has done from the beginning to the end."*

It is hard to see the timing in everything... maybe my definition of time is twisted.

We are here for such a short time on earth and yet we make each day seem as if it is the most important. When things do not go the way we want them to, we worry, we stress, we cry to God. If we remember that we are eternal beings, maybe things going bad for a year or two or five would be easier to put into perspective.

God is who created us. He is the one who hung the stars and moon in the sky along with all the planets and then created the largest animal and the smallest leaf!

He is a God of love and beauty, he is creator of all and we are called to sit in awe of him. I am guilty of questioning God and his path for me. Join me in contemplating the timing and the eternity of God.

Lord,

Forgive me for thinking I might ever be able to wrap my mind around you. We like to think we have things under control but we deceive ourselves. Help us to see your hand in this day, this moment in time. Help us see that you are the creator of all and that your creations are suitable in your time. Thank you for giving us this time, this earth, this journey. Guide us on the journey so that we may be led closer and closer to you. Amen.

Apr 19 - *Romans 6: 10-11 "The death he died, he died to sin, once for all; but the life he lives, he lives to God. So you also must consider yourselves dead to sin and alive to God in Christ Jesus."*

Passages that talk about being dead to sin confound me.
In our human nature, living this life on earth, I know I am never going to be completely without sin. It is not possible for us to be sin free but it is completely possible to be free from sin.
Even though we step out of bounds or commit infractions, even though we sin by action or inaction, we are not slaves to our sin. It is in this way that we are free from sin. We call on the name of Jesus to forgive us again and to help us step forward in grace. The Word reminds us that grace is forever and unending.
He has set us free, removed the chains of bondage, and we can step out of darkness into light every day because he died to sin, once for all. He calls us to come out and live with him.
I begin and end each day searching my heart and asking forgiveness for the sins I find with his help. When I do this, it allows me to step out into the light, leaving my chains behind me and living in and for God.
Come be alive in the light and love of God through Jesus, the Christ!

Lord,
It is a brand new day and I give thanks to you for it! Let my heart sing and my feet dance in joy for the love and forgiveness you so freely give. Help me be a light to others and bring your grace and love to them today. Thank you Jesus, thank you for your gift of life! Amen.

Apr 20 - *2 Corinthians 5:20 "So we are ambassadors for Christ, since God is making his appeal through us; we entreat you on behalf of Christ, be reconciled to God."*

After I looked up the word ambassador in the dictionary this verse made so much more sense to me.

I knew (kind of) what an ambassador was but I haven't really needed to know the purpose of an ambassador or what their role really was. The online dictionary's second definition seemed to fit the best; it says an ambassador is "an authorized representative or messenger."

So, as followers of Christ, he is calling us to be his representatives and share his message of reconciliation with others. I know that it is usually counter-productive to shout it out on a street corner or make speeches at the top of our lungs. Most people who try to get the message across that way are looked at strangely or ignored.

We can share our message of reconciliation by living it out in our own hearts and lives. Seek reconciliation in your own heart, and then with those closest to you. As we move into reconciling relationships one by one, the world receives the message and is blessed by it.

Lord,
The message I hear is to love others as you love me. Help me do this. As I love more and hate less, I am being reconciled to you and to others. Heal my old battle scars and build a deeper trust so I can be a true ambassador of your message and your love to my family, friends, and community. Amen.

Apr 21 - *Psalm 30:11-12 "You have turned my mourning into dancing; you have taken off my sackcloth and clothed me with joy, so that my soul may praise you and not be silent. O Lord my God, I will give thanks to you forever."*

These verses express so well how it feels when the clouds of separation from God have lifted.

When our souls are crying out in anguish it is hard to imagine ever dancing or feeling joy again. We experience the darkness, the wailing and mourning people have felt throughout history, the damage we humans have done to our relationship with the Divine. It can seem never ending and overwhelming.

This is not the end of the story though. God redeems us and our relationship with him. He pulls us to our feet and lifts our hearts out of sadness and brokenness into joy and wholeness.

Take off your sackcloth today because you know the happy ending! Dance and sing in joy for the redeeming love of God!

Lord,

Thank you! Praise your Holy and Almighty name! Thank you for bringing us out of the darkness and mourning times into joy and dancing. Thank you for taking sadness and turning it to joy. I give you all honor and glory for the things you have done and will do in this world. Use me as you will in fulfilling your kingdom. Amen.

Apr 22 - *Matthew 8:19-20 "A scribe then approached and said, 'Teacher, I will follow you wherever you go.' And Jesus said to him, 'Foxes have holes, and birds of the air have nests; but the Son of Man has nowhere to lay his head.'"*

I wonder how Jesus' ministry would unfold in the world today. When he traveled this earth he walked and rode in boats because those were the modes of transportation. Would he drive a car, ride city buses, or continue to walk? Where would he sleep? I imagine he spent many a night sleeping under the stars of the desert.

Would he be taken into homes of friends and family, homes of disciples today? Would he receive blessings for his ministry and funds to continue on his path? Would he come and sit in the pews of our churches or be teaching down by the South Platte River?

In my cushy warm house, with my coffee pot brewing and breakfast a fingertip away how can I understand what he and the disciples gave up to serve?

I type my words of encouragement after sitting in my comfortable rocking chair while others are huddled together in a cardboard box on this chilly morning. What do I give for his ministry?

Lord,
Forgive me for my fickle heart. Each person I see is a child of yours; open my ears and my heart to hear how you would have me love them. Help the drop in the ocean that I do to serve help them feel loved. I pray that someday everyone will know they have a home in you. Amen.

Apr 23 - *Hebrews 13:8-9 "Jesus Christ is the same yesterday and today and forever. Do not be carried away by all kinds of strange teachings, for it is well for the heart to be strengthened by grace..."*

A few days ago it was sunny and 60 degrees, this morning I look out my window and see about 3 inches of snow and icy frozen streets. This is Colorado in the springtime.

Who am I kidding? This is Colorado. There is a saying here: "if you don't like the weather, wait a few minutes."

The one constant in this life is change. It seems nothing stays the same. Change can be a good thing. When we allow change in ourselves, we grow. When we embrace change, we learn to be flexible and allow others to grow. The important thing to remember is our foundation.

Regardless of our growth and flexibility there is one thing that remains constant and keeps us grounded. Jesus and his teachings, from the beginning to the end, have remained constant. As we reach out to others and embrace change and growth, let us keep our feet firmly on the teachings of Jesus, the Christ.

Love God, love one another, and enjoy the changing world around us for the wild ride that it can be.

Lord,
I am simply an extension of you. You created me and I am here to serve you with my life. Help me not lose track of you, my Rock and my Redeemer, as I seek to serve. Thank you for your steadfast love and constant presence guiding and teaching even today. Open our ears to hear you. Amen.

Apr 24 - *2 Corinthians 12:8-9 "Three times I appealed to the Lord about this, that it would leave me, but he said to me, 'My grace is sufficient for you, for power is made perfect in weakness'. So, I will boast all the more gladly of my weaknesses, so that the power of Christ may dwell in me."*

Paul talks about his struggles, the things he has been through while in service to the Lord. It would be interesting to truly understand the word "boast" because I suspect it does not mean what our English word does.

Even so, there will never be a trial that I go through, never a temptation or a suffering that can compare with what Jesus went through. When I feel down-trodden, unappreciated, broken, I need to come back to this passage.

It is in weakness, in brokenness, that we call on the Lord. It is easy to rely on our own strength when life is grand but when things fall apart, we realize we need God and his power to survive. If you are suffering, call on the Lord.

If you are joyful and life is good, give glory to the Lord.

It is only through his power and grace that we live.

Lord,

Thank you for perspective. I take my burdens, small as they are and lay them at your feet. I know I cannot manage them by myself, You know I try. Free my soul from the brokenness these things make me feel so that I can spend my day praising your name and glorifying your kingdom. That is why you created me after all. Thank you for your grace and love, thank you for reminding me you are all powerful, forever reigning in Glory. Amen.

Apr 25 - *Psalm 139:1-2 "O Lord, you have searched me and known me. You know when I sit down and when I rise up; you discern my thoughts from far away."*

I picture a master woodworker or stone carver.
They know before they begin what their creation will be. They pick a seemingly random piece of wood or rock and see beyond what we see; they see what it is on the inside. They carefully hew and chisel and then softly sand it to smooth polished beauty. The difference is this; they may see a mar or blemish and they work around it if possible. They may have to completely abandon that piece and start again.
God knows us beyond anything we can imagine. He created us exactly how he needed us to be so of course, he has searched and known us. He placed his breath and spirit within us so of course he knows when we sit and rise, because he is with us always.
He is omnipotent and ever present and as our thoughts drift toward fruition he has already seen them and is aware of them. There is nothing he does not know or see and yet, he loves us. He loves me and he loves you.

Lord,
I come to you in humble praise this morning. I find comfort in these verses and I hope others do too. I know there are times we wish we could hide but those are the times we need you most. Help us realize this truth of your presence and knowledge and open our hearts to embrace your presence and knowledge. You abide with us, help us abide with you. Amen.

Apr 26 – *1 John 2:9-10 "Whoever says, 'I am in the light,' while hating a brother or sister, is still in the darkness. Whoever loves a brother or sister lives in the light, and in such a person there is no cause for stumbling."*

Darkness lurks in the corners or wherever it is allowed and looks for the opportunity to overtake the light.

We go through our days on auto-pilot most of the time and life seems to go at its pace without a lot of input from us. We don't even see the darkness looming. Hate seeps in slowly like an unseen cloud until it blocks the sun completely.

It is important to consciously walk in the light because when something happens that derails us a bit, darkness swoops in and throw us into trial if given the chance.

Release the grudges, the judgments, and other negative things that fester in your souls. Let God pour light into your whole being so that you may be in the light fully and wholly.

When we are in the light, we can see clearly and also be a beacon of light for others.

Lord,
Shine your light in me this day. Take away any darkness that is lurking in me so that I can truly be in the light. Bring your divine love to a new, deeper level in me so that I may share that love and light with others. Shine your light in me so that I may see your path clearly and stay true. Amen.

Apr 27 - *Genesis 28:16 "Then Jacob woke from his sleep and said, 'Surely the Lord is in this place – and I did not know it!'"*

Jacob ran away from his brother after stealing his birth right and he lay down with a rock as a pillow. After dreaming about a ladder from earth to heaven with angels going up and down it and hearing the voice of God, this is his response.
I have not dreamed of a ladder from heaven but I do have dreams that make me want to proclaim that the Lord was in this place! I wake up with a song or a scripture in my heart that is unexplainable other than the Lord putting it there. I love to wake up feeling the presence of the Lord with me right then or knowing he was with me while I slept.
The thing I so easily forget is that he is always with me. How often do I go through my days thinking I am awake but in reality I am asleep to the presence of God? Our God is ever present; he knows no bounds and is wherever we are.
Whether we are using a rock as a pillow in the wilderness or snuggled up tight in our warm covers, he is there. Whether we work in an office building or in our homes, he is there. Hallelujah!

Lord,
You promise to be with us wherever we go and this passage in Genesis is only one of many reminding us of that. Do not let us sleep any longer. Wake us up so we are fully aware of you in our midst and let us sing praise to you for your faithfulness and unending love. Thank you for the comfort of your presence. Amen.

Apr 28 - *Matthew 6:26-27 "Look at the birds of the air; they neither sow nor reap nor gather into barns, and yet your heavenly Father feeds them. Are you not of more value than they? And can any of you by worrying add a single hour to your span of life?"*

God takes care of his creation. The flowers bloom, the animals are fed and given what they need to thrive, and God takes care of us. This thought soothes me.

I know God will take care of me because he always has. The second verse is one I need written on my heart right next to the first one. I know that worrying does no good and in fact, it causes harm to our minds and our bodies. Worry allows fear to enter and it is a slippery slope down to torment.

By grace I keep most of my worries within grasp, laying them at Jesus' feet. I often come back and grab them away to let them fester in me again, but God is gracious and I bring them back to him again. He is always there for me. He is always there to infuse his peace in me when I will accept it.

Lay your worries down and let your soul fly like the birds of the air. This is how we can glorify our God!

Lord,
Open my eyes to see the world and all your creation. Remind me that you care for these as well as me. Tear these burdens from my tight-fisted grasp so I can be open handed to accept your love and grace. Hold me in your everlasting arms until I am soothed and ready to face what comes with light and life, beaming your love and grace to others. Amen.

Apr 29 - *Psalm 34:17-19 "When the righteous cry for help, the Lord hears, and rescues them from all their troubles. The Lord is near to the brokenhearted, and saves the crushed in spirit. Many are the afflictions of the righteous, but the Lord rescues them from them all."*

When I am in the midst of my troubles, my brokenness, I know I can cry out to the Lord and he will bring his peaceful presence to soothe me.

He comforts me and holds me up when I am crushed. He renews my strength so that I can continue the battle and he delivers me from my struggles.

He does not take them away, for struggles teach me so much. Brokenness brings me closer to God. Being crushed reminds me that I need God to continue on my path.

Without those things, I would likely become self-reliant, proud, and maybe even arrogant. I know through these times of struggle, that it is only by the grace and love of God, that I come through them a better, stronger person.

Lord,
Send your peace to those of us struggling, feeling broken, or crushed. Consume the pain with your love and then gently, lovingly pick us up and walk with us once more, through these times of peril. You are faithful and you deliver us, we simply need to call to you, to cry out, for you are listening, waiting, hoping we will turn to you again. Thank you for your faithfulness and your everlasting love. Thank you for your forgiveness. My heart sings your praise this day because of all you are to me. Amen.

Apr 30- *John 1:11-12 "He came to what was his own, and his own people did not accept him. But to all who received him, who believed in his name, he gave power to become children of God"*

It is hard for me to wrap my mind around being rejected like this. I come from a family that embraces each other regardless of how and who we are.
We do not agree on everything or believe all of the same things yet we love each other because of and despite these differences. We know we are cut from the same cloth and we bring beauty to the quilt with our various colors and textures. The Word, the Christ, came to be with his own and he was rejected by most. He was not invited to their tables for meals or to the family gatherings to share in the fellowship. He was not invited to share his thoughts and insights but he was pushed away as an outcast.
I am so grateful that some treasured few heard and listened. I am thankful that John writes these words for us to ponder and embrace.
Our creator came to us; he came to bring love and grace, guidance and redemption. If we open our hearts to him, we become more like him. We grow in him and become true children of God.

Lord,
Your word teaches us that you created all things. All people are your children but not all of your children acknowledge you. Soften our hearts and open our eyes to finally accept you and see you in truth. Guide our steps as we learn and grow into the children you created us to be. Amen.

May 1 - *Jude vs. 21 "keep yourselves in the love of God; look forward to the mercy of our Lord Jesus Christ that leads to eternal life."*

I woke up with the phrase "can you feel the love tonight" going through my head over and over. There is a bit of a disclaimer here since yesterday evening was rehearsal with my handbell ensemble and we are playing songs from Broadway musicals including this one.

I tried to get it out of my head but then I realized that I could listen to that phrase and use it to lure me closer to God. I feel like I write about love all the time but when I think about the message in the Bible, I guess there is a reason for that.

This passage in Jude calls us build our faith, pray in the Holy Spirit and stay in the love of God looking for the mercy of the Lord. Not only does he want us to stay in his love, he wants us to be agents of his love so that everyone can experience it and join us in looking forward to the mercy of our Lord Jesus Christ. On this first day of May, whether the sun is shining bright and glorious or snow is falling, bringing moisture to the earth, we can feel his divine love showering down into our very souls.

Keep that feeling of Love and go out into the world being a light in the darkness, bringing warmth to the cold, and bringing love to the love starved soul.

Lord,
Thank you for filling up my reserves of love. Open my heart and soul to share this love you give to me with others so that all may find your mercy and eternal life. Amen.

May 2 - *Ephesians 5:22-25 "Wives, be subject to your husbands as you are to the Lord. For the husband is the head of the wife just as Christ is the head of the church, the body of which he is the Savior. Just as the church is subject to Christ, so also wives ought to be, in everything, to their husbands. Husbands, love your wives, just as Christ loved the church and gave himself up for her,"*

These verses came to me a couple of days ago and I have been praying about it but I had not looked them up. This morning when I was led to these verses, I had to relent.

I had been told there is more to the passage than "wives, submit to your husbands" but I hadn't checked. This passage is a gift to marriage.

If we look at our partners in this new light, peace and happiness could become truth. When I submit to Christ, I am not a doormat. Christ desires dialogue, questions, confirmations, and most of all service. When Christ loves the church he loves it with his whole being, giving his life for it.

We are to serve one another in the love of Christ so that we feel divine love in our marriages. Join me in praying for a renewed view and a renewed heart in this service.

Lord,
Please work in my marriage so that we serve each other and we glorify your name in our marriage. Touch suffering marriages and heal them in your holy name. Bless marriages that are strong and healthy and help those people be an example to others in your name. You are my Savior and Redeemer; I ask all these things in your holy name. Amen.

May 3 - *Jude vs. 22-23 "And have mercy on some who are wavering; save others by snatching them out of the fire; and have mercy on still others with fear, hating even the tunic defiled by their bodies."*

The Christian radio station I sometimes listen to in the car was recently talking about a mission trip.
They went to a country where it is against the law to preach or teach Christianity. The way they were able to "preach" was through serving, helping with medical treatment, and giving food and clean clothes.
There are so many ways to share the love of Christ beyond words. The word is vital to the growth of our faith, I will not discount that. We can still show mercy and love to everyone regardless of whom they are and what they believe without endorsement to their lives or beliefs. God is in charge of turning a person's heart.
Let God lead you in your service and he will use you to the glory of his kingdom.

Lord,
Help me separate the person inside from the actions and what I see on the outside. Make me your servant of mercy, of love, of teaching, of healing; make me your servant in the way you know I would be used best. I pray for all those who are in doubt; turn them to you this day and let me be one to embrace them, bringing them from the darkness into the light so that we can rejoice together. Amen.

May 4 - *Psalm 31:3 "You are indeed my rock and my fortress; for your name's sake lead me and guide me,"*

When I picture a fortress I think of the castles I have seen in the British Isles. Massive stone castles standing against time; they are still strong and seem impenetrable.

When I head west into the Rocky Mountains of Colorado, the majesty and grandeur of them speak of God to me. These towers of rock hold life in their palm. They are shelter for creatures of many kinds.

This is a reminder to me again that God holds us in his palm, protecting us and taking care of us. He is my rock and fortress but he is not stone. He is alive, warm, and always present. His arms hold me close, out of harm's way and in this embrace, I find strength. I wonder if my kids collect rocks because somewhere inside of them, they want to hold a small reminder of the strength and beauty of God.

The Bible tells us the rocks will cry out in praise if we do not, so let the rocks we see today remind us to seek him and praise him. Seek his strength, protection, and guidance. He will not turn away from us.

Lord,
We do not always see your presence or even feel it but you are there. Open our eyes to see the reminders you set before us, guide our vision to see you in our midst. As we move into our day, protect us from straying away; keep us focused clearly on you and your path of righteousness. I ask all these things in your name and for your glory. Amen.

May 5 - *Hebrews 10:23 "Let us hold fast to the confession of our hope without wavering, for he who has promised is faithful."*

People used to say their word was their bond and most people were good to their word. If they made a promise they kept it. Trust in each other has diminished; a verbal contract nowadays is a rare thing indeed.

You might be able to make a promise to a friend or neighbor but certainly not a stranger or business. Our word can no longer be our bond. Really, who can we trust at their word besides a true friend? It is a big risk to take someone we don't know at their word.

There is one who never breaks his word; someone we can hold fast to their promises forever. God's word is truth and he is faithful. We can trust him with our hearts and lives because he never lets us down.

All this came to me in a reminder through another song running through my head as I woke up. The word of the Lord holds true, we can trust God! Let us go out in celebration of the steadfast promises of our Lord and our Redeemer!

Lord,
Thank you for your promises and your truth. Thank you for showing us how to keep promises. Forgive us for our failings when we break a promise to you or to another. Help us mean what we say and stay true to our word and our faith in you. Give us this new day to start fresh again, holding fast to our hope in you. Amen.

May 6 - *Revelation 21:4 "he will wipe every tear from their eyes. Death will be no more; mourning and crying and pain will be no more, for the first things have passed away."*

I am missing my Mom today. Over the last week a few things have jogged memories of her and I just miss her.

Last week in Sunday school the kids and I were talking about this passage. We talked about scrapes and bruises but we also talked about disease and death. As we come closer to Mother's Day and the celebration of having Moms and being Moms the knowledge that my Mom is not around seeps in.

I so look forward to the day when there is no more war, no more sadness or anger. The day when the lion lays down by the lamb and spears are broken down into plowshares will be a glorious day indeed.

In the meantime, I am blessed to have people in my life that wipe my tears and bring love and joy in the midst of mourning and crying. These are the glimpses we have of the new Heaven and the new Earth.

I rejoice in these gifts of love from God.

Lord,
You know I relish the day when you come again and your new Heaven and Earth are fully and completely established. I can taste it now but can hardly wait until you come. Thank you for my Mom. Thank you for the blessings she brought to me and thank you for the people that help fill that void and bring blessings straight from you. Use me in your kingdom today so that I may be a vessel of your blessings and healing to others. Thank you for wiping our tears. Amen.

May 7 - *Proverbs 16:18 "Pride goes before destruction, and a haughty spirit before a fall."*

Last night was the annual talent show for the homeschooling group I belong to. There were acts up on stage and works of art and other projects on display as well.

My daughter chose to hand out programs but as the evening went on she asked me if she could change her mind. She wanted to perform. I can't help but wonder at her motivation. I had to explain that the docket was full; she would have to wait until next year.

As I thought back on all of the talent I saw last night I realized how easily we fall into the sin of pride. There were really good musicians, dancers, and artists showing their talents. There was good stage presence shown by some. Only God knows their hearts and motives, I did not see anyone gloating over their performances.

I know how hard I work to prepare for my performances but when the time comes I need to turn it all over to God. He is the one who inspires me to share music with others. I need to remember to give him the glory and honor in all I do. When I feel pride sneaking in, and it does, I recall this verse.

Lord,
Thank you for the many gifts you have given your people. Your word says you have given each of us gifts to use for your kingdom and your purposes. Help us strengthen the gifts you call us to use, whatever they are, and keep our hearts true in remembering to give you the glory in everything we do. Amen.

May 8 - *Ecclesiastes 3:5 "a time to throw away stones, and a time to gather stones together; a time to embrace, and a time to refrain from embracing;"*

Here is a snapshot of my devotion this morning.
I was sitting trying to listen for his word and this verse in Ecclesiastes popped into my head. "Really? It is such an obscure book, is this really you or am I randomly picking books and verses? Okay, I will look it up."... "Oh. It is you." Then I went back to sitting and began pondering what I need to throw away and what I need to gather. What am I embracing that needs to be released and what do I need to embrace?
Before this verse was given to me I was thinking about a dear friend who is going through hard times. I was asking God about the ebb and flow in life and how some stay in the practice of discipleship regardless of the ebb and flow and some do not. Why? Then I received this verse. Verse 12 says only God knows the beginning to the end and we cannot.
I leave you with this: seek to learn what stones you hold that need to be tossed aside and what stones you need to gather. Seek to embrace and refrain from embrace by the leading of his Spirit. When we seek he leads.

Lord,
Open our hearts and minds, our hands and eyes; so that we may clearly see and do however you guide us. Help us hold only what you would have us hold and release what we no longer need. I ask this through You and in You. Amen.

May 9 – *2 Thessalonians 2:13 "But we must always give thanks to God for you, brothers and sisters beloved by the Lord, because God chose you as the first fruits for salvation through sanctification by the Spirit and through belief in the truth."*

What would we do without our network of friends and family? During hard times, they are the ones who minister to us, support and love us, help us get back on our feet. During times of celebration, they are there cheering with us, laughing and dancing with us.

These people, the ones who share our lives and our faith, are present and ready to be with us in rain and in sun.

This verse talks specifically about Christian brothers. I love the times I spend with my Christian friends and family. There is an added dimension to our relationship that is not there with others. I am thankful for those people in my life because when I am in a place where I need their faith support, it is a treasure. It is a blessing that I can call on them to pray with and for me. What a gift.

Lord,
Thank you for the work of the Spirit in people around me and around the world. It is this work that calls us to believe and it is this Spirit that calls us to share with others our belief. Help us recognize each other with open eyes and hearts so that we may commune with all believers, lifting each other up and supporting each other in these days. It is in this fellowship that we have renewed spirits, and that your Spirit can pull us together for even greater good. Thank you for all this. Amen.

May 10 - *Philippians 4:9 "Keep on doing the things that you have learned and received and heard and seen in me, and the God of peace will be with you."*

This week in school, my daughter made a WWJD bracelet. It was interesting to talk about what it means and when we might ask ourselves "what would Jesus do?" Later that day and during the rest of the week I could see her working on that in her mind. It has been years now since so many kids were wearing those bracelets and most everyone knew that catch phrase but this verse calls me to bring that phrase back into our home. Jesus came to earth to teach and show us how to live in the love and light of God. He came as a living example to guide us in truth and the way. My daughter offered to make me a bracelet and I declined but I think I will let her make me one too. It would serve as a little reminder to ask myself "what would Jesus do?" Write it on the palm of your hand for a day, stick a note in your pocket, or hang a note on your mirror. Let's renew an old fad and follow the ways of Jesus. Peace be with you.

Lord,
Thank you for this wonderful reminder that you showed us the way and you continue to show us through your word and your Spirit. Help us receive the blessing of your guidance with open arms and open hearts. As we learn to walk with you, let us spread the peace we receive to others around us so that there will be peace on earth as it is in heaven. Amen.

May 11 - *Ephesians 2:20-22 "built upon the foundation of the apostles and prophets, with Christ Jesus himself as the cornerstone. In him the whole structure is joined together and grows into a holy temple in the Lord; in whom you also are built together spiritually into a dwelling place for God."*

This morning I woke up with the children's song about building your house on a rock or on the sand.
The wise man built his house on a rock. The very next song to jump into my head was the "Church's One Foundation." There seems to be a theme here...
As I prayed about the songs and then read this passage I was reminded that he needs to be the cornerstone of all my life. Every aspect of my life needs to have God at the foundation or it risks falling apart; my family, my work, my finances, my friendships, my chores, everything. When I make God the base in all things, they are so much better.
I encourage you to take time with someone you love and add God to the mix. Pray with each other and for each other and watch the transformation.

Lord,
Give me the courage I need to ask. Touch our lives where we allow you in, and open us up so we allow you into everything. I ask you to be the foundation of my life. When I stand on you, when you are my support, I can do anything because I am doing what you will have me do. Guide me today, please. Call us together in unity, as one building standing on the Rock, so we can be stronger in you. Amen.

May 12 - *John 2:14 "In the temple he found people selling cattle, sheep, and doves, and the money changers seated at their tables."*

My purse seems to be a place to collect stuff.

It is designed to carry things I need but along with my wallet, keys, and a couple of other necessities there are crumbs from a cookie that my kids brought home from church, receipts from grocery shopping, an old lotion bottle...

Just as my purse has a specific purpose so does the temple in Jerusalem as do our souls. Jesus reminded the people that this temple was to be a house of prayer as he cleared out the sellers, animals, and money changers that were defiling the temple.

Later in this passage when the Jews questioned his right to do this he referred to his body as a temple.

If we are a temple for God then what needs to be cleared out to bring our temple back to its intended purpose? What have we let seep in or creep in because it seemed easier or convenient or enticing but then it took root and grew out of proportion?

Let us ask Jesus to clear out the grime and clutter that defile our temples.

Lord,

It brings me comfort to picture you coming in and clearing out all that defiles. It is a daily process and I am so grateful that I can call on you and you come. Cleanse me and renew me to be a true house of prayer and worship for your glory. Thank you Jesus! Amen.

May 13 - *Romans 8:26 "Likewise the Spirit helps us in our weakness; for we do not know how to pray as we ought, but that very Spirit intercedes with sighs too deep for words."*

I have to admit when I read this verse tears started streaming down my cheeks.

There are times the Word speaks so clearly and so deeply that I cannot deny that God is with me, speaking to me at that moment. I am in a time of searching in my life. What should I be doing, how is God calling me to serve him? What of my loves are my weaknesses? What do I need to lay aside for now and maybe pick up in another time?

Now I know, even in my weakness, in my searching and not knowing, the Spirit is praying for me. The tears on my face are tears of relief and gratitude.

I have heard this verse before, today I own it.

Lord,

I am blessed. I don't know how else to thank you but my heart sings praise and my eyes weep in love and gratitude. I know you will show me my path. I know even now in my feelings of floundering, the Spirit is there, stepping in for me, asking for what I need. So many times, and once again, I am in awe of your love and grace. I praise you and lift your name on high. You are Almighty and you love each of us as your own. Hallelujah and Amen.

May 14 - *Mark 11:23-24 "Truly I tell you, if you say to this mountain 'Be taken up and thrown into the sea,' and if you do not doubt in your heart, but believe that what you say will come to pass, it will be done for you. So I tell you, whatever you ask for in prayer, believe that you have received it, and it will be yours."*

My first thought when I read this is "that would never really happen" so I already do not have the belief without doubt. Deeper thoughts are about the will of God.

Why would I ask a mountain to move? Is praying for something only if it is God's will a cop out? Does that allow me to justify something not happening because it was not the will of God? If I pray for something and it does not happen does that mean I was not faithful or did God do what I ask and I cannot see it because it manifested in a different way than I perceived it would?

I definitely feel like a disciple looking at these words and lacking understanding to grasp the message.

I know this without doubt, I take everything to the Lord in prayer and I trust him to do what is right. That works for me as my faith continues to grow.

Lord,
In reality I have seen you move mountains. I have seen you bring healing and wholeness and I have seen you redeem the worst of circumstances. What more do I need? Help me believe and see rather that see and believe. Amen.

May 15 - *Philippians 4:13 "I can do all things through him who strengthens me."*

I think my calendar threatened to overtake me again yesterday. As I looked through it and made note of the things I have coming up my heart got heavier and more anxious by the moment.
The frustration is that most of the things on my calendar are fun. Camping with my dad and kids next week, VBS at the end of June, trip to Tennessee with one of my best friends and our kids; all those things are things I am looking forward to.
I tend to get caught up in the planning phase and trying to make sure I don't forget anything. I want to make sure there is down time for me and the family so we can just sit at home and play too.
It seems wrong that I rejoice at the blank space on my calendar for today. This verse reminds me to review my calendar through the eyes of Christ. If the things on my calendar can be used to serve and honor him or to celebrate the blessings he has given me, it will be fine. He has never failed to support me in my endeavors that bless him and I know he will never fail me going forward either.
I take a deep breath and go forward into my day knowing he guides and strengthens me for whatever he has in store.

Lord,
Thank you for reminding me that I am not on this journey alone. I am not in charge. Lift the burden of worry from my shoulders and help me dance in the day to celebrate your strength and support. This is your day, I rejoice in it! Amen.

May 16 - *Acts 4:10-11 "let it be known to all of you, and to all the people of Israel, that this man is standing before you in good health by the name of Jesus Christ of Nazareth, whom you crucified, whom God raised from the dead. This Jesus is 'the stone that was rejected by you, the builders; it has become the cornerstone.'"*

There are so many people in this world that suffer from so many things.

During Jesus' ministry, he healed many people from physical, mental, and spiritual disease and when he commissioned his disciples they carried on healing people in his name.

God's divine energy heals.

Because Jesus broke the wall between our sinful nature and God's divine nature we can approach him and ask to be healed. It is only God's divine nature that decides how healing takes place and we, in our human sort-sighted view, so often miss it.

Search for healing, ask for healing and know that God hears you. Trust our Sovereign Lord that he will do what is good.

Lord,

It is easy to question, to ask why so many suffer and die. I cannot understand and do not pretend that I deserve to understand. You have called us to love, to serve, to heal. We often look to you for miracles and I suspect you look to us and ask why we are not willing to be the channel for your miracles to unfold. Make me a willing servant. Open my ears to hear your call; open my eyes to see the pain and open my hands to do what I can to heal, serve, and love. Amen.

May 17 - *Exodus 4:11-12 "Then the Lord said to him, 'Who gives speech to mortals? Who makes them mute or deaf, seeing or blind? Is it not I, the Lord? Now go, and I will be with your mouth and teach you what you are to speak.'"*

In this passage, God has called Moses to go to the Pharaoh and bring the Israelites out of Egypt. Moses, like me, tries to tell God he cannot do what God says he can. In the end, we know that Moses does, in fact, do all the things that God told him he could do.

As I feel the pull of God in my life, there are moments I question God. Is he really sure he wants *me*? The promise is there, in verse 12.

He created all, he makes each person with intent and he is with each of us as we do what we are called by him to do. He does not leave us ill equipped. Take a moment today and reflect on the wonderful things God has done with you and for you in your life.

He will do more, we simply need to listen, trust, and obey.

Lord,
Thank you for your encouraging word today. In all that I do and say, may it be by your guidance and teachings. The limitations and gifts I have are given to me with purpose in mind directly from you, my creator. May all that I am and all that I do honor your holy name and further your kingdom as you would have it do. Amen.

May 18 - *1 Corinthians 3:16-17 "Do you not know that you are God's temple and that God's Spirit dwells in you? If anyone destroys God's temple, God will destroy that person. For God's temple is holy, and you are that temple."*

My spouse works for a company that has an incentive plan to be healthy.

They encourage their employees and the spouses to eat well and exercise as well as seek counsel for habits and struggles that keep us from optimum health. As I log the foods I eat and the amount of water I drink it causes me to be more conscious of what I put into my body. As I log the amount of exercise I did and choose what kind of exercise I do, it makes me more conscious of how I treat this body.

I printed out a spring cleaning checklist from the internet last week and I have plans to use it this month to clean the things I don't think about. As I go through this process in my home, I also plan to go through this process in spirit and body as well.

As I meditated on these verses and the passage right before them, I thought of the people I see in society that do not seem to honor their temple.

The question I ask myself and I am led to ask you is this: How can I bring light and love to my temple and then in turn share that light and love to build up the temples of others?

Lord,

Thank you for reminding me that we are your holy temples. You abide in us and we are called to build these temples with care and love. Guide me in building so that the building is strong and well built upon your foundation. Amen.

May 19 - John 15:5 *"I am the vine, you are the branches. Those who abide in me and I in them bear much fruit, because apart from me you can do nothing."*

Have you ever tried to make coffee without plugging in the coffeemaker and turning it on or tried to cook a pot of soup without turning on the stove?

Let me tell you from experience, that these things do not work without their power source. When I read this passage this verse jumped out at me. I thought about electricity. Can we accomplish daily tasks without electricity? Yes, but things are so much more efficient with the power of electricity to help them.

I liked this analogy for a bit but then I came back to the one Jesus used to begin with. As much as electricity is necessary for certain tasks and certain appliances, God is more than that.

We need more than to be plugged in with God, we need to be intertwined; we need to be one with him. The branch is not a separate entity plugged into the vine; they are a part of each other; one in each other.

Do more than plug in, allow yourself to grow in God. Become a part of him and allow him to be in you. This is how we are fruitful people.

Lord,
As we go into this day, open our eyes to see little reminders of you being in us. Whether it is a coffeemaker or a tree, a bush or a computer, remind us that we are useless without you and that, with you, we can bear much fruit for your kingdom. Thank you for being our life source. Amen.

May 20 - *Galatians 6:2 "Bear one another's burdens, and in this way you will fulfill the law of Christ."*

Christ said we should love our neighbor as we love ourselves and I believe this is what Paul is talking about in this verse to the Galatians.

The law of Christ would be to love God with all that we are and love our neighbors as ourselves. When we love someone we willingly carry their burdens, we pray for them, we serve them, we cry with them in times of trouble and when things are good we rejoice with them. We are called to love our neighbor.

Who is our neighbor? As we go through this day let us look around and truly seek to find our neighbors. Try "paying it forward" or a random act of kindness. These little tokens of love may lift a burdened soul and show God's love to someone that hadn't seen it in a while.

I also need to remember my neighbor is as close as someone in my own house.

Lord,
Thank you for your reminder to care for each other. You care for the sparrow, the lilies of the field, and us. We are called by you to love and serve. Help us see the neighbors in our days that need to have a burden lifted from their shoulders. Give us the strength we need to assist and carry the burdens with them or for them. You sustain us; help us sustain those we love and those you love through us. Amen.

May 21 - *Psalm 145:10-11 "All your works shall give thanks to you, O Lord, and all your faithful shall bless you. They shall speak of the glory of your kingdom, and tell of your power,"*

As a late spring snow melts and the earth warms again my tulips breathe a sigh of relief for the moisture and begin to open their colorful blossoms in the morning sun. The sun comes over the horizon dispelling darkness and bringing light and day in a glorious beginning again moment.

Fresh coffee smell fills the kitchen and our bodies remind us that we need nourishment for the day. In all these moments and the many more that come today we can thank the Lord. He is faithful to us and his kingdom will never end. Every morning we trust that sun to be there and God is even more faithful than that. He has blessed us beyond our ability to know from the time he conceived us and into our last day on this earth; he has blessed us. His kingdom is already established and glory shines from it drawing hearts and souls into the Divine Love and Almighty Power.

As one tiny piece of his creation I strive to serve his kingdom and bring blessings to his name. All glory, laud, and honor to my Redeemer King...

Lord,
Thank you for another glorious day to praise and serve you. Open my eyes to see all of your creation as a small manifestation of you. The beauty and creativity that surrounds us is unimaginable. Let us lift our hearts to bless and honor you, our creator and Redeemer. Amen.

May 22 - *Micah 5:4-5 "And he shall stand and feed his flock in the strength of the Lord, in the majesty of the name of the Lord his God. And they shall live secure, for now he shall be great to the ends of the earth; and he shall be the one of peace."*

I cannot tell you how often I pray for peace.
I pray for peace in my soul, my home, my church, my neighborhood, my state, my nation, this world. I know there will not be infinite peace until the coming of the Lord but when I see glimpses of it, it is refreshing.
The still calm of the sunrise, the gentle breeze, and the sound of water lapping at the shore near a mountain lake, the quiet time I have in my devotion; there is true peace in those moments. I relish those; savor them, for they are a sustaining gift from God.
The Lord, Jesus the Christ, is our shepherd; he protects us and leads us, takes good care as a good shepherd does.
He is all powerful and nothing can overcome him so sit back and breathe, relax a bit, and rest in the powerful peace of our God.

Lord,
Peace on earth-the angels proclaimed it so long ago. Send your blanket of peace to us this day. Envelope us, infuse us in your everlasting peace. Compel us to share and spread that divine peace to others and soon peace will abound in spite of the work against it. Thank you for your promise in the word today. It is reassuring to remember that you are my shepherd, you are almighty and your greatness cannot be overcome. Let this message bring peace today. Amen.

May 23 - *Jeremiah 5:31 "the prophets prophesy falsely, and the priests rule as the prophets direct; my people love to have it so, but what will you do when the end comes?"*

Without knowing what God is saying how can we know what the truth is?

We see and hear in the news that preachers and priests are just as susceptible as anyone else to fall into the deception and then lead others down that path of trouble as well. We are all very good at rationalizing things and turning things to see that God must approve; these things must be the truth because it seems so good. This path of deception and lies, so easy to follow, really called me back into the Word of God daily.

As I have moved more and more to that, it is easier and easier to discern between lies and truth; God's authority and man's lies. It is also easier to feel at ease in God's path and so uncomfortable in the lies.

Listen; hear the call of your shepherd and turn to follow our one true shepherd once again.

Lord,

Only you know when the end will be here. Open the hearts of your wayward sheep; open our ears to hear you calling. Guide us back to your safety and truth so we know, without doubt, what we will do in the end. I pray we are all ready and waiting on that day and until then, move us to do your bidding. It is in following your call that we find true meaning in life. Amen.

May 24 - *Romans 13:10 "Love does no wrong to a neighbor; therefore, love is the fulfilling of the law."*

Today feels like a day of foundations.
We are at the end of the school year so the kids and I will join some friends and visit a conservation center that depicts living in the plains in the 1800's as our last field trip. I woke up with the words "in Christ alone" running through my head over and over again. Now I am led to this verse in Romans. All of these things seem to point to a bottom line, to my roots; the foundations.
There are many places in the Bible where we are told to love God and love our neighbor. We are told that if we love like this, the law is not abolished but completed.
How can we love like this? In our human eyes, we see differences and separateness. We see aversions and dislikes. In Christ alone, we are able to see our neighbors in love. In Christ alone, we are able to come to the God of all and love as he taught us to love.
Let us break down barriers and simply reach out in love. Search for the deep love of God in your heart and soul then let that love reach out to others.

Lord,
Thank you for teaching us how to love and how to live. Fill us up with your love and grace and guide us out into this world today to spread these precious gifts to those around us. Let us each be a beacon of light and a lover of souls. In this way, we fulfill your law and further your kingdom. Amen.

May 25 - *John 14:5 "Thomas said to him, 'Lord, we do not know where you are going. How can we know the way?'"*

This morning I have been thinking about all the different paths that I see people on. There are so many different religious practices out there, even more than I can imagine.

In the Bible Jesus is referred to in many ways. He is called Emmanuel, Prince of Peace, Light of the World, King of Kings, Lamb of God, and the list goes on.

As I lift people I know and love in prayer to God because I do not know that they see him in truth, I realize I do not know their heart or their path. Only God can know who they are, who they will become, and what their path is. I do not know the heart of God or the hearts of others, I only know the desire that all would be with him in the end.

I trust his word when he says he seeks out even one lost sheep; his desire is that none would be lost. I trust his power and that he reigns over all this; he is omnipotent.

I believe that he is so much bigger than I can fathom that I turn my prayers over to him and allow him to do the work he knows needs to be done. He is the way... I choose to follow and trust him to lead.

Lord,
So often I feel blind to your ways. I know you are at work in the world, I have seen evidence of it and yet I struggle. Help me let go, placing my prayers for my friends and this world in your mighty hands knowing that you prevail. Show me the way and I will follow you for you are Light, Love, and Life. Amen.

May 26 - *Daniel 6:27 "He delivers and rescues, he works signs and wonders in heaven and on earth; for he has saved Daniel from the power of the lions."*

Bad things happen to good people. I have heard this many times but when I read this story, there is more to see.

Daniel was a righteous man and followed the laws of God regardless of consequences. It starts out well; he was placed third highest ruler in the kingdom but treachery and trickery put him in the den of lions. I imagine it would be easy, sitting in a lion's den, to wonder where I went wrong.

Have you ever been accused of something and paid the price when you did nothing wrong? We are blessed to read this story without the hungry lions pacing at our feet. God protected Daniel; the lions did not touch him. After a long night sealed in the den, Daniel was released and the people who were responsible for his imprisonment were thrown to the lions to be "overpowered."

We can trust in God regardless of circumstance. This story gives us hope to persevere. He will save us and he will bring justice.

Lord,

Thank you for your word today. This story is just one that shows your unending power and love for your people. Help us to live as servants to you. Help us trust that you will rescue and restore us. Daniel went through this trial to bring glory to your name and draw the earthly kingdom he was a part of to you. May we also bring others in our world to you through our circumstances and our service. Amen.

May 27 - *1 John 1:6-7 "If we say that we have fellowship with him while we are walking in darkness, we lie and do not do what is true; but if we walk in the light as he himself is in the light, we have fellowship with one another, and the blood of Jesus his Son cleanses us from all sin."*

I was wondering this morning – where do I draw the line?
I really wanted to include verses 5-10 and then go into chapter two because this whole section of 1 John was leaping off of the page into my heart but alas, if I included all that text on this page of devotion, there would be no room for my meditations and that is important for me to write as well. I would encourage you to read this passage and see what speaks to you.
God is light. As the sun breaks over the horizon this morning I am rejoicing in the Light. He dispels all darkness and brings light and love into the deepest darkest places. He brings healing and grace to those places of hidden secrets; the dungeons of our souls.
Open the creaking doors and allow the light to come in. Do not fear; he is our comfort and our friend, our Healer and our Savior. As he comforts, soothes, forgives, and heals, the light floods the darkness and we all rejoice in truth and love.

Lord,
Thank you for all you have done for me and every reader and for all those who do not read. I cannot abide in your light by my own strength. I do not have what it takes but because of your love and sacrifice I call on your grace and forgiveness and step into the light once more. Hallelujah! Amen.

May 28 - *Psalm 119:76-77 "Let your steadfast love become my comfort according to your promise to your servant. Let your mercy come to me, that I may live; for your law is my delight."*

As I was sitting in my prayer time today I was compelled to lift the people and situations in my prayers journal in love. When I pray I ask God to be with them, to heal them, to guide them... whatever they have asked for in their requests.

It is the pure love of God poured out onto and into us that brings us what we need. His Divine Love brings comfort, healing and guidance. His steadfast love holds us steady when we falter and brings mercy to us when we fail. He is always there with us, never leaving our side. He is truly and honestly steadfast in his love for us.

I delight in his law because his law is love. Love him, love each other. Today I lift my prayers to the Lord in love. I surround those people and situations in love and I go into this day filled with the steadfast love of the Lord. There are many struggles all around but if I can feel the love of God with me and pray for the love of God to fill those struggles, I will be able to continue in delight of the Lord and his law.

Love to you all.

Lord,
Let love songs fill my heart today and as I sing away, let each of them draw me to you and your Divine Love. Fill my heart and my home so that it overflows into my neighborhood and my world, bringing your love and mercy to all. I pray all this in your holy name and to your glory. Amen.

May 29 - *John 3:4-6 " 'Nicodemus said to him 'How can anyone be born after having grown old? Can one enter a second time into the mother's womb and be born?' Jesus answered, 'Very truly, I tell you, no one can enter the kingdom of God without being born of water and Spirit. What is born of the flesh is flesh, and what is born of the Spirit is spirit.'"*

The children's song about bullfrogs and butterflies both being born again was running through my head. This passage seems so appropriate!

We often hear about new life, being born again and living in Christ. The thing is whether a bullfrog, a butterfly, or a Christian, new life is not instant change. There is no switch to flip; there is metamorphosis. The bullfrog grows and changes, little by little from tadpole to bullfrog. It must continue to swim, eat, and sleep if it is to complete its change. The butterfly also must do its part to change from caterpillar to chrysalis, and then finally after much work, come out a new creation!

The path in Christ is a life long journey. I encourage you, strive to grow, get your spiritual nourishment, and work in Christ. This is how we embody the new creation we are in Christ!

We have been born again in Christ, praise be to God!

Lord,
Thank you so much for the gift of change. Open our eyes to see the metamorphoses around us each day and encourage us to morph into the spiritual beings you have called us to be. Give us hearts of endurance and patience as we slowly, painstakingly blossom in your glory! Amen.

May 30 - *Ephesians 2:10 "For we are what he has made us, created in Christ Jesus for good works, which God prepared beforehand to be our way of life."*

We are created by God, created new in Christ.
God gives us each the tools we need to do the jobs he calls us to.
As we continue our life long metamorphoses, he continues to give us talents, gifts, callings. These come when they are needed to fulfill his kingdom.
He did not create us to do our own short sighted will. We fall down regularly, taking hold of our lives and trying to do what we think we should be doing. Take a moment to quiet your mind and heart. Listen; hear the voice of God calling you?
He wants you, he created you, and he is still creating you. Come back to him and do his bidding. He built you to do specific works for his glory.
When we follow his lead, we are fulfilled, complete.

Lord,
I hear you, yet there is so much noise, so many distractions.
Create moments in my day that are still and quiet. I need your
reminders; I need to hear you continuing to call me, to lead me
on your path. I wander into the brambles far too easily. Thank
you for your creations. Thank you for creating gifts in me so that
I can glorify your name. Make those gifts apparent to me and to
those around me so that I may be used in the best possible way,
in the way you created me. You have prepared me, Lord. Please
use me. Amen.

May 31 - *Psalm 135:3 "Praise the Lord, for the Lord is good; sing to his name, for he is gracious."*

It does not bode well for a quiet day at the Garwood house. Both kids are not feeling very good and both were up before I even got up for my "quiet" time. I started my prayers with laments to God about the lack of quiet and missing my alone time with him when this passage was given to me.
I could barely utter the prayers asking for healing of my children's colds knowing there are other children lying in hospital beds with deadly illnesses ravaging their bodies. I turned my heart around pretty quickly after that.
As I sat in meditation I felt the grace of God settle into my soul. In the midst of this little Garwood chaos, he brings peace. He will bring healing and rest to my children and all children. We cannot know his ways or his time but I know he is good and he brings wholeness and blessings to his people.
As the sun breaks over the horizon I am singing praises to the Lord. He has removed the dark cloud of selfishness and replaced it with the sunshine of love and blessedness.
I pray that you are filled with this light and love from God today as well.

Lord,
Open our hands so we release the struggles that keep us down.
Let us see your goodness in our hearts and in our world so that
our voices cannot help but sing praises to you for you are,
indeed, good and gracious to us all. Amen.

June 1 - *Hosea 4:6 "My people are destroyed for lack of knowledge; because you have rejected knowledge, I reject you from being a priest to me. And since you have forgotten the law of your God, I also forget your children."*

I have been one of these people.

I am blessed to have grown up in the church, been exposed to and even memorized scripture over the years, but it seemed I always took it with a grain of salt. I do not believe, in hindsight, that the word was written on my heart because I would not embrace it to be. Knowledge comes from diligent regular study of God's word.

God has been calling me for years and years and I have finally heard him. You who read this and other devotions, those of you who study the word, are striving for knowledge. I take this moment in the day to encourage you.

Steep yourself in his word. Strengthen your knowledge in the Holy One. Let's not ignore his law any longer, let us have it written on our hearts and then lead others to hear, embrace, and gain knowledge. In this way we can praise our Holy God.

Lord,
Forgive my lack of knowledge and the lack of understanding that still lingers. Thank you for guiding me into your word; thank you for using me to share your word with others. Help us all take time to study and share your word so that we can all become more knowledgeable in you. The more I learn about you from your word, the more I am humbled by you and your everlasting love, enduring mercy, and grace. Thank you Lord, thank you! Amen.

June 2 - *1 Peter 4:10 "Like good stewards of the manifold grace of God, serve one another with whatever gift each of you has received."*

It must be time for a stewardship drive in my life.
My husband and I recently talked about changing our pledge amount to our church and now this passage comes to me. There have been other signs I have received as well. I am not talking about money but about the gifts Peter is talking about in this passage. What are your gifts?
We all have them; things we are good at and enjoy doing. I have always enjoyed writing and felt like I was pretty good at it. I have the ability to put my thoughts down on paper. I never imagined I would use this gift to benefit God's kingdom and serve others but he had a plan and here I am. I really enjoy teaching and at one point in my youth thought I would teach elementary school. I never dreamed I would be teaching my own children in homeschool but God had a plan.
Search your life and see if you are using the gifts God gave you. Allow him to guide you forward in the process of becoming a better steward of his grace, using your gifts to serve him and others.

Lord,
Thank you for calling me back into focus. When there are days that do not go as planned, I tend to get derailed and this verse has put me back on track. Help me use what I have been given for your glory and to serve your children. Amen.

June 3 - *Joel 2:1 "Blow the trumpet in Zion; sound the alarm on my holy mountain! Let all the inhabitants of the land tremble, for the day of the Lord is coming, it is near-"*

I haven't been downtown in quite a while but I can still remember seeing someone preaching to repent for the end is near. Back then I thought they must be a little off of their rocker and maybe they were. I wonder how many people thought Joel was off of his rocker.

It seems like the people of old, in the times of the Bible, took notice and, to a degree, respected prophets. I do not know of one nation's leader that has called on a prophet to tell them what they should do. Do we no longer have true prophets in this world? Has media grown so vast that word of mouth is no longer effective? There was a poll on the news recently that forty percent of the people polled believe the end of the world will happen within forty years.

People have thought the end was near for thousands of years now but here are two things I am sure of. The "end" is closer than it was and it is the day of the Lord, so this is not the end for me. Let's all continue to turn to the Lord in every way we can so that when this day comes we are ready to be embraced with open arms.

Lord,
I know you know the perfect time to come in all of your glory. Let us not sit idly by waiting but help us continue to do your work and spread your love to others until that day we see you face to face. Amen.

June 4 - *Psalm 119:33-35 "Teach me, O Lord, the way of your statutes, and I will observe it to the end. Give me understanding, that I may keep your law and observe it with my whole heart. Lead me in the path of your commandments, for I delight in it."*

The Lord impresses this message on me in so many ways: Bible study, raising my children, walking the path I feel called to. In every aspect of my life I am led to listen and obey.
There is a song; the only part that I remember says - trust and obey, for there's no other way than to trust and obey, trust and obey. We know as parents when our children listen and obey life goes pretty well, with a lot less bumps along the way. When they choose not to listen and obey, life can be much harder because of the consequences we enforce or because of life's natural consequences.
We are taught in the book of Proverbs that children should obey their parents. Are we not the children of God? When we choose to disobey or ignore the guidance and decrees of God, we pay for it with consequences too. When we trust and obey, we do find delight.
Let us delight in the Lord today!

Lord,
Teach me, direct me, and give me understanding. I want to hear you; I want to obey with all my heart. There is the disobedient child in me still. Quiet the restlessness in me, the defiant child that thinks they know what is best. My heart and soul know that you lead me down true paths. Let me listen and obey that I may find delight. Amen.

June 5 - *Acts 6:8 "Stephen, full of grace and power, did great wonders and signs among the people."*

I don't expect to be a person doing great wonders and miraculous signs.
I sit in my home, with my kids and spouse, a little money in the bank. I didn't expect to be sending out daily devotions to my family and friends either but here I am, doing the unexpected. I didn't expect to have a child 2 days shy of 43 years but I have a healthy little boy that has blessed my life beyond measure. God gives us gifts and tasks that we never expect.
I wonder if Stephen expected to be doing great wonders and signs. I wonder what God could achieve if we would simply allow ourselves to be full of God's grace and power.
Take a moment and ask God to show you the gifts and blessings he has for you.
Be willing to embrace the tasks God has for you, knowing he gives you what you need to accomplish them. Allow yourself to be used, for God's glory, among the people. Let God rock your world so we can rock the world around us.

Lord,
I know you are always with me and have blessed me beyond my imagination. I hear you calling me to do more, to be more, and to give more. I am here to say, Lord God, show me the talents and gifts you have for me, open doors for me to use them to your glory, remind me that you are there, never leaving me to work for you on my own. I am ready to heed your call. Amen.

June 6 - *2 Chronicles 5:13 "It was the duty of the trumpeters and singers to make themselves heard in unison in praise and thanksgiving to the Lord..."*

This verse comes from the story of bringing the Ark of the Covenant into the new temple.

When I read these stories it strikes me as odd that there is so much ritual in what they do. I do not think the church I attend has very much ritual but someone from the outside may see that differently. We have a specific order to our service. We stand when we sing and for certain prayers. We have specific responses to the worship leader based on what they say and the list goes on. I used to think ritual was just pomp and circumstance and if not treated properly it could be.

Rituals serve to bring us into focus. The rituals here serve to remind everyone that the Holy of Holies was coming to be among them. The rituals we observe in church serve to call us into the presence of that same God. We can do it by rote or we can do it with intent.

As I go into this day of bell ringing and music making, I go with the intention of praising and thanking God with music. I encourage you to go into your day with intent.

Lord,
Help us be present in our lives today. It is easy to slide through the day without thinking or feeling anything. Guide our intentions so that we serve and honor you in whatever we do. Thank you for the rituals that draw us to you. Amen.

June 7 - *Colossians 4:2 "Devote yourselves to prayer, keeping alert in it with thanksgiving."*

The last couple of days I have been battling a cold to beat all colds. I haven't done my exercises, my sleep is not as good, and I have not been as diligent in my quiet time either.

This morning I turned to this verse and read it along with verse three and four. I lifted a prayer for the people sharing in the Word of God today all over the world and then I plopped into my rocking chair. A little nudge about faith came to me from Hebrews then and so I had two passages to ponder in my sleep deprived heart. I admit I went back to bed and got a little more sleep.

Now that I am slightly more awake, I can say what I received in these verses. There are many things that can get in the way of our time with the Lord. Sickness, bad nights of sleep, busy days ahead... When I don't spend time with the Lord I feel it. I have been reminded so I remind you as well- be faithful and devote yourselves to prayer.

Give thanks for all we have been given through the love of our Lord and his faithfulness to us. This morning I lift a prayer for each of you to be healthy in heart, body and spirit, thanking God for the blessings he has already given each of us.

Lord,
You know my heart and through your strength I persevere
through the distractions and excuses to find time with you.
Thank you for being there when I finally come to be with you.
Thank you for giving us prayer. Amen.

June 8 - *Isaiah 40:7-8 "The grass withers, the flower fades, when the breath of the Lord blows upon it; surely the people are grass. The grass withers, the flower fades; but the word of our God will stand forever."*

I have heard people say the Bible is just a book or translations that have been too badly marred to be true. The Bible was written by people, not God. There have been times I have pondered these thoughts as well.

Over the last couple of years, since I have been bathed in the Word of God daily, I have been transformed. I have read many other books, a lot with good and helpful information, but none have the power his word does. God used frail, broken humans to write his word and God is bigger and more powerful than any deviations in translation. We are on this earth for "a blink of an eye." We wither quickly like flowers and the grass.

I pray that I have brought someone healing or knowledge of the Holy One. I hope I have drawn at least one soul back to the Almighty God. Even so, I rest in the knowledge when my days are done the Word of God stands forever.

With his Word, people have the ability to communicate and commune with the Divine. What blessing! Praise be to God!

Lord,
I cannot express my joy for being drawn into your Word. Through your grace and love, I heard you and have immersed myself in your Word. You speak in many ways but thank you for this written guide of love, grace, conviction, forgiveness, teaching... for your word I give you thanks! Amen.

June 9 - *1 John 3:1 "See what love the Father has given us, that we should be called children of God; and that is what we are. The reason the world does not know us is that it did not know him."*

Do you remember the first time you held a tiny baby in your arms?

They are so precious with their soft new skin and their little wrinkles. They have tiny little hands and they just snuggle into you. Do you remember the first time children you love spoke words and the first wobbly step? The joy and pride that comes from those moments are a treasure.

Even now as I watch my kids learning and growing, I am taken aback by the amazing gift they are to me. God has blessed us with the children in our lives. Whether they are our own or ones dear to us, they are a reminder of how God loves us. The love we feel toward these children is a tiny mirror image of how much God loves his children.

I love to sit in the rocking chair and hold my son. I am a little sad that my seven year old daughter is too big for my lap but I love that she wants to snuggle.

As they grow and change, my love does not diminish. As we grow and change, God's love for us does not diminish either. What an amazing love!

Lord God,
Thank you for embracing me in your love and for the blessing of knowing your love never ends. Thank you for helping me see, through my children, the love you have for your children; for me. Guide me as I grow and learn, help me guide my children too. Amen.

June 10 - *James 5:7 "Be patient, therefore, beloved, until the coming of the Lord. The farmer waits for the precious crop from the earth, being patient with it until it receives the early and the late rains."*

It is so neat to watch the plants in my garden grow from seed to fruit in a season. We have strawberry plants that came back this spring in spite of the birds and other creatures trying to destroy them last year. The beans have sprouted and will soon begin to wrap themselves around whatever they can reach.

I have an empty spot in the garden though. It looks like nothing is planted there but I know I must wait and be patient. Carrots take a long time to germinate and I know from last year that if I water and wait, they will grow. Just as I cannot expect to plant seeds and have a mature plant and fruit the next day, so it is with my soul.

Each day I receive the nutrition I need from the Lord and I grow a little more. I am not the only plant in the garden. He waits for his precious crop to mature and the harvest will be soon enough. He is patient with each of us, so I must be patient with myself and others.

Today I thank him for the growth he has provided and the growth yet to come.

Lord,
Your words seep into my heart like the gentle rain seeps into the roots of a little seedling. Help this food nourish our souls so we continue to grow in you. Thank you for nurturing us. May the fruit I produce glorify and praise you. Amen.

June 11 - *Mark 14:38 "Keep awake and pray that you may not come into the time of trial; the spirit indeed is willing, but the flesh is weak."*

Jesus and his disciples had finished the Passover meal and walked to a garden. Jesus asked them to sit and keep watch while he prayed. They fell asleep three times! Three times he came and woke them up.

Mark reminds us to watch and pray every day. In all we do, in our rest, in our work, in our meals, in everything, we need to watch and pray. Our Redeemer sent the Spirit after his death so that we have a guide and protector at our fingertips. Through the Spirit of God our spirit is strengthened but we need to remain diligent.

God wants to be first in our lives. He used to ask for the first born calf, first crops, and our first earnings for sacrifice. He gave his only Son as the ultimate sacrifice. What are we willingly sacrificing now for him?

On this day, take a moment to ask what you could be sacrificing in thanks for the blessed gift of salvation? We love because he first loved us. Find a way to show him your love today.

Lord,
Forgive my callousness. Please change my heart to share the love and mercy you share with me. Other people learn about you through the love they see in me. Fill my heart with your love until it is bursting, so that I have no other option than to let it flow from me to those around me. Thank you, my Redeemer and my Lord, for your amazing grace. Amen.

June 12 - *Colossians 1:11-12 "May you be made strong with all the strength that comes from his glorious power, and may you be prepared to endure everything with patience, while joyfully giving thanks to the Father, who has enabled you to share in the inheritance of the saints in the light."*

I love to watch the Spirit at work in the world.

A while back bombs exploded in Boston. People were killed and many were injured, another senseless act of violence in a seemingly ever growing sea of violence.

The love and beauty that poured out in that moment overcame any darkness that loomed. Even before the smoke had cleared marathon runners and bystanders alike were running to help the people affected by the explosions. They were not running away from danger, they were running to help each other.

God gives us each the strength we need to endure whatever comes. When we allow his Spirit to guide our hearts we are filled with his power and patience so we are able to move forward rather than run away. We are able to see the beauty from ashes and give thanks to the Father, for that beauty.

We can rejoice that the violence is not the end, darkness does not overcome and we, the sons and daughters of the Father revel in the fact that we will remain in his light and love forever.

Lord,
Thank you for your healing love. Thank you for the bravery that was shown in Boston and is shown around the world. Your light and love remain. Hallelujah and Amen.

June 13 - *Luke 1:18-19 "Zechariah said to the angel, 'How will I know that this is so? For I am an old man, and my wife is getting on in years.' The angel replied, 'I am Gabriel. I stand in the presence of God, and I have been sent to speak to you and to bring you this good news.'"*

There are stories in the Bible where God speaks and the person questions. There are stories where God speaks and the person responds with obedience.

Zechariah couldn't believe his ears. He questioned the message and he was not able to speak for the whole pregnancy because of his lack of belief. The blessing from God was given but Zechariah paid a price for not trusting.

The hard part of listening to God is truly hearing God. The more we allow God to be in us the more we recognize his voice. Zechariah was blessed to hear so clearly, he was close to God and yet he still faltered. This is one of many messages showing God's grace. He does not give up, he does not quit. His plan unfolds and he wants us to be a part of it.

He invites us into the story, calls to us, waiting for us to embrace the fact that he is our Father and his plan for us is so much better than we can imagine. Just as Zechariah could not imagine a baby, we are clueless at the wonders that God has in store for us.

Lord,
You are with me, you are in me and I am in you. Let my will be softened so that my will is simply your will always. Thank you for speaking to me, help me to listen; to listen and obey. Amen.

June 14 - *Ephesians 3:5-6 "In former generations this mystery was not made known to humankind, as it has now been revealed to his holy apostles and prophets by the Spirit: that is, the Gentiles have become fellow heirs, members of the same body, and sharers in the promise in Christ Jesus through the gospel."*

I love a good mystery. I have been known to sit up into the wee hours of the night reading to get to the end and find the solution to whatever that mystery holds.

When I am up late, burning the midnight oil, I tell myself only one more page or just to the end of this chapter... then the next thing I know I have passed that stopping point without realizing it. I get so involved in the story it is nearly impossible to put it down.

What would it be like if we read the mystery of the gospel with such voracious appetites? Why is it so easy to set this story aside and move on with our day? Is it because the mystery is so big it is beyond our full grasp? Is it because it is so familiar that we do not see the mystery that still exists?

God is a God of mystery to me. He reveals what he will and in his time. God is also a God of faith. I cannot prove to others what I believe but I know he continues to reveal himself and so I go into the day of mystery.

Lord,
Help my sense of adventure guide this day. There is no mystery in the fact that your love is steadfast and true. You leave no question of your Almighty power and presence among your creation. Help me find you today. Amen.

June 15 - *Proverbs 20:27 "The human spirit is the lamp of the Lord, searching every inmost part."*

I was just thinking about my baseboards.
It is almost summertime and the deep spring cleaning for my house has been calling my name for a while. I have no idea when I will fit in all those tedious things. Dusting the high places, scrubbing the baseboards, washing windows... it must be done or it becomes dingy, dirty, and grimy. Sigh.
This verse calls me to allow some spring cleaning in my spirit. I know I hide "dust" and "grime" even from myself so that when I think I have confessed everything there are still things hidden in the shadows.
The lamp of the Lord searches everywhere, every corner, every baseboard, every high place. I call on him to search, find, and scrub it clean so that my spirit may be cleansed and righteous in his sight again.
As I clean my baseboards, windows, and high places, I hope they remind me to have the Lord search and cleanse me.

Lord,
Search my spirit, search and cleanse. I desire nothing more than to be fully in your presence and I know I cannot be without being clean and righteous in your sight. Thank you for the salvation of Jesus. It is through his sacrifice that I can come to you for healing, cleansing, and wholeness. Search my inmost being Lord. Only you can bring to light the hidden things and then they, too, can be cleansed. All glory and honor are yours, forever and ever. Amen.

June 16 - *Psalm 27:11 "Teach me your way, O Lord, and lead me on a level path because of my enemies."*

It has been quite an experience to see all this construction out my front window.

Yesterday there were even more trucks and workers, more noise and restoration of cement. I found a note on my door that today they begin work on the asphalt. I already have to walk my kids across the street just to be safe and now I wonder how much trouble it will be to get anywhere in my neighborhood while they tear up the street.

When we go get the mail around the corner, will I have to step around even more wet concrete or avoid the flying debris of torn up asphalt? Will I be able to get my car out to run the errands I need to?

Worry and anxiety are two of my biggest enemies. They left me alone for quite some time but they are back again. As I look out my window and watch the path and road being torn up and then restored I hold hope in that vision.

I know the Lord makes my path level and he holds my hand through the rubble I encounter. He will not let me be run over with anxiety or worry but leads me in love and peace.

That is his way.

Lord,

Thank you for this message today. Post it on my forehead and on my arm; write in on my heart and soul so I can feel it at every moment. Thank you for the rest and restoration we all received during the night. Hold our hands and keep us all on level ground today. Praise to you, O God. Amen.

June 17 - *Romans 14:12-13 "So then, each of us will be accountable to God. Let us therefore no longer pass judgment on one another, but resolve instead never to put a stumbling block or hindrance in the way of another."*

Who am I to know the heart of God?

When I look at others and condemn them for their behaviors, character, or any other thing, it places heaviness on a part of my heart. If I continue down the path of judging others, it continues to darken my heart until I am so closed off from the grace and mercy of God that I do not know how to come back.

In my experience, not only does judging place stumbling blocks and obstacles in my brother's way it also places them in my way. Only God can know a person's heart and only God knows the path he calls them on.

Join me in asking for stumbling blocks and obstacles to be removed from our hearts and our paths and let us encourage and love one another as we are called to do in Christ.

Lord,

Forgive my judging heart. Open my eyes to see others in the love and light of Christ, our Redeemer. Please remove the obstacles and stumbling blocks we have in our path and I ask that you remove any that we have placed in the paths of others. Give us hearts of love and mercy so we are able to see each other as you would like us to. Help us to love one another in you. Amen.

June 18 - *John 8:7 "When they kept on questioning him, he straightened up and said to them, 'Let anyone among you who is without sin be the first to throw a stone at her.'"*

Apparently I am a rabble rouser.

I posted what I thought was a thought provoking video on Facebook yesterday and the next thing I knew some of my dear friends, who disagree with each other, began degrading each other and calling each other names. I am so distressed by this but, unfortunately, not surprised.

We are a passionate people and we believe what we believe with all our hearts and souls. Just as these people believed the woman who was caught in adultery did not deserve to live because of her sin, we often slam and dehumanize the people we disagree with until we have stoned them to death.

Jesus calls each of us to review our own hearts before we condemn someone else. When we run into a democrat and we are republican, or vice versa or when we run into an unbeliever and we are a believer should we condemn them because they are "wrong" or misguided or...

Join me today in asking the Lord for forgiveness of our close-mindedness and hardheartedness. We all struggle with these things at times.

Lord,
Please forgive my lack of love for my brothers and sisters. Help me see you in them regardless of our differences and open my ears that I may hear what they really have to say instead of picking apart their words and their hearts. Help me be an agent of love for you. Amen.

June 19 - *John 1:5 "The light shines in the darkness, and the darkness did not overcome it."*

It is moth season in Colorado.

About this time every year, we have a few weeks filled with birds diving through traffic intersections catching a bounty of moth snacks and young children squealing in fear at the sight of a moth.

We have one in our house now; we haven't been able to catch it. They seem to hide during the day and only come out when the lights are on. It is strange to me that they don't come out during the day since they are drawn to the lights when it is dark outside. If they like light and warmth I would think they would be out when the real light and warmth from the sun is out. I guess they do not recognize or appreciate the true light from the sun.

As the sun rises this morning there are many reminders that I can use during the day to remind me of God's true light dispelling darkness. The sun chases away the darkness of the night. During the evening we flip a switch and a light comes on in our home so we can see, the light dispels the darkness. The stars and the moon dispel darkness in the night sky.

If we look around, we see light shining and clearing away darkness all around us. Take a moment to praise the Lord for his light because the darkness did not overcome it!

Lord,

Thank you for your light! Thank you for shining it eternally so we can see it and come to it. Help us receive and share your light around the world in whatever way you call us to. Amen.

June 20 - *1 Thessalonians 5:16-18 "Rejoice always, pray without ceasing, give thanks in all circumstances..."*

"Rejoice always" sounds hard and it can be.
When I am tired or sick, when the day is not going well for one reason or another, it is very hard to feel joyful. The next part of this passage is so important though. Pray continually, give thanks...
When I take a moment to sit quietly and refocus in prayer, when I turn my heart to the things I can be thankful for, it changes my weariness or illness. It makes those things less important, they have less impact on me. When I can pray and be thankful, my heart finds joy in spite of the other issues I am having.
Lay your troubles down, pray about them and let them be gone from your heart. Turn your troubles over and release them, then it is much easier to be thankful and joyful. It is easier, not easy, but less hard. This is God's will so I encourage you to try.
He will not fail you.

Lord,
Thank you for this message today. There are many things I could choose to worry over but I choose to give thanks for the blessings and the struggles you have given me this day. My heart sings songs of praise, thanksgiving, worship, and then my heart is filled with joy for you. When this is hard, please strengthen me to keep at it. When I follow the path of your commands, it does bring me delight! Amen.

June 21 - *Psalm 57:7-11 " My heart is steadfast, O God, my heart is steadfast; I will sing and make music, Awake, my soul! Awake, O harp and lyre! I will awake the dawn. I will give thanks to you, O Lord, among the peoples; I will sing praises to you among the nations. For your steadfast love is as high as the heavens; your faithfulness extends to the clouds. Be exalted, O God, above the heavens. Let your glory be over all the earth. "*

Music brings my soul to God like nothing else.
When the sun is just beginning to warm the sky the birds can no longer contain themselves, they lift their song to praise God in the new day. When children feel happy, it never crosses their minds to contain their song. I remember times my children sang as they played and how many times I shushed them.
Too often we close down the joy. Maybe if we would allow the joy from our souls into the open there would be more reason for songs of joy and praise.
As the day nudges us into action, find a song of praise to bring along. Let it carry you through your day. Let songs bring exaltation from your heart to God because his love is beyond abundant. Soak it in and sing to him.

Lord,
You are the Almighty, Everlasting, King of kings, and Lord of lords forever and ever. Your presence settles in us every moment we allow it. As I walk through this day let my soul sing and praise you all day long. Let song transform me and those around me into beings of Light and Love, singing and praising you all day in all we do. Amen.

June 22 - *1 John 3:14 "We know that we have passed from death to life because we love one another. Whoever does not love abides in death."*

I recently read a story about degrees of light and dark, degrees of warmth and cold.

The argument was that there is no darkness or cold there is only absence of light or absence of warmth. The less light or warmth we have the closer we are to the complete absence of light or warmth. When I read this verse I could apply that theory to this statement as well.

If we live in love we have fullness of life and as we have less love we have less life. Death is the complete absence of life. If I watch the news or read news stories on the internet it seems the world can suck the life right out of me. It is a slippery slope from being informed to abiding in death. Our world does not ooze love and light – according to the news stories I see.

God clearly calls me, all of us, to be agents of love and life. Seek to please God, seek to live in the flow of his everlasting love and life will abound.

In this world of snuffed out light and dampened life, I encourage each of us to be one who spreads life and love, leading our hearts and those around us away from the absence of life in to the fullness of his life and love.

Lord,
Forgive the destruction I have caused by drawing others away from love and light. Direct my words and my deeds in love and light so that your kingdom is strengthened and we step ever closer to eternal life with you. Amen.

June 23 - *Deuteronomy 8:3 "He humbled you by letting you hunger, then by feeding you with manna, with which neither you or your ancestors were acquainted in order to make you understand that one does not live by bread alone, but by every word that comes from the mouth of the Lord."*

Do you ever read a scripture passage that just leaves you without words? This one spoke to me like that today.

When I review my life I have wandered in the desert, searching, never finding enough, never feeling satisfied. When I realized that I was still hungry, and was blessed to finally, truly, hear the words of God in my heart, I was deeply humbled.

The Word of God has taught me, guided me, and challenged me but more than anything else has pulled me into the presence of the Almighty and there, I have found satisfaction. Now I hunger for his word, his presence, his guidance. I know he gives me everything I need and more.

The manna he gives is life giving and sustaining. Blessed is he.

Lord,

Thank you for never deserting me when I wandered around searching; never heeding your call. Thank you for bringing me to life, awakening the need for You in my heart so strongly that I could not stay away. Your word; your divine guidance sustains me. Oh Lord, help me share this blessed sustenance with others so they may find "manna" that you so lovingly provide. Where would I be without your Word? Lost! Thank you God, thank you so much. Amen.

June 24 - *1 Peter 3:14-15 "But even if you do suffer for doing what is right, you are blessed. Do not fear what they fear, and do not be intimidated, but in your hearts sanctify Christ as Lord..."*

I spend a fair amount of time lamenting over the state of our world.

On the surface it would seem I worry or fear for the world and maybe to some degree I do. I see the suffering and the brokenness everywhere. I know most of that is needless but we are blind to the Divine love that waits to fill the world and bring everlasting healing.

In this verse Peter reminds us that we may not be free from suffering during our lives here but even in our suffering we are blessed. I know the suffering this world is enduring is temporary just as any suffering I may go through. God has a plan and he has sent his Spirit to live in us and encourage us.

Regardless of the sufferings we endure, we know in our hearts that Christ is Lord and he is the ruler of our hearts and our world. In this we can hold on to the blessings we have been given and release any fear we may harbor.

In all things we can praise his holy name as ruler of all!

Lord,
Forgive my short sighted vision; it seems to come back again and again. I hold your hand and your hope in my heart as I go forth into this day filled with your love and your blessings.
Thank you for all you give us and thank you for the reminder that we are simply called to sanctify you, the Lord and the Christ.
Strengthen our hope in you today. Amen.

June 25 - *Psalm 34:5 "Look to him, and be radiant; so your faces shall never be ashamed."*

I love the picture this verse draws in my mind.
I see our faces lifted up to the rising sun, glowing with joy and warmth. There is no shadow of sorrow or grief on anyone's face and there is not a cloud of despair to be seen. Someday this will be our reality.
The good news is we can have experiences like this even now, today. As I take the time to let go of all my prayers of concern and petition, let go of all my plans for the day and thoughts that crowd my mind, it is then that I can truly look to him. When I have released all those things my vision becomes clear and I can see him without anything getting in the way.
At those moments, I am certain that I am radiant because I am simply filled with his love and light and there is no greater joy to experience. When we acknowledge and feast in the presence of the Lord, we glow; we radiate his love.
Take a few moments today to look to (not at) the sun and ponder the bright light and warmth it provides to us each day and then remember that it is nothing compared to the light and warmth God provides. Hold that feeling in your heart and radiate it through your day to all those around you.

Lord,
Thank you for your presence, thank you for being there when we finally look to you. Empty us of darkness and despair, sickness and fear, and fill us with your light and love until we are truly radiant. Lift us into your light and love so that we are beacons of you in this world of shadows. Amen.

June 26 - *Matthew 7:9-11 "Is there anyone among you who, if your child asks for bread, will give a stone? Or if the child asks for a fish, will give a snake? If you then, who are evil, know how to give good gifts to your children, how much more will your Father in heaven give good things to those who ask him!"*

God gives us what we need and so much more.

Sometimes we come to our Heavenly Father and ask for a stone instead of bread, we ask for the snake instead of the fish. We are so focused on what we think we need that we ask for things that are not good for us at all. God will say no.

We do not give our children things we know are harmful even if they ask and God does not either. When we come to him, asking for things, we need to clear our selfish desires from our minds; focus our hearts on him and then, with the guidance of the Holy Spirit, we ask. There have been many times in my life that I have been thankful that God did not give me what I asked for in my selfish short sighted vision.

God is gracious; he gives us what we need and so much more.

Lord,
Thank you for not giving us stones and snakes even when we ask for them. Open our hearts and eyes so we can see what you give us, and we can be truly thankful for the blessings you have given and continue to give. Help us ask for things that strengthen, build up, feed, and renew us. Continue to give us what you know we need and help us see that these things are good! Amen.

June 27 - *Genesis 1:29 "God said, 'See, I have given you every plant yielding seed that is upon the face of all the earth, and every tree with seed in its fruit; you shall have them for food.'"*

I am becoming more and more aware of the food I eat.
Our society talks about it, the shelves of the grocery store are stocked with all kinds of new and improved, healthier, etc... We have junk food in our house though.
I am disappointed with cereal, bread, and crackers. The additives in these foods are amazing. I have not come to the point of eating all natural, it would cost a lot, but I need to do something. This passage is the story of creation. In this perfect world, even the "beasts" are all given grass to eat.
I have reduced the amount of processed food I eat (a little). As I read and meditated on this passage I realized I need to study this much more before I stop eating anything but vegetation. I am encouraged to stop eating store bought cookies and ice cream though. This will be a very gradual change for me but I will move to a healthier and more holistic diet.
What is one food item you could drop that is not on the natural food chain? Are you willing to give one thing up to move closer to the Eden God wanted?

Lord,
You know my weaknesses and you know what is in my pantry. Remind me of this verse and my desire to treat my body in a better way. Give me strength to resist "junk" and replace it with good food. I ask this in your name. Amen.

June 28 - *Psalm 33:4-6 "For the word of the Lord is upright, and all his work is done in faithfulness. He loves righteousness and justice; the earth is full of the steadfast love of the Lord. By the word of the Lord the heavens were made, and all their host by the breath of his mouth."*

This morning I wish I could crawl back into bed, nice and warm, close my eyes, and sleep in late.

My boy is already awake and full of life this morning so there is no sleep for the weary (me). As I would find comfort in my bed, I find comfort in these words.

As I search the word of the Lord, it is comforting to know his word is right and true. It never leads me astray, he always walks with me and guides me; he is faithful to the end. This faithfulness, this love, this power that God brings us through his word, is evident in everything. The clouds, the sun, and planets are hung in the sky simply by his word. He speaks and it is so.

I wrap these words around me instead of my blankets as I walk into his world. I listen for creation singing thanks and praise for his word. I join in the singing today, singing praise and thanks for the power, love, and righteousness of his word.

Lord,
With just a breath you create or condemn. Open my ears, my eyes, and my heart that I may take you in through my whole being. The breath of your mouth created all creation. Let me hear your breath guiding me and loving me today. Your love abounds, infuse me with it and hear me as I join with all the earth in singing praise to you. Amen.

June 29 - *Mark 6:42 "And all ate and were filled."*

How many times have I heard the story of Jesus feeding the five thousand?

I know this story from childhood so when I was led to read it again this morning I wondered what the purpose was. What would God bring to my heart from this story today? I woke up this morning with the thought "I am sufficient for you" running through my head and I know there are verses in the Bible that talk about that. This verse leapt off the page when I read it because it says the same thing to me.

Have you ever eaten until you were so full you hurt? Sometimes we use food to fill an emptiness that is not hunger for nutrition. Have you ever been at a meal where the conversation and company is such a blessing that you hardly ate and yet you were satisfied? I picture that scenario in this story.

We need food for fuel and to sustain our energy and bodily health. We need God to sustain our spirits and our souls. When our souls are filled our needs are so much less in every other part of our lives.

Join me in seeking to be filled with the presence of God and only eating enough to sustain our energy and bodily needs. Allow God and his word to be food for your soul.

Lord,
Help me place food in proper context today. You are my true sustenance, food is simply fuel. Help me enjoy the food you have provided and help me enjoy the fullness that your Spirit provides to my soul. Thank you for your word today. Amen.

June 30 - *Psalm 103:10-12 "He does not deal with us according to our sins, nor repay us according to our iniquities. For as the heavens are high above the earth, so great is his steadfast love toward those who fear him; as far as the east is from the west, so far he removes our transgressions from us."*

I love camping with my Dad.
When I sit under the blanket of stars with the sky so dark I can see the Milky Way, the heavens seem within reach, like I could touch the stars. When I see the azure sky during the day, airplanes flying, birds flying, the sky seems so far away.
God's love is like this. It is not only way up high in heaven. It surrounds us, it is everywhere and it is never ending, going on forever just as our sky does. The heavens we gaze upon are just a glimpse of what is out there and this is how his love is. It is because of love he separates us from our sins.
How far is the east from the west? There is no tangible measurement for how far God takes them from us. Thank God he does not lay the crushing load of our iniquities upon us; he loves us and removes our sins from us.
Praise him and thank him.

Lord,
Your name is above all names and I praise you. When I step outside today, help me remember your unending love when I see the unending sky. Remind me that my sins are no longer weighing me down but have been removed as far as the east is from the west and let the warmth of the sun remind me of the warmth of your love and grace. You are my God; I praise your name and thank you with all my heart. Amen.

July 1 - *Acts 12:24 "But the word of God continued to advance and gain adherents."*

In spite of the persecution of the disciples, in spite of those who fought it, the Word of God continued...

As I sat contemplating this, the sprinklers were running. The Word of God nourishes us, refreshes us just like sprinkled water. The water gently rains down to the blades of grass and it seeps down into the roots, giving each blade a much needed drink. Some water hits the driveway or sidewalk but there is nothing taken in; no refreshment to the concrete because it is hard and dead.

Which are you? Are you a blade of grass, thirsting, drinking, and taking the word in to the very roots of your being? Are you growing and becoming lush and green because of his word? Are you concrete; hard and unchanging? The word falls gently but it sits on the surface, dries up, and evaporates.

Let God's spirit make you a blade of grass. Allow him to gently nourish you to your roots with his word. When we are nourished we are able to grow into the beauty God created us to be and we can let his word permeate the very heart of us.

Let the word increase and spread throughout you and your day.

Lord,
Thank you for my daily refreshment; the nourishment you bring to me. There is nothing like receiving your grace and just soaking it in allowing it to reach to my very roots. Let me feel your word spreading and increasing in me; let me be a vessel to spread and increase your word around me. Amen.

July 2 - *Luke 18:16-17 "But Jesus called for them and said, 'Let the little children come to me, and do not stop them; for it is to such as these that the kingdom of God belongs. Truly I tell you, whoever does not receive the kingdom of God as a little child will never enter it.'"*

As I was sitting in my rocking chair trying without success to sit and simply listen and be in the presence of the Lord, I heard the familiar thump, thump of my little boy coming down the stairs. I sighed because now my quiet time was effectively over even though I was not done. Right then is when this passage came to my heart.

When children are small they come without reservation, fully expecting to receive what they need, and never doubting that they will be taken care of. They are untainted by the world of nuance and innuendo so when they speak it is in their truth. Maybe this is what Jesus meant when he said these words to his disciples. Children come with pure intentions, pure desires, and pure faith that it will happen.

How would our view change if we would come to the Lord in that same way?

Lord,
Our vision is clouded by the disappointments of this world. When we look beyond this world and see the truth of your love and grace we are ashamed at our lack of trust and faith. It is clear that you have never let us down; you have always given us everything we need and much more. Help us see clearly what you have for us so that we can truly lift our hearts in praise. Thank you Lord, thank you! Amen.

July 3 - *James 5:15 "The prayer of faith will save the sick, and the Lord will raise them up; and anyone who has committed sins will be forgiven."*

There are many references in the Bible with sickness and sin being almost interchangeable.

When I think about this it is understandable. When we are in sin, we are sick. Sin is like mold and mold can definitely make us sick! It starts small and almost invisible but if it is allowed to continue, it grows and can take over an entire house!

Our houses cannot ask to be cleaned. It is up to each of us to be diligent in cleaning and keeping mold and dirt at bay. The worse we let it get, the harder we have to work to clean and make our home livable again.

Sin is the mold of our hearts. Do not let it grow and take hold. We simply need to ask in faith and he cleanses, he heals and he raises us up, renewed.

It is like handing God the sponge; knowing in all our being that he will clean the mold from our hearts and we will be whole, shiny and sparkling once more. Praise God!

Lord,

Thank you for bleach. As I clean my showers remind me of this verse. I do not need to get my hands dirty to clean my heart; I need to get on my knees and hand all that grime over to you. I need to ask you to clean because I cannot. Cleanse my heart today Lord. Please make me pure as snow. Let me gleam in the Son so I may shine your light. Let me dance for joy with a renewed heart! Amen.

July 4 - *Romans 6:22 "But now that you have been freed from sin and enslaved to God, the advantage you get is sanctification. The end is eternal life."*

I struggle with an understanding of human slavery.
Even our founding fathers owned slaves. If the owner was kind, maybe it would be okay. You had a place to live, food to eat, and work for the day. It would almost seem normal but you had to earn your keep for sure.
Some slave owners were not so kind. They treated their slaves worse than animals. During that time in US history freedom was a luxury not everyone knew and it certainly wasn't free.
Our soldiers today still fight for freedom. Freedom from sin is a gift from God. Sin shackles us, chains us, and keeps us down with weights threatening to drown us. When we follow God we are freed from those chains and shackles.
Being enslaved to God is not God locking us down, it is a choice to live in him. We are free to run to him and we are free to run away. The question is why would we run away?
When we stay "enslaved" to him, we experience true freedom and when we turn away, we become enslaved to the chains and shackles of sin again. I choose God, I choose his sanctification, and I sing praises today for all my freedoms!

Lord,
Let me not take freedom for granted, you give it freely but there was a price paid by Christ for my freedom. I live in the land of the free, help me honor the freedom I have been so graciously given. Amen.

July 5 - *Psalm 23:4 "Even though I walk through the darkest valley, I fear no evil; for you are with me; your rod and your staff – they comfort me."*

There are road hazards all along life's highway.
In my life, the "highway" has often seemed a barely visible path in the middle of a forest. Following a forest path can be relaxing, the shade of the trees, the damp coolness, and a stream running near the path with soothing sounds of water.
The path in the forest can be arduous. Tree roots and hidden rocks in the path trip me and cause me to fall. There is a steep embankment and I surely do not want to fall for fear of life and limb.
God is with me on this journey, whether it is a stroll or a trial of a hike; he is with me and he has brought along his crook. The shepherds crook has a curved handle to fit around the neck of a sheep, allowing a herder to catch any stray and reroute them in a new direction. This is the rod and staff that comfort me.
He keeps me safe pulling me back from the edge of danger, guiding me, and nudging me to correct my way.

Lord,
Your rod and staff bring me comfort. You never leave my side; you guide my steps and keep me safe. I need to pay attention to your nudges and your voice calling me back in, drawing me close to your side once more.   Lord Jesus, thank you for being our shepherd. Bring obedience to my heart and soul that I always hear your voice and leap to be close to you, knowing you are the good Shepherd. Amen.

July 6 - *2 Timothy 2:23 "Have nothing to do with stupid and senseless controversies; you know that they breed quarrels."*

Just yesterday I found myself picking apart words that were said to me.

I didn't jump in and spout out words that would have escalated the situation into a quarrel but I could have. I watch these senseless controversies happen every single day in my home between my children and sadly even in the news and on social media.

I have even, inadvertently, been an instigator recently to one of these senseless controversies and it surely did breed quarrels.

Isn't it amazing how someone can take what we said and twist it around to something completely different? They actually do not hear the same thing we meant even though the words are not changed. I have seen it and experienced it and it is strange and troublesome every time.

This verse calls us to step back from those moments. Do not jump from the frying pan into the proverbial fire. I know the only way I can manage to keep myself from getting burned is to keep my eyes and heart focused on Love. Maybe then, I can be a guide for others to keep away from these follies too.

Lord,
We sure do like to be right and sometimes that desire gets in the way of truth and love. Hold us back from stepping into trouble and being a part of a silly or senseless quarrel. Guide our hearts and our words so we are careful with them; so that our actions and speech honor you and your love. Amen.

July 7 - *1 John 3:18, 23 "Little children, let us love, not in word or speech, but in truth and action...And this is his commandment, that we should believe in the name of his Son Jesus Christ and love one another, just as he as commanded us."*

I love my garden. I love to watch it grow and I love the joy of eating fresh fruit and vegetables from my own backyard. If I do not love my garden with action, it will not grow.

My actions start in preparing the soil for the growing season. I must gently lay seed or seedlings paying attention to where and how they are laid in the ground. I make sure they receive the water they need and sunlight that helps them. I pull weeds to keep them from choking out the good plants.

This is how Christ showed us to love one another. If I love others like I do so easily my garden, how wonderful the results would be! Tend to those around you today like a gardener; gently caring and nurturing. Tenderly prune if necessary but with the care of a gardener.

Pray and allow Christ, the true master Gardener, to guide you and he will. He loved us all those years ago and he continues to love us in action and truth through his Spirit.

Lord,
Let me love as you have called me to. Move me to do love, not just say love. Use the world around me, my children, my spouse, my garden to remind me that love is action, not simply a feeling. Give me a servant's heart to love as you show me to. Let me hear you, so I may truly follow your command to believe and to love. Amen.

July 8 - *2 Corinthians 5:9 "So whether we are at home or away, we make it our aim to please him."*

There is no place like home.
When I go on a trip it is fun to travel, see people and places but as the journey comes close to an end I am usually ready to be home. Sometimes I miss seeing the enjoyment in the journey remaining because I have already begun to focus on home.
This is also true in my spiritual life. I cannot count how many times I have said that I am ready to go home.
I long for the day when I sit in heaven, worshiping and praising my Lord with no sadness, no strife; only joy and love beyond my imagination. Yet, the Lord has placed me on this journey in this time and in this place for a reason.
I will not lose the longing for home but I need not lose the blessing of the journey while I am away. I cannot fully please him if I am not living the journey as he has designed it for me.
As I journey, I receive joy in my children and my spouse. I worship and praise him in my prayer and my music. I honor him in my teaching and my work. I seek him in the midst of this journey and he is here.
We are not alone in this journey away from home. Let's join together in seeking to please him in this time away from home.

Lord,
Thank you for this verse. Thank you for reminding me again that wherever I am, I aim to please you. Help me find pleasure in the journey more and more each day until the day when you bring me home. Amen.

July 9 - *1 Timothy 1:14 "and the grace of our Lord overflowed for me with the faith and love that are in Christ Jesus."*

As I was visualizing the grace of God overflowing on me I thought of fountains that people have on their desks or end tables.

A pump recycles water from the pool at the bottom back up and the water runs down over the little rocks and sculptures to the pool and then back up again. Next I picture a river.

The water is crystal clear and the river rocks that sit in the bed are washed gently over and over with a never ending massage from the running water.

This seems like the grace of our Lord to me. We are rough and ragged when we come to Jesus. His grace "flows" over us, never ending. It smooths out the rough edges and the ragged broken parts until we are smooth and soft. When we have been infused with God's grace, his love fills; faith is strengthened.

Let the grace of our Lord pour out over you in abundance today. Take a moment and allow the gentle massage of his love and grace to renew and soothe you. Let it soften the rough edges and then, in faith, go out and allow his grace and love to flow from you to those around you.

Lord,
Without water we would die and without your grace we would die. The sacrifice of Jesus was the greatest act of love. Let the sounds of water remind me that your grace is here. Let this world receive your grace in abundance today and then let us praise you eternally! Amen.

July 10 - *Psalm 107:20-21 "he sent out his word and healed them, and delivered them from destruction. Let them thank the Lord for his steadfast love, for his wonderful works to humankind."*

A few times a day we nourish our bodies to stay healthy and have energy to thrive.

We need to feed our spirit regularly to keep it healthy so it can continue to thrive. When we are too busy and do without, our spirit runs down, becomes weak and is susceptible to sickness. We are more likely to ignore our spiritual nourishment but it is so much more important. Our bodies will not survive forever. They continue to break down and grow old.

Our spirit is eternal and we need to treat it with more intention so we are living eternity where we would like to. God waits for us to call. When we call out from our distress he sends forth his word and we are healed.

This beautiful passage is about all the ways God brings relief to us. I encourage you to read it; it is not long but gives so much encouragement in how much God wants us to be whole. Give thanks to the Lord for his steadfast love and his wonderful works for us.

Lord,
Thank you for your healing word. When we call in distress you are there instantly with your word and power. Help us remember the Bible is your word at our fingertips. Open our hearts and minds to communion and wholeness through your word and your unfailing love. Thank you for rescuing me, thank you for loving me, thank you for using me. Amen.

July 11 - *James 2:8-9 "You do well if you really fulfill the royal law according to the scripture, 'You shall love your neighbor as yourself.' But if you show partiality, you commit sin and are convicted by the law as transgressors."*

Who of us does not show partiality?
We all have people we do not understand and really do not wish to understand. We all have people that repel us that we have no desire to know and in fact, turn away from knowing for whatever reason.
When I read these verses another pops into my mind right away. Paul writes that all have sinned and fall short of the glory of God. Here James tells us the same thing in a different way.
On our last day of co-op classes for the school year, in the preschool class, the Bible story I shared was when Jesus charged his disciples to go out and spread the good news. I had the preschoolers give each other hugs and tell each other "Jesus loves you." It was so cute to watch and participate in. The shy ones took a moment to participate but in a moment all of them were doing it.
Today I want to share a hug with you and remind you that God loves you. Feel his embrace around you and let it lift your heart so you can go out and love your neighbor today.

Lord,
Your love never ends and you wait to pour it out into anyone who will receive it. As you fill me, your vessel, pour your love out of me as you will to whomever you will. My neighbor is not for me to choose. Let me see others as you see them so that I can share your love without reservation. Amen.

July 12 - *Acts 12:7 "Suddenly an angel of the Lord appeared and a light shone in the cell. He tapped Peter on the side and woke him saying, 'Get up quickly.' And the chains fell off his wrists."*

When Peter came to he knew without a doubt the Lord had rescued him.

I wonder how often the Lord sends angels to us and we choose not to listen and be rescued from our chains. We get so comfortable, so used to our chains that the thought of being free can be scary. We get used to carrying our burdens. We can't imagine what it would be like to walk freely, without chains.

I know my chains of "control" are hard to leave behind. They are tempting; so inviting. The great deceiver can even make them look like beautiful bracelets but they are imprisonment. Wake up, leave your chains behind, and walk with the Lord. Trust that the Lord guides and strengthens you as you leave your chains. I can assure you he will protect and guide you.

Lord,

Thank you for releasing my chains. Open my eyes so that I always remember the truth of them being imprisoned, not in comfort, not in security. I can only find true comfort and security in your love.

In my freedom, guide my steps away from my prison, keep my heart and mind focused on your light and remind me to acknowledge the amazing power you have in rescuing me from my chains and bringing me into freedom so I may dance and sing, so I may walk and serve in your love and light. Amen.

July 13 - *Isaiah 42:20 "He sees many things, but does not observe them; his ears are open, but he does not hear."*

It has been brought to my attention that I am not the most observant person.

My husband recently asked me the color of one of our friends' houses and it took me a full day to come to an agreement within myself as to what color it really is. I go there several times a year, I park in their driveway and yet the color of the house eluded me at first.

Someone asks me if I noticed the outfit on a person or the color of their hair and I didn't even see the person much less any of the detail of them.

Then there is my hearing. A couple of years ago I actually went to get my hearing checked because I needed to make sure I wasn't losing it. My hearing is just fine yet I still do not hear well, especially on the phone. I suspect this is, in part, that I am not listening well. Distractions like my children or the noise around me don't help but I suspect the noise in my head and the distractions in my mind do not help either.

Needless to say, this verse in Isaiah broke through all that blindness and deafness to remind me to observe and to truly listen.

Lord,
Open my eyes to the point of being truly observant. Open my ears and tune them in to truly listen. Let us all look and listen so that we see and hear you in our midst today. Thank you for breaking through to us, for always being there when we finally turn to you, seeing and hearing you after all. Amen.

July 14 - *Joshua 1:8-9 "This book of the law shall not depart out of your mouth; you shall meditate on it day and night, so that you may be careful to act in accordance with all that is written in it. For then you shall make your way prosperous, and then you shall be successful. I hereby command you: Be strong and courageous do not be frightened or dismayed, for the Lord your God is with you wherever you go."*

My daughter learned how to ride her bike this weekend.
I knew she could ride a bike but until she knew she could ride it, it wasn't going to happen. My husband and I had given her instruction, guided, and encouraged her. She finally let go of her fears and within one hour, she was riding, turning, stopping.
Now that she figured it out, there is no stopping her.
We have instruction and encouragement from God every day.
The Bible is always there as an instruction manual. If we meditate on it day and night we will hear him and his commands. Trusting him, we can release fear, take courage, and go forth. When we step forward in faith, with the Lord, we find that we never want to stop.

Lord,
I know you are always there, guiding and encouraging me. Help me release fear; my small voice says I cannot but your Spirit tells me that I can with you. You created me, you called me; I release my fears and myself to you. Let me ride like the wind, free and joyful, never turning back and always feeling your divine guidance and presence there encouraging me and cheering me on. Amen.

July 15 - *Acts 5:20-21 " 'Go, stand in the temple and tell the people the whole message about this life.' When they heard this, they entered the temple at daybreak and went on with their teaching."*

This story of the apostles is hard for me to imagine.
They are preaching, telling the story and message of Jesus to everyone that will listen. They bring healing to so many people and the church leaders are worried and jealous. They get thrown in jail and then an angel of the Lord breaks them out in the middle of the night and tells them to go out and spread their message.
I know nothing of persecution for anything I do or say.
In the news this week, there is a Rear Admiral in the Armed Forces of our nation who is stepping forward in faith.
There has been a push to stop military personnel from sharing their faith in the last few weeks and this man is refusing. I pray for this military man of God. He is a soldier for our country and he is a soldier for God.
As I write my devotions and seek to increase the depth of my faith walk, I wonder what will come of it. He gives me the strength to withstand whatever comes.

Lord,
Please protect our military and give them voices to honor you in the midst of this push to quiet them. Protect us as we seek to further your kingdom in a world that does not seem to want it. Encourage us to trust in you and share your message wherever you call us to. Amen.

July 16 - *Deuteronomy 4:39 "So acknowledge today and take to heart that the Lord is God in heaven above and on the earth beneath; there is no other."*

Monopoly is fun to play.

You go around the board collecting "salary" and buying up properties. Then you add houses or hotels to make property worth more and anytime someone lands on your property they have to pay rent. The game is over when one person owns everything. They have a monopoly.

We live this game. There are so many things we want or need. We try to collect as much as we can and make what we have worth more. If we are not careful those things become gods to us.

God is the banker and holds the monopoly on earth and in heaven. The one true God is not ruthless and he does not charge more "rent" or raise the cost because of what he owns. He is merciful and loving.

I take heart; the Lord of heaven above and earth below is my God, the one and only true God. He is the only one I want to hold a monopoly on me.

Lord,

Your power and might are infinite. You created all things and are above all things and yet, you do not run your world with malice and control. You love it, you guide it, you protect it, and you correct it. All your ways are filled with love for your creations. Thank you for loving each of us. Thank you for the hope and peace that comes from this verse today. Amen.

July 17 - *Psalm 34:12-14 "Which of you desires life, and covets many days to enjoy good? Keep your tongue from evil and your lips from speaking deceit. Depart from evil, and do good; seek peace, and pursue it."*

I was talking with my sister about happiness.

I told her that happiness would not be found on this earth and searching for it by means of other people leads to heartache. My jaded view, with broken marriages and destroyed homes, may not be the best one to share.

When I finally moved past the darkened view, past the destruction that I caused and that I had come through, I realized that I have only survived through the grace of God. When I finally turned my daily focus to the Lord I began to love life.

I cannot keep my thoughts and desires from evil unless I keep my thoughts and desires focused on God. It is through his peace and my seeking it to fill my life that I can keep from speaking lies.

Peter says there is a war against my soul. I am so thankful that God is fighting with me in the war. I love life, I love God. I seek to "do good" and I seek peace; I pursue it.

I have found happiness in the Lord. Glory to him, forever!

Lord,

The battle continues. We are such easy prey without your protection. You call to us, you tell us to seek the life only you can provide. Turn us away from evil so that we can do good for your kingdom. Guide us to peace; compel us to seek it. It is through your path, your guidance, and your life we can see many good days. Then we will find true happiness. Amen.

July 18 - *Acts 4:31 "When they had prayed, the place in which they were gathered together was shaken; and they were all filled with the Holy Spirit and spoke the word of God with boldness."*

I have a routine I like to follow.

I like to get up, get my cup of coffee, and then do my quiet time. I eat breakfast, shower, and get the kids ready for the day. Next we sit and "do" school. Lunch and chores follow that... you get the idea.

The reality rarely follows my desired routine. Almost every day there are little things that shake my routine up and change the course of the day. Are these moments of shaking one of God's ways of trying to wake me up?

Life is not routine as much as I would like it to be. If it were as routine as I think I want it to be, it would probably be so boring. I look to the Lord this morning and ask this; when I have my daily routine shaken, remind me of this verse.

Shake me out of my stupor, wake me from my slumber. Stir the Holy Spirit in me and compel me to go into this day boldly serving your kingdom as you lead me to.

Lord,
You do not call all to the same service but I hear you calling me to be bold in my service. Ruffle my feathers. Bring new energy and shake it up a bit so I remember that you are here. Fill me with your Holy Spirit so I go boldly forth in my day and remind me that you are God and if anything, you are not routine. Thank you for bringing newness to my days. Help me embrace that newness so I may continue to grow in You. Amen.

July 19 - *Mark 4:18-19 "And others are those sown among the thorns: these are the ones who hear the word, but the cares of the world, and the lure of wealth, and the desire for other things come in and choke the word, and it yields nothing."*

The kids and I planted the garden a couple of months ago. I dug the holes and the kids placed seeds in the soil covering them quickly so the wind wouldn't sweep them away. Then my daughter took off to go play.

When she came back with her friend to water the garden it had already been done. We have a lot of chances to water and weed the garden.

As I tend the plants in my garden, I hope I tend the word and my soul even more. We hear the Word of God in church or we sing praise songs to God. We need to plant the word, covering it so the wind doesn't blow it away. We need watering and nurturing so the word can grow and produce fruit.

My garden does not grow well if I plant seeds and leave them. Neither does our faith grow well if left on its own. Weed the deceitful desires and nurture the seeds of faith. If you are willing to take time in God, you will have fruit beyond your imagination.

Lord,
Let my garden be a reminder to be diligent in my time with you. It needs care but my faith needs daily care more. There is nothing more valuable than my salvation and my life in you. All things I do need to be reminders of you to me, they need to be calling me to You. Use my daily tasks to call me closer to you so that I may become fruitful and bring blessings to others, so that I may be blessed by You. Amen.

July 20 - *1 Corinthians 12:4-6 "Now there are varieties of gifts, but the same Spirit; and there are varieties of services, but the same Lord; and there are varieties of activities, but it is the same God who activates all of them in everyone."*

I am glad to say I do not have the same gifts and services as the governor of my state. I am glad I do not have the same gifts and services that a TV or movie star has.

It is interesting how I look at others and sometimes I really cannot fathom how they could do what they do, or why they even want to. The orchestration of the world and all that is in it is mind boggling if I stop to think about it. Each person created for a specific time and a specific space, placed just so by the Creator of all things.

Just as in a symphony orchestra there are a few stray notes and things don't always go perfectly, so it is with life on earth. The Maestro knows what gifts we have and what services we are created for. He helps us find the instrument that fits us best and then beautiful music begins to happen.

No matter who we are, where we live, and what we do, the same God who created me created you. God of all placed the desires to serve and the gifts to serve within your soul and mine. Listen to the music as we all practice our parts today.

Lord,
Thank you for music in my soul. Help me see and appreciate all the gifts you give others that work in conjunction with mine to make music in your world. I pray that we make beautiful music for you today. Amen.

July 21 - *John 1:16-18 "From his fullness we have all received, grace upon grace. The law indeed was given through Moses; grace and truth came through Jesus Christ. No one has ever seen God. It is God the only Son, who is close to the Father's heart, who has made him known."*

There is a song that I like to sing during my quiet time. It focuses my mind and my whole being.
The journey I have embarked on over the last year or two has been nothing short of amazing to me. This morning is no different. I was singing "I want to know you" and then I come to this passage at the beginning of John.
Jesus the Christ came so that I might know God. As I study the Word more, I know God more. He is not just this Divine being *way* beyond my grasp, so holy I dare not gaze to see him. He is God the Son, who came to this earth.
He came to that which was his own bringing grace upon grace. When we receive his grace, when we embrace him and his truth, we know God. Be with God today and take delight in his love and grace.

Lord,
So very often I come to you humbled and amazed. You sent your Word as flesh to walk among us, to teach us to share your unending grace. I cannot find words to express the awe I experience when I sit in your presence infused with your love, grace, and light. I pray that your light, your grace, and your truth would radiate from me today blessing those around me and drawing more people into your Word, into Christ, and into knowing you. Amen.

July 22 - *Acts 8:30-31 "So Philip ran up to it and heard him reading the prophet Isaiah. He asked, 'Do you understand what you are reading?' He replied, 'How can I, unless someone guides me.' And he invited Philip to get in and sit beside him."*

Do you remember a subject that didn't come easily?
My challenge was geometry. When I used to study it, things just didn't make sense. I needed someone explain it to me. In school we have teachers and tutors to help us understand things that are difficult.
In our spiritual growth we have teachers and tutors as well. An angel of the Lord tells Philip to go south to the road to Gaza. He met this eunuch reading Isaiah. God sent an angel and God sent Philip.
God sends guidance and understanding if you seek it. The man reading this scripture wanted to understand. I need to be open to guidance and teaching that God brings me. When there are Scriptures that I struggle to understand, I need to seek understanding. If I seek, I will find.
I encourage you to seek; gain knowledge and understanding of the Holy One.

Lord,
Thank you for your guidance and teachings. I cannot imagine something more precious than understanding more of you. Come teach me and guide me through my lessons. Give me the courage to be like Philip. When I hear your voice, I want to go follow your directions and maybe I will be blessed to sit with someone else; explaining what I have learned through your blessed teaching. Amen.

July 23 - *Mark 6:34 "As he went ashore, he saw a great crowd; and he had compassion for them, because they were like sheep without a shepherd; and he began to teach them many things."*

Compassion is a beautiful thing.
Just saying or thinking the word brings softness to my heart and focus to my mind. I get wrapped up in my daily tasks, wanting to check off each thing on my list and get things accomplished. I get irritated when things or people get in the way of those tasks being crossed off.
What would it have been like if Jesus came to shore with my mindset? He would have been annoyed that the people would not give him his quiet time. He would have been frustrated that they were so needy and couldn't seem to get along for even a little while without him. I am glad that he was filled with compassion for them and that he is filled with compassion for us today.
I hope this story guides my heart today as I teach my children, as I clean my home, and as I prepare to make music for others this evening. All these things can be done with a heart of compassion. We, too, are like sheep.
Let's follow our good shepherd and share the compassion he gives us with those around us.

Lord,
Thank you for your teachings and your unending compassion for us. Write your message of love and compassion on our hearts so we learn it well from you. Soften our hearts in compassion for others as we follow you. Amen.

July 24 - *Leviticus 23:22 "When you reap the harvest of your land, you shall not reap to the very edges of your field, or gather the gleanings of your harvest; you shall leave them for the poor and for the alien: I am the Lord your God."*

Generosity does not come easily to some.

Kids struggle with it on the very basic level. They cling to their toys and "fight to the death" to keep them. I see it with my own kids and I see it with their friends. As we grow and learn to share we realize that it makes our hearts feel good to share with someone else. Seeing the gratitude on someone's face eases our desire to hoard.

I don't personally know very many people who actually harvest fields but the principle in this verse still holds true. We have been blessed beyond words and whatever we have received in blessing, we are called to share first with God and then with our neighbor. The verse uses the words poor and alien but I believe this is synonymous with our neighbor in today's world.

As we care for our gardens, receive another paycheck in the bank, or prepare our evening meal, let us remember to share.

Lord,
Thank you for the blessings you have given to us in such abundance. Help us see and remember those who have less or none and compel us to reach out in love and share. Open our hearts and our hands to receive the blessings of generosity by being generous to others. Amen.

July 25 - *Psalm 23: 2-3 "He makes me lie down in green pastures; he leads me beside still waters; he restores my soul. He leads me in right paths for his name's sake."*

Lying down in green pastures brings a peaceful picture to my mind's eye.

Soft green grass warmed by the sun is relaxing me like being wrapped in a warm blanket. The sky is deep azure blue with a puffy white cloud or two floating by, catching my gaze so I can ponder their shapes. I hear a brook gently flowing in a nearby glen. It is a nice shady area where I can get a cool refreshing drink.

Once I have lingered in this spot, I realize that God has indeed restored my soul. I can more easily see the path that has always been there. He raises me with his hand and we walk together on the right path so that I may go forward glorifying his name.

Lord,
Thank you for the beauty on this earth. You have created peace on this earth and this picture in my mind's eye is the closest I can come to what I imagine heaven being like. All these things are images of you and what you give to me. You bring me healing and restoration so that when I am ready, you will hold my hand and guide me once more to the path you have created for me. Thank you for your word. Thank you for being Jehovah-raah: The Lord my Shepherd. Amen.

July 26 - *Psalm 24:1 "The earth is the Lord's and all that is in it, the world, and those who live in it."*

Rain is falling in Colorado. The ground is soaking it in, the grass is drinking deep, and the earth around me breathes a deep sigh of thanksgiving and satisfaction.

As I sat at my kitchen table this morning I could not block out the overwhelming songs coming from the birds outside. I cracked the back door for a moment just to sit and listen to the soft drum of rain falling and the birds singing their songs of praise and jubilation. In my mind I could almost see them dancing and playing in the rain like children; they sounded so happy! Yesterday my kids were out playing in the rain with the neighbors.

What some don't realize is that rain in Colorado is cold! After they were thoroughly soaked I brought them in for a bath to warm them up and a nice cozy supper for their tummies. Even the kids are celebrating this moisture for the Lord's earth.

Step away from the news of the day with me and soak in the rain just as the earth is doing. Let the moisture refresh our souls and lift our spirits until we cannot help but sing like the birds and dance like children.

The earth is the Lord's and all who live in it!

Lord,
Thank you for the blessed moisture on this thirsty earth. Thank you for the song of birds to draw me into the beauty of the morning. Help me see the beauty of your earth and to be a part of caring for it rather than a part of destroying it. I rejoice in you and your world today. Amen.

July 27 - *Colossians 2:6-7 "As you therefore have received Christ Jesus the Lord, continue to live your lives in him, rooted and built up in him and established in the faith, just as you were taught, abounding in thanksgiving."*

It is not the season for thanksgiving; we are still in the height of summer today.

Tradition has one day a year set aside to give thanks for all we have been given. We usually gather with loved ones, sharing a meal and stories of blessing. These times fill us with love; we go back to our roots where we feel safe and grounded.

Today I can picture the wonderful moments of Thanksgiving Day and because of my life in Christ I know I can experience those moments every day.

I spent time this morning releasing old hurts, searching the corners of my soul for hidden chains of sin. Jesus shines his light and cleanses all when we release it to him. This is how we can be rooted and built up in him. When we have faith in him and his healing grace, faith in his forgiveness and redemption, we cannot help but be thankful.

Renew your walk with him. Live and work with him and thanksgiving will abound.

Lord,
When I look at all I have in you, my heart is filled with thanksgiving. I can never stop singing your praises for all the blessings in my life. You bring abundance of joy, light and love to any who will have it. I pray for all those who do not have Christ, that they hear your call and come to be filled with your blessings too. Amen.

July 28 - *1 Timothy 2:8 "I desire, then, that in every place the men should pray, lifting up holy hands without anger or argument;"*

Without prayer, I am nothing.
Without prayer I am easily distracted, frustrated, and argumentative. We, as humans, are a selfish bunch. It is in prayer that I find compassion and forgiveness for myself and for others. It is in the prayers for others that I am brought to a place of peace and love for my neighbor.
There is much in the world that we can justifiably be angry about. There are injustices and atrocities in the news every day. We can choose to dwell on those and let the poison of their darkness seep into our souls bringing us back to angry and argumentative places, or we can seek the Lord.
We can lift up our hands, calling on the Lord to make us holy. We can bring those things that break our hearts to the Lord knowing that he is all mighty and all knowing.
Just as children cannot always see the plan a parent has and they think life is unfair, we cannot know the heart and mind of God. We can pray and trust.

Lord,
Thank you for Paul's words to remind us to come to you in prayer. Through our salvation in Christ, we are made holy and so we can come in prayer, lifting our holy hands to you. Help us release anger, frustration, and bitterness and receive grace, mercy, and compassion in place of those. I ask these things in Jesus' name and for your glory. Amen.

July 29 - *Leviticus 23:3 "Six days shall work be done; but the seventh day is a sabbath of complete rest, a holy convocation; you shall do no work; it is a sabbath to the Lord throughout your settlements."*

I have been looking at my calendar and shaking my head. Every day has numerous things written on it to remind me of appointments and commitments so I don't forget something. The other day I went to pick up my son from preschool. When I got there all the parents were in the room, visiting and eating treats with their kids.

I must have had a look of horror my face and I know I was near tears thinking I forgot something on my calendar. His teacher came to my rescue quickly assuring me that this had been only on the note handed to me that very morning, the note I didn't read. I had too many things to do and set it aside for a later time. We are all so busy all the time that the idea of a Sabbath day seems absurd if not a waste.

I used to think I didn't have time for an hour with the Lord but now that I do it regularly I cannot imagine not having the hour each morning to spend with the Lord. I know a day with the Lord would be even better... now to put that on my calendar...

Lord,
Thank you for the rest you graciously give us despite our lack of time with you. When we have a day of rest, call us into your arms of love; infuse us with your presence. Entice us to make this a habit so that we follow you more closely and receive even more blessings from being with you. Amen.

July 30 - *Psalm 104:24 "O Lord, how manifold are your works! In wisdom you have made them all; the earth is full of your creatures."*

God uses music to speak to me because He knows me and He knows I hear messages conveyed through music.
As I sat enjoying the beauty of God's creation this morning I could not help but feel praises and joy glorifying his name.
There are so many things that bring me to my knees when I look at his beautiful creations.
The peace and sweet innocence on the faces of my children when they are asleep is just one tiny gift of beauty in my world. The softness of flower petals and the fragrance they bring to my nose send me calm, gentle caresses of love from God directly.
We have been given this day, a new day to be in the presence of God regardless of what our day holds. He is wherever we are.
Take time today to find the beauty in your world and in yourself as well.
God created all things in wisdom, let us enjoy and rejoice in his wisdom and in his creation.

Lord,
The beauty of your creation is awe inspiring. People try to create music, poems, and art to convey the beauty they experience but I have found myself lacking any means of communicating the feelings you bring to my heart in your creation. Thank you for creating me. My heart sings praises to you this day because, in your wisdom, all things are created. Thanksgiving and unending praise belong to you. Amen.

July 31 - *Daniel 3:17-18 "If our God whom we serve is able to deliver us from the furnace of blazing fire and out of your hand, O king, let him deliver us. But if not, be it known to you, O king, that we will not serve your gods and we will not worship the golden statue that you have set up."*

When I read the story of Shadrach, Meshach and Abednego it lifts me up and it humbles me.

These men would not bow to a false god. They stood up for their faith and God. Do I have the strength of character to follow in their footsteps?

I am disturbed at how often I falter at the slightest bump in my walk with God and I have never faced anything like a fiery furnace. Are the subtle tests of faith harder to fight because they are subversive?

I only know this; God stands by my side, he protects and delivers me from any test of faith, any trial or tribulation if I stay by his side. I hope I never have to walk in a blazing furnace but if I do, when I walk in the furnace of my faith, I will call on the Lord to walk with me and deliver me for his glory.

Lord,
It is easy to get burned in this world of temptation and "easy" life. Please remind us of these men of faith whenever we are struggling with temptation to take the easy way out. You call us to be faithful to you and you have shown us so many times that you will never let us down. Send your protection, be my fortress, strengthen me so that I never let you down either. I want to serve you, I want to know you. I want to walk hand in hand with you, my Lord and Savior. Amen.

Aug 1 - *1 John 4:15-16 "God abides in those who confess that Jesus is the Son of God, and they abide in God. So we have known and believe the love that God has for us. God is love, and those who abide in love abide in God, and God abides in them."*

"... and they'll know we are Christians by our love, by our love..."
The divisiveness in the church is heavy on my mind. We try to force our thoughts and beliefs onto others and we shut them out if they do not believe as we do. We confess Jesus is Lord but we do not live as he taught us to live.
Who are the tax collectors and prostitutes of today? There are many who do not walk in the light and there are many who think they walk in the light but are deceived. Instead of condemning them, let us love them.
The moment we believe we are better, piety and pride take over; we have sinned once more. When I feel pride sneaking in, I remember it is ONLY because of God's grace and love that I do anything at all.
It is his love abiding in me that has brought me back from darkness.

Lord,
Please bring encouragement and peace today. Seep into our souls so that we feel your presence there. When we stop to feel your presence, we feel your abundant love filling and renewing us once more. When we acknowledge your presence, we can live in you. Bring me to my knees so that I take a moment to state, without doubt, that Jesus is your Son. You abide in me and me in you. Hallelujah! Amen.

Aug 2 - *2 Corinthians 3:18 "And all of us, with unveiled faces, seeing the glory of the Lord as though reflected in a mirror, are being transformed into the same image from one degree of glory to another; for this comes from the Lord, the Spirit."*

It is very easy for me to get caught up in getting to the destination, reaching the end of the journey. Just let me get where I am going and be done with it.

Life is not like that and neither is our walk with God. There is a long, sometimes arduous journey to experience before we ever get to the destination. It is in God's wisdom that he does not allow me to rush forth, skipping the journey and the lessons to be learned. Without walking, step by step, we cannot be transformed from one degree to another. We would miss some beauty along the way. Without gradual transformation we cannot be prepared for the full glory of the Lord.

Slow down a bit and take time to learn the lessons God has for you. Look for the beauty he has woven into the path along the way. I will try to heed this advice as well.

Lord,
Thank you for teaching and transforming us by degrees and small increments. Even those are sometimes so hard. Thank you for your grace and mercy. Thank you for your Spirit and your Word to guide our steps. I want to get so close to you, to know you beyond anything I can imagine. Keep me focused on this journey so that someday I reach the destination and live in full glory with you. Amen.

Aug 3 - *Hosea 6:1 "Come, let us return to the Lord; for it is he who has torn, and he will heal us; he has struck down, and he will bind us up."*

I really don't like to put my kids in "time-out" but there are times that it must be done.

They push the boundaries, make bad choices, and disobey so there must be some kind of discipline invoked before they get completely out of control. I am sure, based on their reactions, that they feel like I have "torn" or destroyed them when they are sitting on that stair or in their rooms. It is only a short time and then we talk about it, hug, and move forward in a new way.

This verse reminded me of this scenario so much. How often do we turn our backs on the ways the Lord has taught us, defying his word and guidance, disobeying his commands?

Before we get completely out of control, he "tears" us down and disciplines us. He tries to get us to turn around and focus on him and his path again. When he has disciplined or torn, he also heals. When he takes us down a peg or two he picks us up again. I search my heart today to find how I am disobedient to the Lord so I can turn around before I get out of control.

Lord,
Thank you for never quitting on us. Just as a parent with their child, you continue to guide, reprimand, and correct. You continue to love, heal, and pick us up to start again. Thank you for your words in Hosea to call us into action before you must act on our behalf. Help us stay true to you in this world of deceit and distraction. In Jesus' name, Amen.

Aug 4 - *James 4:7-8 "Submit yourselves therefore to God. Resist the devil, and he will flee from you. Draw near to God, and he will draw near to you. Cleanse your hands, you sinners, and purify your hearts, you double-minded."*

My kids love to play outside.

They ride bikes, play in the sand box, make mud soup and more. It is hard to stay clean when they are playing and exploring and when it is time to come in they have a hard time listening and giving up what has been a fun time.

This is how it seems to me for us adults too. The world is full of "fun"; it is easy for us to become double-minded and forget to submit to God. We want what we want and when God calls us to something different, it is hard to come in. It is only when we come in, wash up, and cleanse our hearts that we realize the real goodness in God.

When we send the devil packing and we curl up in the arms of our Heavenly Father, there is nothing better. It is great to go into the world and participate but we need to heed the call when we hear it.

We need to focus on God where we are; whatever we are doing. When we do this, we can resist the devil and be near God. We will no longer be double-minded; he will cleanse our hearts and our hands and draw us near.

Lord,

Our world is a messy place and if we are not careful we get messy too. Keep us from trouble. Please send the devil away so we can be wholly focused on you. Open our ears so we hear you call us. Let me be a shining light in this world for your glory. I ask all these things in your name. Amen.

Aug 5 - *Isaiah 45:11-12 "Thus says the Lord, the Holy One of Israel, and its Maker; Will you question me about my children, or command me concerning the work of my hands? I made the earth, and created humankind upon it; it was my hands that stretched out the heavens, and I commanded all their host."*

These verses do two things for me this morning. First, they bring me to my knees in humility. Second, they lift me up in praise for his work in me.

It is so easy to question the workings of God. I come to him asking for understanding and sometimes questioning him. When I have received blessings beyond my imagination I question him again.

Here it is, cut and dried; he created all things, every living thing including me and those people around me. The Creator does what he will with his creation, and in his sovereignty, he gives us grace and love. He continues to create in us and if we stumble, crack, or mar he heals us.

I come to the Lord on my knees today. I know I need to be melted and molded once again to be a worthy vessel.

Lord,
You created me just as I am. Forgive me for the lack of trust I find in my heart. Forgive my rebellious ways that cause you and me pain. Create me anew today, Lord. Bring me forth as a renewed vessel, filled with your Spirit and trusting you to use me as you will. All these things I ask are only for your glory and honor. Amen.

Aug 6 - *1 Corinthians 13:12 "For now we see in a mirror, dimly, but then we will see face to face. Now I know only in part; then I will know fully, even as I have been fully known."*

Mirrors must have been a fraction of what they are today based on Paul's description.

I know when I look in my bathroom mirror I can see every gray hair and every wrinkle or line in my face. What came to my mind when I pondered this verse were transition sunglasses. You know the ones that are clear when you are inside and turn dark when you go out in the sun?

I think Paul might use that analogy... for now we see through dark sunglasses in a dark room but then we will see face to face. Now I know through a blinding fog, then I will know fully...

We are set for another sunny and hot summer day in Colorado. I can clearly see the sun already over the horizon as I write. We deceive ourselves if we think this verse is really about our eyes. We must see with our souls.

Clear the fog; take the shades off of the eyes of your soul so you can see more clearly the face of the Lord. As we continue to seek with our soul's eyes, we begin to see more clearly. What a blessing that is!

Lord,
Thank you for this verse and thank you for cleansing our soul's eyes to help us see better. Keep our focus on you so we can learn to trust even more that we will see clearly. You promise us if we seek we will find. Bless us with a clear vision of your kingdom in our world today. Amen.

Aug 7 - *Psalm 119:41-42 "Let your steadfast love come to me, O Lord, your salvation according to your promise. Then I shall have an answer for those who taunt me, for I trust in your word."*

I want to clarify that I do not have people, in reality, taunting me because of my love of God or my faith in Christ.

I am so blessed to live where I do so I do not face the persecution that exists in other parts of the world. Sadly, it is my inner self, and the deceiver, Satan, that taunt me.

His evil goal is to cause me to stumble and fall. He delights in the hope that I will lose heart and give up my faith and he stops at nothing to try and win this battle in me and in you.

There is hope in these verses. God promises his love and salvation. When we call on his name, he is there to rescue and save us, to love and heal us. The Word of God is our sword to fight the taunting voice of Satan and he cannot stand against it. Jesus used it in his temptation and so can we.

The more we study the word, the better equipped we are to stand in God against the enemy. God redeemed all of humanity. Believe it, own it, and stand for it.

Lord,
Pour your healing love into my heart and renew me again. Quiet the voices that tear me down and bring me to peace. Your word brings hope and guidance. It feeds me and strengthens me; I know that you will not forsake me. I am a redeemed child and you fight for me forever. I praise you and thank you with all my heart. Amen.

Aug 8 - *Ezekiel 33:16 "None of the sins that they have committed shall be remembered against them; they have done what is lawful and right, they shall surely live."*

How would a butterfly flutter if it had to carry the cocoon around? How well would a bullfrog jump if it neglected the legs it had grown and tried to use the tail it used to have?
This is how it is when we try to live in God, carrying around the baggage and burdens of the past. We are weighed down but not really.
As people of God, we confess our sins and he forgives us and makes us new. We humbly bring our sins to God, lay them at his feet and we promptly (or maybe eventually) come back to the throne and pick up the weight of a sin that no longer exists. We walk around with bent backs, stumbling around, unable to dance in praise because we think we still have a burden.
Leave your burdens, real or imagined. None of these are remembered against you so let's lay them down once and for all. When we have received and accepted forgiveness it is hard not to dance in the light of God.
Join me in celebrating the light, join me in praising God at the new creation he is working in us. Dance in joy, for surely we shall live!

Lord,
Forgive me for my lack of trust and my unaccepting heart.
Teach me to embrace your forgiveness and to turn in humility;
dancing with renewed spirit. You are creating me new each day.
Help me leave yesterday where it belongs and be present in this
new and holy day. Amen.

Aug 9 - *John 15:3-4 "You have already been cleansed by the word that I have spoken to you. Abide in me as I abide in you. Just as the branch cannot bear fruit by itself unless it abides in the vine, neither can you unless you abide in me."*

I used to picture God near me, sitting in the chair next to me or hovering just above me. It is still fairly new to me to picture God *in* me and me *in* God.

This verse reminds me that this is the more accurate vision. We are connected, a part of each other. Another analogy that comes to mind is this; I am a part of my family. I am not my family but we are connected and a part of each other. I am a part of God's family. God calls us to be a part of him, live with him, abide IN him.

When I trim back, or prune, the plants and trees in my yard, they flourish. God also prunes his fruitful branches so that they may become more fruitful. When we live in him, he nurtures us and feeds us. He prunes us and guides us.

Let's go into this day remembering that we are in God as a tree branch is in the tree. We are attached, intertwined. We grow and are kept healthy because of his roots. We would wither without him.

Lord,
The roots and grounding you provide through your word are refreshing. They strengthen us; they feed us and bring us new life. Help us turn those gifts you give us around and give to others so we may be fruitful branches. Fill us with your presence today so we do not doubt that you are in us and we abide in you. Amen.

Aug 10 - *Psalm 23:6 "Surely goodness and mercy shall follow me all the days of my life, and I shall dwell in the house of the Lord, my whole life long."*

I love the message of this verse; I have known it for years and have clung to it during challenges in my life.

When I picture goodness and mercy I see myself walking on a sunny path that is surrounded by beautiful wildflowers and soft puffy white clouds in azure skies. That is what mercy looks like in my mind. As I turned this verse over in my meditation this morning a new view came to mind.

God's goodness and mercy are always with me but if they follow me they are also behind me. What do I leave in the wake of my journey? As I move forward, striving to follow as a disciple of God, do I leave goodness and mercy for others or do I leave brokenness and selfishness in my path?

The more I seek the Lord and his ways, I trust and believe I will dwell with him for eternity, for my whole life. Now I also am aware that I need to strive to bring goodness and mercy for others to follow as my legacy to the love I have for my Lord. Goodness and mercy might follow me because I leave some as a trail for others to follow.

I can only hope for this.

Lord,
As I receive your gifts of goodness and mercy, help me open my heart to give those gifts to others as well. Protect me from being a person of destruction and damage and guide me to be a vessel of mercy, bringing a piece of your kingdom to others each day. Amen.

Aug 11 - *Matthew 6:6 "But whenever you pray, go into your room and shut the door and pray to your Father who is in secret; and your Father who sees in secret will reward you."*

This instruction from Jesus has always intrigued me.
I think about all the times my family gets together on holidays or birthdays and the prayers that have been lifted over those meals.
I can hear the voices of family members saying "you should pray, you do a much better job than I do." I have yet to be a liturgist in my church; partly because I am such an introvert at heart the desire to get up there and speak in front of the congregation is not very strong. Also the prayers they read are fluid and deep. I love listening to those words with my heart instead of reading them with my eyes and mouth.
I see people, on occasion, praying over their meals at restaurants.
I used to think that was awkward or strange but as I grow in my faith I think I feel like I am intruding in their prayer if I don't grant their privacy, yet if they are praying in public do they desire privacy?
I think the message Jesus was giving here is this: when we pray, we need to seek God and not the accolades of other people.
When we pray in public we risk receiving praise from others.
The purpose of prayer is to commune with God.
Now I need to go pray about this more...

Lord,
I love our private times of prayer. Help me teach my children how to pray as you taught me. Help us all keep prayer in our hearts and love in our hands as we seek to serve you. Amen.

Aug 12 - *John 17:3 "And this is eternal life, that they may know you, the only true God, and Jesus Christ whom you have sent."*

We have been placed on this earth for just a fraction of time but our souls live on.

As we walk the journey of this life, we are aware that there is more. I listen to the rain falling this morning giving the ground a much needed drink. Then I realize that this too, is a cycle. Rains fall, plants grow, and the sun brings warmth and dries the earth. All these things will fade away eventually...

Our souls live on. The only place we can find true, deep peace is in knowing God. When we search and find him, when we begin the relationship of knowing God, the only true God, we begin to see the edges of eternity. When we are with God, eternity brings a sense of light and joy, peace and love.

Stay true to this call; continue striving to know the only true God and Jesus the Christ whom he sent.

Lord,

It is so easy to get caught up in this trap we call life. Help us release the worries and troubles of this earthly life because we know, in you, we are not here forever. Give us the courage to step forth seeking to know you more deeply each day. You have called us your own, you know us and you want to be known. I want to know you. Help me seek and find you today and all days. Amen.

Aug 13 - *Galatians 2:16 "yet we know that a person is justified not by the works of the law but through faith in Jesus Christ. And we have come to believe in Christ Jesus, so that we might be justified by faith in Christ and not by doing the works of the law, because no one will be justified by the works of the law."*

Can I keep the letter of the law? I know, beyond a shadow of doubt that I cannot.

When I think about the laws and precepts that exist, it is disheartening to say the least. It would be easy to lose hope in reviewing and trying to live letter perfect.

I cannot express the relief I have knowing that I do not have to be perfect and even if I try I will be humbled and reminded that it is not because of my works but because of my belief in Jesus that I live.

On the days I am convicted of my transgressions, I can come to my Savior in humility and in confidence because I have confessed my trust and love for him. He washes me and sends me out a new person to work for his kingdom again. I grow strong only because of my faith in him; I serve him because of my faith in him.

He is my all and all. Amen.

Lord,
I come to you often with my cross heavy on my back only to find that you have already removed it. Your love for me is renewing and healing; it lifts me once again. I pray that all I do serves to build your kingdom. Forgive my shortcomings and my failures. I know you will rebuild me and use me again. Thank you Jesus. Amen.

Aug 14 - *Psalm 117:2 "For great is his steadfast love toward us, and the faithfulness of the Lord endures forever. Praise the Lord!"*

This morning when I woke up I was already singing praises. That does not happen every day but when it does I take joy in that moment. I spent my prayer time trying to praise and thank the Lord for the people and their situations instead of petitioning for them.

I thanked the Lord for medical care, for support systems, for friends, and for faith. I praised the Lord for the freedom of religion, freedom to homeschool, and freedom to seek knowledge. I praised the Lord for the founding fathers and the vision they had for this country. I thanked him for downtime and inspiration, energy and rest.

It was hard not to ask the Lord for anything but to turn each request in to a prayer of thanks and praise. This verse called me to do that today. His steadfast love is great toward us and he is always faithful; forever and ever.

Praise the Lord!

Lord,
I am filled with praise and joy for the love and grace you give me every moment, every day for eternity. I have seen your hand working in my life and in the lives of others. The evidence is clear; you are truly faithful and loving. Thank you for filling me with those blessings and allowing me to be a servant of yours, spreading joy, praise, and love to the world around me. Amen.

Aug 15 - *Philippians 1:27 "Only, live your life in a manner worthy of the gospel of Christ, so that, whether I come and see you or am absent and hear about you, I will know that you are standing firm in one spirit, striving side by side with one mind for the faith of the gospel."*

Christ lived here to show us how to live.

We are to love God and love each other as he loves us. Our human desires get in the way of this charge and muddy the waters of our faith. When that happens we come to the foot of the cross and repent, asking God to forgive our shortcomings and our failures.

This brings me to the second part of living the gospel; living in the light and joy, the true and deep freedom that God granted us in the death and resurrection of our Lord, Jesus Christ. If we do not release our sins fully, we are rejecting grace.

Let's step forward together, side by side, encouraging each other and supporting each other in the faith and love of Jesus Christ. Listen for the Spirit guiding you to live in a worthy manner. Praise God for this Word and go forth in freedom and celebration.

Lord,

How do I begin to thank you for the grace you pour out onto me? I give you my life and then I end up taking it back and living in my selfish ways again. This cycle is perpetual and yet you are there, always willing to forgive me once again. Teach me to follow this life without fail so that I can be a beacon of your love and grace glorifying your name and kingdom in every moment. Amen.

Aug 16 - *Hebrews 4:12-13 "Indeed, the word of God is living and active, sharper than any two-edged sword, piercing until it divides the soul from spirit, joints from marrow, it is able to judge the thoughts and intentions of the heart. And before him no creature is hidden, but all are naked and laid bare to the eyes of the one to whom we must render an account."*

The passage talks about the rest God promises to the faithful. When we are rushing around like chickens with our heads cut off, it is likely that we have lost any Godly intentions we had. The time I spend resting in the Lord is invaluable.
I can be laid bare and held accountable for my thoughts and intentions. His living word can divide my selfish soul from the true spirit. I am so grateful that the God who holds me accountable, he whose word guides and corrects my path, is a God of grace and mercy.
I have never felt freer than after the times I have spent with God searching and judging, then cleansing and forgiving me. He brings things to me that I had not seen or realized, but when I have asked to be forgiven for all those things I see and he sees; it is a fresh new day again.
Take a risk; sit with God and allow him to divide and judge. Lay bare before him so that you may be fully renewed in him.

Lord,
Open our eyes to see that you know and see; we are already laid bare to you. Teach us to trust, to willingly release those hidden things to you. Open our ears and our hearts that the living, active word would cut to the very heart of us so that we may be truly changed in you. Amen.

Aug 17 - *Psalm 147:3 "He heals the brokenhearted, and binds up their wounds."*

I am encouraged and relieved by the message in this verse and in this passage of Psalms.

I was feeling discouraged by the lack of trust or faith I must have in the Lord when I came to this scripture. I know God has given many people the gift of healing; physicians and nurses, psychologists and pastors, to name a few. There are many tools we have today that assist us in physical and mental healing and I praise the Lord for those people and those tools.

For myself, I know that my biggest malady is not physical, it is spiritual. I seek the Lord to fill me up as I have written about so many times and yet it is all too easy for me to seek human fulfillment for a spiritual hunger.

I can spend time with my family and friends and I am blessed by the love I receive from them. I can get hugs and kisses from my kids which are a treasure to me. All of these people are gifts from God that ease my heart most of the time. There is an emptiness that cannot be filled by humans.

I need him. Only he can bring wholeness to any spiritual brokenness, only he can bring the balm of Gilead.

This verse promises just that. He heals our brokenness...

Lord,
I thank you for the healing you have brought to my heart and to the hearts of so many. I thank you for the gift of our Savior, Jesus Christ and the Spirit you sent to guide our every step. Call our hearts into your presence so that we may receive your healing touch today. Amen.

Aug 18 - *Hebrews 6:1 "Therefore let us go on toward perfection, leaving behind the basic teaching about Christ, and not laying again the foundation; repentance from dead works and faith toward God,"*

Our spiritual journey is like school in a way.
Just as small children begin with the foundation of the alphabet and counting we begin with learning about Jesus Christ and our salvation. Children cannot learn to read and add unless they have the foundation of letters and numbers and we cannot learn to live toward perfection unless we have the foundation of faith in Christ and God as our Redeemer.
As the school year ramps up again the foundations and steps my kids have learned are on my mind. I do not want them to slide back down but when they have a few months off, not really using those skills, I know we need to step back and review.
The same is true in our spiritual walk. If we do not use what we have learned we slide back and have to review and relearn what we already knew. This passage in Hebrews encourages us to continue learning and growing. Use the knowledge we have gained and strive to learn and grow even more.
This is how we "go on toward perfection."

Lord,
There is no summer break in your kingdom. Your Holy Spirit came to the disciples and has never withdrawn for a break. Renew our strength and desire to learn and serve. Help us build onto what we already have and continue growing in you. Amen.

Aug 19 - *Psalm 96:2-4 "Sing to the Lord, bless his name; tell of his salvation from day to day. Declare his glory among the nations, his marvelous works among all the peoples. For great is the Lord, and greatly to be praised; he is to be revered above all gods."*

What a glorious morning today.
I went for a walk during my quiet time this morning. As I listened to the different bird songs and the gentle stream I could not help but to praise God. He created each bird with their own unique song and they sing without fail. How often do I fail to sing the song God put in my heart or try to sing the song of someone else?
When I got close to the playground on my walk I noticed trash along the path. How often do I ignore the trash in the world, hoping someone else will take care of it?
As I headed back home I heard the rhythmic sound of my steps and the rhythmic beat of my heart. All these beautiful things I saw and heard along the path of my walk are the marvelous works of God.
God is great; join me today in praising him greatly!

Lord,
Let my song declare your glory and tell of your salvation. Give me courage to sing the song you have given me and to glorify you. Grant me strength and wisdom to clean up the trash I see without crushing anything in the process. I pray that I bless you and I would be filled with your love and grace so that I can share all these things with the people I come in contact with. Amen.

Aug 20 - *1 John 5:3-4 "For the love of God is this, that we obey his commandments. And his commandments are not burdensome, for whatever is born of God conquers the world, And this is the victory that conquers the world, our faith."*

Conquering the world seems like such a huge and powerful project.
It brings to mind soldiers, battles, and victory. The amazing thing is that in God's love, in our love for God, and sharing the love of God we can conquer the world.
The love of God brings us freedom and light. This freedom, this light is what makes it easy to love him with all we are and love our neighbors as he loves us.
A candle brought into a dark room conquers darkness and brings light and warmth. The love you carry for God is a candle. It is not a bonfire, yet the light of your candle will conquer the darkness in your world. We are in the world; we are not of the world, according to John. Live in the victory of your faith.
Love God, love others, and shine the light of your faith, conquering the darkness of this world.

Lord,
Let my light shine. It is in the freedom of my salvation that I can go forth in faith, obeying your commandments to love you and share your love with others. Each small victory I have over the world glorifies you and your kingdom. Strengthen my faith each day, let my candle of love shine brighter each day until there is no more darkness, no more "world" and we are truly victorious. Amen.

Aug 21 - *Matthew 3:11 "I baptize you with water for repentance, but one who is more powerful than I is coming after me; I am not worthy to carry his sandals. He will baptize you with the Holy Spirit and fire."*

The Holy Spirit that John forecast in this verse was sent in a powerful way to the disciples in Jerusalem and the message of Christ was proclaimed to nations.

At first reading of this verse the baptism by fire sounded ominous to me, but when I thought back to the references of fire in the Bible I realized the fire of God is not the fire I understand and hold in my hearth on a cold winter night.

Moses saw fire that did not consume a bush, it was God. A pillar of fire led the Israelites from Egypt, it was God. Fire did consume the altar completely and powerfully in a display against the god Baal. Tongues of fire rested on the disciples as the Holy Spirit came to rest in them.

The fire of God is purifying, cleansing, and renewing. It is powerful but not destructive. As I think back on my baptism with a little sprinkle of water on my forehead I wonder about a tongue of fire. It may not rest over my head but I have felt it stir in my heart.

The Spirit moves me to action; he moves us all.

Lord,
Your power is unfathomable to me. I only know I have seen your work in me despite my human frailty. You have used me in ways I never imagined and I can only imagine that you will continue to do so. I offer myself to you; I am yours. Amen.

Aug 22 - *John 15:16 "You did not choose me but I chose you. And I appointed you to go and bear fruit, fruit that will last, so that the Father will give you whatever you ask him in my name."*

The passage this verse comes from is talking about Jesus being the vine and us being the branches.

There are many allegories in the Bible to visualize our relationship with God. He is the potter and we are the clay; he is the shepherd and we are the sheep. There is the gardener and the sower of seeds. The list goes on.

This verse brings it all to a new light. He is our creator. He pieced us together with his love and his purpose. He chose each one of us. He chose me, he chose you.

We are each given tasks to do, things to work on. We are appointed to bear fruit, fruit that lasts, according to our purpose in his kingdom. As I sit and ruminate on this verse, I ask: How I am fruitful? Am I bearing fruit that lasts?

Take a moment to embrace the fact that God chose you. He wants you. With the redemption and grace of Christ, he delights in you.

With this blessing in your heart, go forth with me today and bear fruit that lasts.

Lord,
You call each of us to bear the fruit you have created us to bear. Give us the courage and the joy in our hearts to do as you ask us to. Let us go forth in your love today, guide our steps so that wherever we go, we walk in your light and love, sharing this with those we see and meet. Amen.

Aug 23 - *Romans 3:23-24 "since all have sinned and fall short of the glory of God; they are now justified by his grace as a gift, through the redemption that is in Christ Jesus"*

I confess that occasionally I get caught up reading the law written in the Bible.

The downfall of that for me is this; I get caught up in the knowledge of sin and then I begin chastising myself for all my shortcomings. This passage clearly states and reminds me once again that I cannot do any deeds to clear my name with God. There is beauty in this passage too.

Sin is like a barrier between me and God's presence. Through the faith I have in Jesus, and by his grace the barrier is removed and I am blessed to turn, turn, and come 'round right.

We all fall short and we are all welcome to come in faith. It is in falling that we are shown grace and raised up again by our faith. Because of the grace we have been given, we are able to share that grace with others.

Lord,
The words do not always come easy and today is one of those days for me. May the message you have for me and for others be received in spite of the shortcomings in me. I am called to abide in Love, live in God and when I do, I can rejoice. When I do not, please forgive me. Keep my humble heart in your loving arms and help me to remember, because of your grace, I am redeemed. Help me share that grace with others so that they may feel your redeeming love as well. Amen.

Aug 24 - *Psalm 89:11 "The heavens are yours, the earth also is yours; the world and all that is in it – you have founded them."*

It is a crisp morning.
The wind from yesterday has quieted for now but the forecast has it coming back in all its bluster later today. The sun peeks over the housetops across the street and the birds chirp songs of the morning again.
When I read this verse I begin seeing all of creation, every living thing, in the hands of God. Not only did he fashion the sun and the moon, but the stars and planets as well. He created grass and wildflowers as well as towering trees that reach to the sky and the wind that blows through the branches of those trees.
He created my family, my friends, and my enemies; he created me. I am his and all that I see and hold dear are his. We are not his possessions, but because of his love and grace, we are his beloved.
As I go through this day, I want to live as his beloved, and treat all those I see as his beloved too.

Lord,
With my breath I will praise you. You created and founded all that I know. I want to treat all of your creations with the respect and love they deserve as creations of the Most Holy. Help me see you in all I see today, for you are there. Guide my words and my thoughts, my steps and my actions, so that I honor you as one of your beloved. Amen.

Aug 25 - *Isaiah 43:18-19 "Do not remember the former things, or consider the things of old. I am about to do a new thing; now it springs forth, do you not perceive it? I will make a way in the wilderness and rivers in the desert."*

I tend to get stuck on the past.
When things get rough in my world, I look back to see all that has happened and all that I could have done better. I dig up all the skeletons and all that old pain and guilt and wallow in it.
God calls us to put the former things of the past away and do not remember them. When I am focused on the former, how can I see the new?
Turn and look; he is doing a new thing. In his infinite grace, he has done many new things and I should not be astonished that he continues to do new things in my life. He, indeed, has made a way in the wilderness and brought living water to my deserts.
He has brought me forth from wilderness and desert into new and renewed life.
He is doing this same thing in your life; do you not perceive it? He will make a way…

Lord God,
Turn our hearts and eyes to you and away from our past. The past is gone and you have forgotten it. Remove the blinders of guilt and pain so that we can see the new things you are doing. Guide us in our wilderness and renew us with the living water you have brought to the deserts of our souls. In our refreshment, in our renewal, we praise and bless your Holy name. Amen.

Aug 26 - *Hebrews 9:27-28 "And just as it is appointed for mortals to die once, and after that the judgment, so Christ, having been offered once to bear the sins of many, will appear a second time, not to deal with sin, but to save those who are eagerly waiting for him."*

I treasure my family and my friends. I love the beauty of nature and my children. I love music in my ears and in my heart. These things are here on this earth.

Christ came and experienced life on earth. He lived his life teaching us and ultimately dying for our sins. I am blessed because my judgment will be one of the redeemed believers of Christ. While we wait for the day he comes, we work for his good.

Are there people you know and love that might be judged differently? Do they have the blessing of redemption?

As we wait for the Lord to come, let's pray for the hearts of our family and our friends. Let's pray for the hearts in our neighborhood and for our enemies. When God brings his glory to this earth, I pray all are ready.

I cannot know the heart of anyone else, but I can pray for other souls as I pray for mine. I continue my vigilance until the day he comes; will you join me?

Lord,
I wait for the day you come. I pray my heart will be true on that day and I pray for the hearts of all on this earth. Draw us all in so that we can celebrate together. Turn our hearts, open our eyes, and compel us to follow you so on that day we can all rejoice as one. Amen.

Aug 27 - *Isaiah 11:3-4 "His delight shall be in the fear of the Lord. He shall not judge by what his eyes see, or decide by what his ears hear; but with righteousness he shall judge the poor, and decide with equity for the meek of the earth; he shall strike the earth with the rod of his mouth, and with the breath of his lips he shall kill the wicked."*

Jesus came and brought enlightenment and justice. He brought grace, love, and salvation in his death and resurrection. He will come and judge with righteousness and equity. We cannot plead our case at that point.

While we wait for him, what can we do to bring the peaceable kingdom? I search my heart to hear what the Lord is calling me to do. Abide in him as he abides in me. Allow him to guide every step, word, and thought. I allow him to work in me; his kingdom is here and now.

The moments I live and love as he does, I see his kingdom. Can you picture wolf and lamb, calf and lion, all sitting for a group photo? Then they stroll over to the nearby field for a vegetarian lunch, side by side.

I have heard it said we live in a man eat man world today. I think I will strive for vegetarian fare, suffering no one for my needs, and remembering to thank God for all he has given.

Lord,
You have always provided for me and will continue to give me what I need. Fill me with your spirit so that I see others in your eyes. Help me bring love and mercy instead of judgment. Let others see a glimpse of your peaceable kingdom through me. Amen.

Aug 28 - *Colossians 3:1-2 "So if you have been raised with Christ, seek the things that are above, where Christ is, seated at the right hand of God. Set your minds on things that are above, not on things that are on earth"*

For some reason today has started off with my mind running a mile a minute.

When I was going to sleep last night my thoughts were of Kyle turning four next week and of my birthday two days later (which I would be fine skipping). This morning I was thinking of all the things I need to do and the things I forgot to do yesterday and the things that could be done that are not even on my list and...

You get the idea.

Needless to say my quiet time was not very quiet today. When I get like this I have learned that I need to take deep breaths. I breathe deeply three times to center myself again and it forces me to slow down a little bit. In that moment I can set my mind on things that are above and release the tension that surrounds my list of to-dos.

Christ tells us not to worry about tomorrow. Focus on him and things that are above; my to-do list will happen in its time.

Lord,
You know my task-driven personality; you created it. Please pry open my heart and hands to release that list from my grasp. Only then can I grab your hand and let you lead me along the way. When I let you guide me things go much better, so keep my eyes focused on you and let me breathe your love and peace deeply into my soul today. Amen.

Aug 29 - *Psalm 139:14 "I praise you, for I am fearfully and wonderfully made. Wonderful are your works; that I know very well."*

There is beauty in all of God's creations.
The intricacy is amazing. I was not created with a side glance and a wave of the hand but knit together by the hand of God, strand by strand.
Have you seen a potter work with clay? The clay starts out a brown lump on the wheel. It takes the hands of the potter gently coaxing and molding the clay for it to be transformed into a vessel. The potter is focused completely on guiding the clay, feeling for imperfections or flaws that need to be corrected in the process. The pot that is created goes through firing, glazing, and firing again.
This is how it is with God. He lovingly focuses on us, guiding and correcting us. We are put to fire and flame, still carefully and lovingly. We are still being created in God. Each day he is there guiding us, transforming us, and using us as the vessel he created us to be.
Relax in him. Become a malleable piece of clay and allow his loving hands to form and guide you into all he will have you be.
You and I are fearfully and wonderfully made.
Praise God for all he has done and will do with you!

Lord,
Thank you for your verse today. It is good to remember that you created me and I am wonderfully made. Your works are wonderful and because of the beauty in me and all those you created, I praise you today. Your grace and care for us abounds and I can only serve you in thanks. Amen.

Aug 30 - *Matthew 9:20-22 "Then suddenly a woman who had been suffering from hemorrhages for twelve years came up behind him and touched the fringe of his cloak, for she said to herself, 'If I only touch his cloak, I will be made well.' Jesus turned, and seeing her he said, 'Take heart, daughter; your faith has made you well.' And instantly the woman was made well."*

Here is a woman I can identify with.

I imagine she searched for a cure for her suffering in any way possible. She may have just about resigned herself to the fact that this would be her curse.

Then, out of nowhere, comes Jesus. He is a teacher and a healer. She hears and believes that he can heal her but he is surrounded and hard to get an audience with. Besides that, who is she to have an audience with this Jesus?

If she could just touch a piece of his clothing she knows that she will be healed. In his infinite grace and love, Jesus blesses her faith and heals her instantly.

Can you imagine the days after this for her? Each morning waking with the joy of knowing she has been healed? Did she grow accustomed to it and forget the blessings of her healing? Did she even forget she had been sick?

I know I am guilty of this. I forget to be thankful for all the healing he has done and is doing in me.

Lord,
Thank you for all of the miraculous healing you have given to me and to others as well. Let me be a testament to your healing power today. Amen.

Aug 31 - *1 Corinthians 2:12 "Now we have received not the spirit of the world, but the Spirit that is from God, so that we may understand the gifts bestowed on us by God."*

We all have things we are good at and things we are not so good at.

God has given me a gift of communication and only recently have I heard the call to use this gift to the glory of his kingdom. As I watch my children grow, I see glimpses of gifts they have been given. It is tempting to try and teach them how to use those gifts but I realize how arrogant that is.

It is not *my* job to teach them to use the gifts God gave them; it is my job to help them learn to listen to the Spirit of God. It is my job to pray for them and guide them as the Spirit guides me to.

I encourage you to take a few moments today to ponder your gifts.

Sit in stillness and listen for understanding given to you by God's Spirit. I have not experienced anything more fulfilling than sitting in the presence of God and receiving understanding from him. It is because of those moments that you are reading this today.

As you experience your day, watch for the gifts in yourself and others and know that God blesses us all.

Lord,
Thank you so much for your Spirit. Without that guidance; without that voice I would be lost. Through your grace and love you sent your Spirit so that we might understand the gifts you gave us and be moved to use them in your name. Amen.

Sep 1 - *Romans 6:13 "No longer present your members to sin as instruments of wickedness, but present yourselves to God as those who have been brought from death to life, and present your members to God as instruments of righteousness."*

The first things that came to my mind when reading this verse were eyes viewing sinful things or hands doing sinful actions. There are all kinds of people that come to mind that are easy targets for this verse as well.

In deeper reflection though, who of us is free of sin?

When I am seething in anger, is that not sin? When I am feeling jealousy or gossiping is that not sin? When I judge someone else, is that also, not sin?

Our hearts and minds are just as likely to be used as instruments of wickedness as our eyes and hands. The great deceiver uses any part of us that he is allowed access to, and he will drag us down to the depths.

Take a few moments today to offer your body, mind, and spirit to God for cleansing and renewal and then as an instrument to righteousness. Join him in life!

Lord,

Thank you for your redemptive power and your gracious love. It is through these things that we are allowed to come to you and be cleansed and holy. It is through these things that we are allowed to be instruments to righteousness. I ask you to cleanse my body, mind, and spirit once more. Use me, all of me, as your instrument to righteousness. Thank you God, your love endures forever, thank you! Amen.

Sep 2 - *Luke 5:4-6 "When he had finished speaking, he said to Simon, 'Put out into the deep water and let down your nets for a catch.' Simon answered, 'Master, we have worked all night long but have caught nothing. Yet, if you say so, I will let down the nets.' When they had done this, they caught so many fish that their nets were beginning to break."*

I woke this morning with the hymn "Will You Come and Follow Me" running through my head.

I am humbled by the awesome grace of God once again. The last part of this passage says they left everything and followed him. God is with us, he speaks to us and he blesses us in abundance when we listen.

Simon tosses his nets over into the deep, following Jesus' lead. I suspect he was muttering under his breath about a waste of time. He had just spent all night doing this. What was different now? When he began to pull the net in, he found out quickly what was different.

He followed Jesus' instruction. He listened and obeyed and his nets were overflowing! He tells Jesus he is a sinful man and that Jesus should go away.

I know this feeling. When we listen and obey, he blesses us beyond our imagination. He is calling you to toss out into the deep. Will you listen?

Lord,
How much more could you encourage me to listen and obey?
You have shown me in this story and so many others that when I follow, I am blessed beyond measure. Help me share these blessings with others today. Help me cast into the deep waters, trusting your lead. Amen.

Sep 3 - *John 6:26 "Jesus answered them, 'Very truly, I tell you, you are looking for me, not because you saw signs, but because you ate your fill of the loaves.'"*

What do you desire? What do you seek and work for?
This crowd that Jesus was talking to had just received bread and fish from him the day before. When they woke from their camp out and realized the disciples and Jesus had moved on they crossed in boats to search him out in Capernaum. When they find him this verse is his response to them. They came to have their bellies filled again and nothing more.
How often do we come to the Lord for immediate gratification? How often do I ask him for something that is of little or no real value in the eternal world? Do I come to him for my own benefit and my own purpose or do I come to seek his knowledge and wisdom, his healing and guidance, regardless of where it leads me?
I can picture myself in the crowd without a problem and so I know I would easily fit in to the group asking for instant gratification. He promises to provide for us better than he does for the lilies in the field. Why do we ask for those daily needs? As I go out into this beautiful day, I search my heart for motive.

Lord,
Thank you for your word. Protect my heart and soul from selfishness. Open my eyes and my heart to the true value of spiritual growth, trusting that you will continue to give me exactly what I need in the moment I need it. Thank you Lord. I pray I bless your kingdom today. Amen.

Sep 4 - *Colossians 4:5-6 "Conduct yourselves wisely toward outsiders, making the most of the time. Let your speech always be gracious, seasoned with salt, so that you may know how you ought to answer everyone."*

I know a person that was turned away from faith at a very young age and has never been compelled to search it out again.
I have this person and their family in my prayers, not knowing their story, just knowing they are on my heart.
In church, the preacher referenced a saying from St Francis of Assisi "Preach the Gospel at all times and when necessary use words." These verses lead us to do the same thing. Live in grace and be gracious to those you see. Let your words be guided by the Holy Spirit, seasoned with the salt from heaven.
I do not want to turn someone off from God. A song reminds me that I am the only Jesus some will ever see and that I am the only Word some will ever read. Paul calls us to pray, keep alert, and give thanksgiving.
Live as Jesus taught us to live so that we can be filled with his light and be a beacon of his light and love to all those we see and know.

Lord,
You have shown me, so many times, that you are here with me every moment. Let the words of my mouth and the actions in my day lead people to you, only to you. Keep me away from any distractions and keep me from becoming a distraction to others. I am your vessel. Use me to your glory. Amen.

Sep 5 - *James 1:19-20 "You must understand this, my beloved, let everyone be quick to listen, slow to speak, slow to anger; for your anger does not produce God's righteousness."*

I only have to turn on the TV to find anger. I only need to listen to my children bicker over toys or treats or any trivial thing to feel anger in myself.

This morning as I was trying to sit in silence, waiting for the Lord, it became crystal clear to me why this practice is called a discipline. We do not learn this in our society at all. There is no silence and very little listening.

We learn to wait; we learn not to interrupt but that is not the same as listening. I give a direction to my daughter and cannot even finish a sentence before she has begun talking over me. She has pointed out a few times that I also interrupt her. This is how our society works.

As I prepare to teach reading, writing, and arithmetic today I tuck this scripture in my heart so that, by God's grace, I may do better at listening and not so much speaking.

Maybe this will keep frustration and anger at bay...

Lord,
Your word is my guide, thank you! You know each of our struggles and frustrations. Help us stop and truly listen. Open our ears to hear your soothing voice, open our eyes to see your love in each other, and open our hearts to receive the guidance you so freely offer. As I strive to live in righteousness let me remember to forgive others and to receive forgiveness when I fall short. Amen.

Sep 6 - *John 1:38-39 "When Jesus turned and saw them following, he said to them, 'What are you looking for?' They said to him, 'Rabbi (which translated means Teacher), where are you staying?' He said to them, 'Come and see.' They came and saw where he was staying, and they remained with him that day..."*

I wonder if the two men Jesus was talking with were nervous or if they knew they wanted more time with him than a short conversation would allow.

John had just told them that Jesus was the Lamb of God and so they followed him. Maybe they were shying away a bit when Jesus asked them what they were looking for. They answered him with a question. I really believe they wanted to have an in depth conversation with Jesus, Lamb of God; they wanted to know him so they asked where he was staying.

Jesus says "Come and see." They walked with him and remained with him. As I spend time praying on this scripture I come back to the words of Jesus *"What are you looking for?"* Whatever we are lacking, whatever we are searching for, he wants to help us find our true longings.

When we are brought to those longings, he invites us to *"come and see."*

Lord,
Thank you for allowing us to remain with you just as these men did so long ago. You have given your Spirit to abide with us always. Search my heart to show me what I am looking for and guide me to understand that my deepest longings will be fulfilled in you. I want to see, Lord. I want to remain with you. Amen.

Sep 7 - *Jeremiah 3:15 "I will give you shepherds after my own heart, who will feed you with knowledge and understanding."*

Here is another story of God seeking the hearts and repentance of his people.

They cheat, they lie, and they turn their backs on him. He is angry, but he still calls to them, still wants them to come back and be in relationship with him again. Nothing has changed in thousands of years. We still cheat, lie, and turn our backs on him. When I came to this verse in my reading, it nearly jumped off of the page at me.

What an incredible promise and I am eternally grateful that he has delivered and continues to deliver shepherds after his own heart to guide us. He sent Jesus, the Christ, and he sent the Holy Spirit who still resides with and in us. We have his word and his called servants that guide us as well. The Spirit and the word help us discern whether the shepherds are after his own heart, if we listen for guidance.

I take courage through this passage and this verse. In this time of false prophets and fallen shepherds I know God still provides true shepherds and people after his own heart to feed us with knowledge and understanding.

I praise and thank him for this!

Lord,
Your promise elates me today! You are faithful to us beyond the walls of time. Thank you for giving us a continual source of food through your word and your Spirit. Thank you for shepherds to feed us with knowledge and understanding. Help us grow stronger in you each day. Amen.

Sep 8 - *Luke 1:37-38 "'For nothing will be impossible with God.' Then Mary said, 'Here am I, the servant of the Lord; let it be with me according to your word.' Then the angel departed from her."*

Does it take an angel of the Lord in all its glory to make me an obedient servant of the Lord?

I get so frustrated with myself sometimes. I love the Lord, I want to be obedient and follow him in all ways, and then my human selfishness creeps in. Before I am even truly aware, I have stopped listening and started following my wishes instead of God's commands.

As I think about God's servants and their stories in the Bible, I am reminded that we all fall short. We are all human and cannot live perfectly; we are not and will not be perfect in this lifetime. These verses renew my spirit and call me to strive forward because I believe them to be true.

I believe that nothing is impossible with God. Amazing things happen when I walk in his path; when I am with God and not against him. So I come to him on my knees.

I picture Mary, dirty and dusty from her work, young and naïve in the world.

Lord,

Bring my heart to the humble place of Mary's. Fill it with trust and wonder. I come filled with humility to offer myself again. I am your servant, dusty and dirty from my work, truly naïve in the world. I offer myself to you; use me according to your will, for nothing is impossible with you, God. You give me amazing grace and amazing love; thank you! Amen.

Sep 9 - *Matthew 14:31-33 "Jesus immediately reached out his hand and caught him, saying to him, 'You of little faith, why did you doubt?' When they got into the boat, the wind ceased. And those in the boat worshiped him, saying, 'Truly you are the Son of God.'"*

I have read this story many times and always thought about the statement "You of little faith…"
How often have I been saved by Jesus after faltering or questioning and losing trust in his guidance and plan for me? There is another side to this story though.
Peter stepped out in faith, trusting that it was the Lord calling him. When he became afraid, he called on the Lord to save him and when Jesus saved him, Peter and his boat mates worshipped him, proclaiming him the Son of God. It is this trust and faith that brings me hope.
When I lose my footing and falter in my trust; when I drop the ball because I am not sure I am really hearing Jesus, all is not lost. I know I can call on him to save me and he is always right there, waiting to grab my hand and renew my faith and trust in him again. It is because of those failings and rescues through Jesus that I have grown in my trust and faith in him.
He has never failed me and I know beyond a shadow of doubt he will always be there with me, no matter what.

Lord,
Thank you for rescuing Peter and bringing peace to me with this story. Help me hear you clearly and trust in you fully. Thank you for being there to rescue me again and set me on the right path once more. Amen.

Sep 10 - *Proverbs 8:10-11 "Take my instruction instead of silver, and knowledge rather than choice gold; for wisdom is better than jewels, and all that you may desire cannot compare with her."*

We are in the process of sorting through stuff.

When I got married we combined all our stuff and since then we have accumulated more stuff. Every time I go down to the basement the old adage "you can't take it with you" echoes in my mind.

I have collections that have not seen the light of day in years and when I look around my house there is not a place to set them out on display. It seems to be a common desire to want to gather more things, more treasure, and more money. These tangible treasures make us feel worth more, I think.

These verses in Proverbs tell me something different. If everything was gone, all my possessions, my home, and my bank account, what would I have left?

I would have the love of the Lord, my relationship with God, and the knowledge and wisdom he has given me. No matter what happens in this life, we always have those internal gifts that are God given, thank the Lord!

Lord,
You tell us your kingdom is not of this world and these verses clearly remind us of that. Help us seek true treasure through you and your Spirit rather than clinging to the earthly treasure that only lasts for a moment of time. Thank you for your instruction and your guidance. They keep us walking forward to a deeper and stronger faith in you. Amen.

Sep 11 - *Acts 1:7-8 "He replied, 'It is not for you to know the times or periods that the Father has set by his own authority. But you will receive power when the Holy Spirit has come upon you; and you will be my witnesses in Jerusalem, in all Judea and Samaria, and to the ends of the earth.'"*

My friends and I talk about the end times.
There are many days I wish Jesus would come back right now. I do not know when that day will come, whether I will be alive on earth or living in his glorious heaven. If I knew, I would be tempted to focus more on that day than on the call he gives us all.
He tells his disciples and he tells us as well; we receive power through the Holy Spirit. This Spirit lives in us and guides us as his witnesses. The Spirit uses the gifts we each were given by God to further the kingdom. You know what you are good at and what you are not so good at. Allow the Spirit to use the things you are good at and strengthen the things you are not so good at.
It is through the Spirit that all we do and all we say can be used as a witness to the love and grace of Jesus Christ. Be what he calls you to be. Believe in him, live in him, and proclaim him in all you are and all you do.
This is how we witness to the ends of the earth.

Lord,
We all have different gifts that you have given us but we have all been given the Holy Spirit. Make me aware of the movements of the Spirit in me. Set my selfish desires to the side so that all I do and say is true witness to your love and grace for us all. Amen.

Sep 12 - *Numbers 6:24-26 "The Lord bless you and keep you; the Lord make his face to shine upon you, and be gracious to you; The Lord lift up his countenance upon you, and give you peace."*

My heart is with friends today.

I have a friend taking her daughter in for a medical test, a friend preparing for back surgery tomorrow, and a friend that is moving away. I was outside my home with my daughter yesterday and I noticed a young girl down the street that I had not seen before. When I mentioned it to Rachel, she went and introduced herself and made a new friend. A couple of weeks ago she made a new friend that has just moved in at the top of the street. She makes friends so easily!

I, on the other hand, have to talk myself into going and meeting the new neighbors. It takes me time to warm up and when I do, I don't like to say goodbye. This benediction in Numbers has been going in my head all night. I know my friend who is moving does so with a divided heart.

This day, I simply write to share this blessing with each of you. I send it to you with love and hope that you feel it pouring out over and into to you this morning.

Lord,

I love you. Thank you for the blessings you have given me in this life and that you have planned for me on this day. Thank you for the blessing of friendship. As the friends you have brought into my life have blessed me deeply, I ask that you guide me to be a blessing to my longtime friends and new friends as well. All honor and glory are yours. Amen.

Sep 13 - *1 Timothy 4:8 "for, while physical training is of some value, godliness is valuable in every way, holding promise for both the present life and the life to come."*

I have begun riding my bike again.
I hadn't ridden in years, since my daughter was born. It was hard to find the time and other priorities ... life got in the way. Now that my kids are getting bigger, soon my spouse and I will go riding with them. My daughter loves riding her bike and my little boy is learning quickly. The first time I got back on, it was a little wobbly but each time has been easier.
It is tempting to take my quiet time on my bike. I could "kill two birds with one stone." When I do that, I am slighting the time I give to God. Our society is so focused on reducing obesity and getting healthy. We do need to exercise and eat right.
What would it be like if we had as much encouragement in spiritual health? We hire personal trainers for exercise and physical training; do we seek out a personal trainer for spiritual growth? The Holy Spirit will guide us and the Word of God will teach us. I encourage you to join me in seeking out mentorship or direction from others as well.
Is God asking you to move more deeply into life with him?

Lord,
My health and well-being are important. I cannot be all you call me to be if I only work on my physical health though. Use your Spirit to bring me closer to you. Guide my spiritual growth and well-being so that I keep my priorities straight, keeping you first, always. Amen.

Sep 14 - *Ephesians 5:1-2 "Therefore be imitators of God, as beloved children, and live in love, as Christ loved us and gave himself up for us, a fragrant offering and sacrifice to God."*

Kids love to play house.
They love to imitate their parents and role models. If you picture the toy aisle at any store this is clear. There are baby dolls, kitchens, lawn mowers, trucks, tools and tool belts, the list is almost endless. It is in this play, this imitation, that kids learn how to be like their parents.
If we take this stance, imitate living as Christ lived, we learn how to be like Christ. This is a life-long lesson for us and we cannot be perfect like Christ. Yet, we can be perfected in Christ; through his love and redemption. It is in his love, living in his love, that we can imitate him by showing kindness and being tender-hearted to one another. It is by living in his love that we are able to forgive as God, through Christ, forgives us.
Push away the daily distractions and focus on one thing today; be an imitator of Christ.

Lord,
As I go forth today, I pray I am a good imitator of your love and grace. Fill my heart with the joy of knowing that I am your beloved. It is this joy that gives me strength to share your love and grace with others... all others. You gave your life so that I could live. Let me live in you and for you. Help me to live and love like you. Amen.

Sep 15 - *Matthew 26:33, 75 "Peter said to him, 'Though all become deserters because of you, I will never desert you.'...Then Peter remembered what Jesus had said: 'Before the cock crows, you will deny me three times,' And he went out and wept bitterly."*

The hours leading up to the death of Jesus must have been surreal.

There was a whirlwind of activity from the Passover meal until Jesus was hung on the cross to die. I imagine being in Peter's shoes; believing that I would never run away from my Lord. I see Peter and myself telling Jesus that we would die first before denying him.

As the story unfolds, we find Peter with a look of humiliation when he realizes he has denied his Lord, *three times*. In times of reflection dismay and humiliation come as I realize I, too, have denied my Lord. These moments of brokenness are used by God. He lifts us up and heals our wounds.

In his infinite love and because of Christ's redemption, Peter is the rock on which the church was built. Through Christ's redemptive power our brokenness can be used to strengthen us in Christ.

We are his beloved. This is why he died. In spite of our denials, God loves us and he wants to redeem us.

Lord,
I come to you often with tears of humiliation. You wait for me; you hear my cries and you pour your love and grace into me again. It is in awe and wonder that I hear you call me your beloved. I give this day to you, as best as I am able, as a token of my love for you. Amen.

Sep 16 - *1 Thessalonians 5:11 "Therefore encourage one another and build up each other, as indeed you are doing."*

I have lost track now of how long my church has been without a "permanent" pastor.

We had an interim pastor, whom I loved, for about two years and when he stepped down we thought we were really close to having a new pastor seated. Here we are months later with another pseudo interim pastor who has agreed to stay with us another month and again it seems we are pretty close to having a new pastor seated.

It is hard to move forward without leadership. Sheep get lost and wander off without their shepherd to guide them. God has been gracious to my church in providing great leadership in the space between called leaders. God has been gracious in moving people within the church to step forward and grow into leadership roles they didn't think they would do.

As I prepare to help lead worship as a liturgist, I am feeling very much like one of those people. I am so grateful for the people who volunteer to help in the interim times and all the time.

Let us encourage each other...

Lord,
Soothe the anxiety that lurks below the surface. We pray, we work, and we fret. Open our eyes to see the encouragement you have sent through others to ease the burdens we bear and guide us to be ballast for other people's burdens as well. Amen.

Sep 17 - *Psalm 145:8-9 "The Lord is gracious and merciful, slow to anger and abounding in steadfast love. The Lord is good to all, and his compassion is over all that he has made."*

Good news! The sun came up again today!
There are days that I barely even notice the sun, the singing birds, or the laughter of my kids. All those things are there regardless of whether I notice them or not.
God is like that too. He is here, his love and compassion are all around us, whether we notice them or not. We can choose to see the darkness and evil in this world; it is rampant. It is so easy to focus on the things that are going wrong. Take a moment to look further into things.
In the midst of the evil, there is good. In the midst of the darkness, there is light. God moves in all things and he is full of grace and mercy. Look for God's compassion and goodness in the midst of your day.
It is there, for the verse says "his compassion is over all that he has made" and he has made you and everything you see this day.

Lord,
Thank you for your grace and mercy. Thank you for your slowness to anger for I know I test your patience beyond reason. Your love does, in fact, abound. Let the goodness, love, and mercy I have found in you seep to the deepest part of my bones so that I can resonate those things back out to the world around me. Amen.

Sep 18 - *Galatians 5:24-25 "and those who belong to Christ Jesus have crucified the flesh with its passions and desires. If we live by the Spirit, let us also be guided by the Spirit."*

I think about each part of my body.

I remember my mind, eyes, and ears. I think about my speech, heart, hands, and feet. Each and every part of me has been given over to God. It is so easy to let my mind wander and fall into my own passions and desires. It is very easy to let my speech come in waves full of damage and destruction, tearing down instead of building up.

As I reviewed these things, I realized I need to commit my whole self to the Spirit again. I need to release my passions and desires because I know, beyond a shadow of doubt, that the passions and desires God has for me only bring me joy and delight while mine lead me into brokenness and despair.

I encourage you to take a moment this morning to remember your crucifixion in Christ. Remember the moment you turned your whole life over to him. Allow him to release all the wayward thoughts and desires and replace those things with his holy passions and desires for you, his beloved.

Live by the Spirit.

Lord,
Stop the voices of distraction and wayward leading and let me hear only your Spirit's guidance for me today. I live in you and I rejoice in the blessings you have given me through your Spirit. I pray that my mind, eyes, ears; my whole being only have focus on your guidance and not even perceive any other way. You are my all in all. Amen.

Sep 19 - *Proverbs 13:24 "Those who spare the rod hate their children, but those who love them are diligent to discipline them."*

I cannot count the times in my life that I have heard the statement "spare the rod, spoil the child."
Growing up, I thought this was talking about spanking or physical punishment for bad behavior. As I talk with my women friends about our kids (only occasionally, you know) discipline is often a topic of discussion. Only a century ago children were to be seen and not heard; speak only when spoken to.
Expectations have changed dramatically since then and for the most part it is good. As I guide my children in the disciplines of self-control and respect for parents sometimes I think it would be easier if they didn't speak so often...
The rod is not for corporal punishment. It is a tool shepherds use to guide the path of the sheep. We are not called to squash the spirits of our children; we are called to be diligent to discipline.
As I grow in my discipline to God, I pray that learning will bless me in teaching my children discipline as well.
Then we can all step forward as disciples together in the kingdom of God.

Lord,
Help me remember the rod as a tool, not as a switch. Guide my words and my tone to be of your spirit and not of my wrath. As you have been gracious and loving in my discipline, help me be gracious and loving in the discipline of my children. Thank you for these words today. Amen.

Sep 20 - *1 John 3:23-24 "And this is his commandment, that we should believe in the name of his Son Jesus Christ and love one another, just as he has commanded us. All who obey his commandments abide in him, and he abides in them. And by this we know that he abides in us, by the Spirit that he has given us."*

What draws me to the love of Jesus?
My memories and my understanding of Jesus are powerful reminders of Jesus' love for me. He has given me so much grace and love. I live abundantly through his love.
The memories of answers to prayer, the divine intervention keeping me from bad choices, and the love that redeemed me in spite of bad choices draw me to his love. The love Jesus showed during his life on earth also has a big impact on me. He loved in truth and light, he always lived in a way to show God and his love to others. This is a part of how I understand Jesus and his love.
When I keep these things in my heart, it is less difficult to release my will and allow the Spirit to guide and lead me. He does abide in me and the Spirit is always there nudging and encouraging me to follow his commands, believe in Christ, and love one another.

Lord,
Thank you for loving me. Thank you for redeeming me and sending your Spirit to guide my words and deeds. When my will steps in and tries to take over things go awry. Remind me of this when I see my day begin to unravel. Cause me to sit in a quiet space and find you and your infinite love so I can go out believing and loving in you again. Amen.

Sep 21 - *2 Corinthians 5:14-15 "For the love of Christ urges us on, because we are convinced that one has died for all; therefore all have died. And he died for all, so that those who live might live no longer for themselves, but for him who died and was raised for them."*

I am struggling with control.

I say in my mind that I am not in control, God is in control. Yet, as I review my days I see that I fight for control as much as my children do. I may not do it in the same way but the bottom line is this; I like to be in control.

My meditation this morning reminded me that I am not in control, and it does not go well when I try to be. It is Christ's love that needs to propel my actions, not control.

I need to let go; for once and for all, trust in the Lord, with ***all*** my heart. It is the love of Christ that calls me to this. It is his love that urges me to go forward each new day and love. He died for me.

I live in him and because of this I live for him.

Lord,
Transform my view to see the new creation you created in me. Your love and mercy have changed me beyond recognition and yet the old ways linger waiting to jump in at a moment's notice. Let the old ways die away and raise me to live my life in you. Take my life; take all of me and fill me with your love. Urge me on with your Spirit to do all I do in love. Amen.

Sep 22 - *Matthew 26:3-4 "Then the chief priests and the elders of the people gathered in the palace of the high priest, who was called Caiaphas, and they conspired to arrest Jesus by stealth and kill him."*

It is strange how wrong people can be without even seeing it. We can be led astray and down a slippery slope to the depths of darkness and stay blind the whole way.

The Pharisees and Sadducees were leaders of the people. They were the priests and law keepers, the ones to look to for guidance. In his ministry Jesus tried to lead them away from the self-righteousness they held in their hearts but they were blind and deaf to anything he had to say.

In chapter 22 they try to trip him up asking him what is the most important law and his response was "You shall love the Lord your God with all your heart, and with all your soul, and with all your mind. This is the greatest and first commandment. And a second is like it: You shall love your neighbor as yourself."

As they sat in Caiaphas' palace, these words never came back to remind them? Do these words come to remind us today?

Seek redemption and go out in love.

Lord,
Rather than looking at others shortcomings help me look at my own. Search out the darkness that lurks in each of us and redeem us again today. Thank you again for your sacrifice of love. I claim victory through you, my Savior and Redeemer. Amen.

Sep 23 - *Mark 9:23-24 "Jesus said to him, 'If you are able! – All things can be done for the one who believes.' Immediately the father of the child cried out, 'I believe; help my unbelief!'"*

I suspect verse 24 speaks to the heart of every Christian.
We pray for many things using similar words as this passage.
Our prayers have qualifiers like "if it is possible or if it be your will." Have you ever read anywhere in the Bible that God did not wish for us to be whole?
He uses our brokenness but I do not believe he wishes for our brokenness. Maybe when we pray we are uncertain because we have not searched for God's will. I am learning, slowly, how to sit and listen. When I am able to quiet the voices and distractions, it is amazing to sit in silence and wait upon the Lord. He can be heard much more easily and he guides our prayers, our steps, and our actions.
I take comfort in the fact that the Spirit prays in my stead when I do not know what to pray for. As I continue to grow in my life with God, I hope I learn to pray as Jesus taught us.
I want to pray without doubt.

Lord,
Even as my faith grows stronger daily, the doubt is there lurking in the shadows. I lift this father's words to you for me and so many others. I believe, help my unbelief! Teach me to pray in full trust and confidence, knowing you have guided my prayers. Erase any doubt that you will do what we ask in faithful prayer. Jesus says all things can be done for the one who believes. Lord, help me believe! Amen.

Sep 24 - *John 20:14, 16 "When she had said this, she turned around and saw Jesus standing there, but she did not know that it was Jesus. Jesus said to her, 'Mary!' She turned and said to him in Hebrew, 'Rabbouni' (which means Teacher)."*

Have you ever been looking for something and it was sitting in plain view the whole time?

When this happens to me I am a little disgusted with myself. How could I have missed that? My Mom used to say "if it were a snake, it would have bit you." Jesus appears to the disciples after his resurrection and even though he is in plain view they do not see through their despair and worry. Jesus, in love and patience, does not give up on them. He says things and does things; he opens their eyes so they see again.

Jesus is always with us, always in plain view.

I like to see things with my own eyes. I do not like to shop online unless I have first seen it in a store with my very own eyes. When I look around me or when I review my days, it is easy to see Jesus in the midst if I am looking for him, believing that he is there.

I need to see with my heart and my eyes, not just my eyes. Mary knew Jesus when she heard his voice.

How do you recognize Jesus in your life?

Lord,
Open my heart and my eyes to see and know you are here with me. There are so many ways you touch my day, every day and I thank you. Thank you for being patient and persistent in showing yourself to me. I see you with me and I believe. Guide my actions and my words to help others see you too. Amen.

Sep 25 - *2 Corinthians 1:3-4 "Blessed be the God and Father of our Lord Jesus Christ, the Father of mercies and the God of all consolation, who consoles us in all our affliction, so that we may be able to console those who are in any affliction with the consolation with which we ourselves are consoled by God."*

Bless God of all mercy; he consoles us so that we may console others. He gives us mercy so that we may be merciful.
We receive blessing upon blessing from God. We are called to share our blessings with others. When we are suffering, God pours his mercy over us, consoling us so that we feel his love and mercy in the midst of whatever our afflictions may be. We are called to share the mercy we receive with others so that they may feel the presence and mercy of God in the midst of their afflictions as well. When we share the blessings and mercy we have received, we share God.
I encourage you to find a memory where you felt the mercy and consolation of God. Take a few moments to remember the blessing of that and then spread the mercy and love you have received to those around you today.

Lord,
Thank you for your continuous presence, you are always here with us: you never leave our side. Help us see clearly the blessings you bestow on us and the mercy we receive from you. Open our hearts and our hands so that we may share those blessings and mercy with others, bringing you and your love further into the world. Amen.

Sep 26 - *Psalm 89:6-7 "For who in the skies can be compared to the Lord? Who among the heavenly beings is like the Lord, a God feared in the council of the holy ones, great and awesome above all that are around him?"*

In current days as in days of old it is easy to get caught up in paying homage to something or someone other than the Lord our God.

There are little figurines of angels and saints. There is nature, full of beauty and grandeur. The intricacy of God's creatures and creations bring a sense of awe and wonder. Money, status, or a job can become the ultimate goal in our lives. Anything we place first, above all else, becomes our god.

Regardless of what we see in our world, real or imagined, one thing is unshakeable. The Supreme God, the Creator of all, and Almighty King, is above all else. There is nothing that can take his place and there is nothing or no one else that can give us the steadfast love and grace that he does. He is faithful and loving. All other things we put in place in front of him are a farce, a pittance.

Clear the path in front of you so you can run, unhindered, to the throne of the Most High.

Lord,
Forgive me for all the distractions and lesser "gods" I have put in front of you. I know you are the one and only, the true God of all. Do not let me be deceived or drawn in by all the glitter and shine around me but keep my eyes and heart focused on your true light. God of gods, you are my Lord and Savior. I praise and worship you today. Amen.

Sep 27 - *Luke 1:46-47 "And Mary said, 'My soul magnifies the Lord, and my spirit rejoices in God my Savior,'"*

Magnifying glasses are cool.

I remember playing with the one my grandparents had when I was a child. My sisters and I would take turns and it was fun to see how far away we could get and still see clearly. I liked to see if I could find that perfect distance of clarity and enlargement. Boys on my street would use a magnifying glass to concentrate the sunlight in a certain spot, increasing the brightness and warmth of the sun.

When I read this passage the word magnifying practically jumped off the page at me. It begged me to answer the question: Does my soul magnify the Lord? When people gaze through me, do they see the Lord more clearly and larger than they did before? What do I see when I gaze into my soul?

I cannot comprehend Mary's situation but the trust and faith she had in the Lord is clear. I hope that as I continue on my faith journey, I continue to grow so that my soul will magnify the Lord clearly and my spirit will rejoice ever more in my God and my Savior.

Lord,

We have many tools to help us focus on things more clearly. As I gaze into the mirror and as I look through my eyeglasses, let these simple tools remind me that my soul needs to magnify you. Guide my words and deeds in rejoicing so that when others gaze into me, they see you more clearly. Amen.

Sep 28 - *James 5:16 "Therefore confess your sins to one another, and pray for one another, so that you may be healed. The prayer of the righteous is powerful and effective."*

I have seen the power of prayer work in small and big ways. Why is it so hard to come into prayer sometimes?
There are so many verses in the Bible that call us to pray; they encourage prayer and promise blessings and healing from prayers. Yet we hesitate to come to the throne in prayer.
The times I come to the Father in prayer I am changed. There is no doubt in my heart or mind that he changes me because of prayer.
Find a friend or a trusted mentor that you can share your inner self with. Find a prayer partner. It is a blessing to know that someone is praying specifically for you. It is also a blessing to be able to bring someone you care about to our Lord in prayer. The power of prayer is real and true.
There is healing and love that flows when we tap into the heart of the Lord. The verse for today confirms that.

Lord,
Thank you for this blessed day. As I come to you bringing forth my family and friends for your touch of healing and love as well as your protection from the darkness that is in this world, I am blessed. I am blessed to know and love so many and I am blessed to be loved by so many. Help us pray for one another and trust in your word that our prayer is powerful and effective. All blessing, glory, and honor are yours. Amen.

Sep 29 - *Psalm 112:7-8 "They are not afraid of evil tidings; their hearts are firm, secure in the Lord. Their hearts are steady, they will not be afraid; in the end they will look in triumph on their foes."*

Much ado about nothing… I have been known as a master of worry.

There was a time (and occasionally still is) when if I didn't have something to worry about, I would create something to worry about. I lived in fear. I cannot sit here and write honestly saying I never worry or have no fears, but I know my fears are relieved. That knowledge brings me peace and calm in the midst of strife. God has been gracious beyond all measure.

He has sent many messengers to me in my life, sharing and showing me the love and grace that was mine for the taking. When I finally, finally accepted his gift of grace, my heart became steady and I was not afraid. My fear, my awe, and worship are in the Lord. My heart is no longer in my worries of this world.

When I walk in his knowledge, in his grace, my fears are banished and I can look in triumph over my foes, praising and thanking Jesus for bringing me securely to him.

Lord,
You are my rock and my salvation. It is only by your grace that I can worship and praise you without the worries weighing me down. I have been released through you and I am not afraid. You are with me and you keep me secure. Thank you for blessing me so abundantly, Lord. Help me be a blessing to others. Amen.

Sep 30 - *Galatians 5:13-14 "For you were called to freedom, brothers and sisters; only do not use your freedom as an opportunity for self-indulgence, but through love become slaves to one another. For the whole law is summed up in a single commandment, 'You shall love your neighbor as yourself.'"*

Have you ever sat in church and listened to the sermon thinking it must have been written just for you?

Occasionally, I have this experience. It is like the pastor has been reading my mind and heart and knows exactly what I have been grappling with. Paul's letter to the Galatians calls them back to the basics. I do not know what they were doing or how they were changing, but whatever it was, it was not following the gospel message Paul had brought to them.

As I seek a deeper relationship with God, I can see how easy it is to fall into the traps of doing rather than being. Works are not what keep us with the Divine; it is our spirit and his Spirit that are in relationship. We are freed from works and called to spiritual, soul work instead.

We are called to love.

Lord,

Thank you for pastors who are messengers and interpreters of your word. Thank you for freedom through your grace and the life of Jesus Christ. Guide me in the steps of your son so that I may learn to love as he loved and receive the love he gave. Help me show my love for you by loving others. Amen.

Oct 1 - *Colossians 3:12-13 "As God's chosen ones, holy and beloved, clothe yourselves with compassion, kindness, humility, meekness and patience. Bear with one another and, if anyone has a complaint against another, forgive each other; just as the Lord has forgiven you, so you must also forgive."*

As I reviewed my day I was reminded of the times I did not show patience, compassion, or kindness.

I am more prone to be impatient and sarcastic when I am driving and I was in the car all day. I was able to be compassionate, kind, and patient during the day as well so my day was complete.

I know when I start my day with time in the Word of God; I go forth clothed as these verses say. If I see the people I meet as I am called to, as children of God, I am able to exhibit these attributes more easily.

I need to remember when I am driving; they are still a beloved child of God. I am blessed by these verses because I am forgiven.

I am able to forgive and go into the new day newly clothed in Christ.

Lord,
I praise you and I lift your name in glory and honor. Because you forgive, I can forgive. You taught compassion, kindness, humility, meekness, and patience. Clothe me in these things. Cover me in your word and love as I go into the new day. Amen.

Oct 2 - *Psalm 23:5 "You prepare a table before me in the presence of my enemies; you anoint my head with oil; my cup overflows."*

The lavish abundance is amazing to think about.
When I picture the table the Lord would prepare for me and for you, I picture a table laden with delicious and beautiful foods of every kind. I picture a feast fit for a king laid out just for me.
It is a clear statement to my enemies that I am treasured and important, loved and honored by my Lord.
It is enticing and as I prepare to sit with my Lord at this lavish table of abundance, he anoints my head with oil. He lovingly pours his healing, cleansing, and sanctifying oil over me making me new; renewing me. As we dine together, basking in the love and light, I am reveling in the overflowing blessings I receive from my Lord. He completely satisfies my every need and every desire.
I invite you to come and join in the feast of the Lord. His presence, his word, and his love will fill you and complete you like nothing else. Through this abundant love, he fills us up and prepares us to go into the world remembering we are his beloved, his treasured children. He is always by our side guiding, protecting, and loving us.
Truly, my cup of blessing overflows every day.

Lord,
Thank you for your lavish love spread out and poured out for each one of us. Help us come to you and receive the blessings you so freely give. Let us remember how treasured we are in your sight today. Amen.

Oct 3 - *2 Timothy 3:14 "But as for you, continue in what you have learned and firmly believed, knowing from whom you learned it."*

I am troubled by my actions.

Two separate times yesterday I was asked by a homeless person for some money. As graciously as I could I told them no. Now the battle ensues.

I know when homeless people receive money; often they don't use it wisely. I know I give money to my church and it probably filters down somehow to help people like this. I know there are programs and shelters and the list goes on.

I have learned and firmly believe this; I am called to love others with the love of Christ and serve others. I know people who give gift cards for fast food restaurants to homeless folks or even take them to the restaurant to buy them food. I have a friend who carries canned food or prepackaged precooked foods in her car so she can give those to the people that stand on street corners. The question in my heart this morning is this: Do I live what I have learned and believe? How can I do more?

Lord,

I live in my little sheltered world most of the time. Thank you for opening my eyes a bit more. Guide my steps going forward so I can answer, without a doubt, that I live what I have learned from you. Amen.

Oct 4 - *Isaiah 41:9-10 "You whom I took from the ends of the earth, and called from its farthest corners, saying to you, 'You are my servant, I have chosen you and not cast you off': do not fear, for I am with you, do not be afraid, for I am your God; I will strengthen you, I will help you, I will uphold you with my victorious right hand."*

I am so blessed to read this encouragement.

I have been reflecting on my life and the poor choices that have ended up teaching me lessons the hard way. Many times I heard the voice calling; I ignored it or thought I knew better.

I do not know better and I hope by God's infinite grace I will remember that he knows better, always. In spite of my false starts and faltering steps he is faithful.

Verse 9 confirms that he calls us to be his servants; he has chosen each of us and has not cast us off. I hear the message from verse 10 clearly: I am with you, I will strengthen you, and I will help you.

Take joy with me this morning in this message because it is for each of us, we are all his beloved; we are all called to him.

Lord,
I come to you again and again in humble adoration and in awe of your mercy and grace. Thank you for your words in Isaiah, they bring peace and comfort to me this morning. I pray these words whisper in my ear all day and that these words bring encouragement and comfort to those who read them with me. Your word brings you close to my heart and my soul and I am blessed because of it. Thank you. Amen.

Oct 5 - *John 4:37-38 "For here the saying holds true, 'One sows and another reaps.' I sent you to reap that for which you did not labor. Others have labored, and you have entered into their labor."*

I am reminded of the saying "It takes a village to raise a child." Each child is changed by any relationship they experience. Parent, teacher, and neighbor all play a role in how that child is formed.

We plant seeds when we show and share the love of God. We water and nurture seeds when we serve as the Lord calls us to. We are all working as a team, on God's team, to further his work in this world.

As Sunday school is under way in my church, I am reminded that I am not in charge of what the children walk away with. I am in charge of listening for the guidance of the Lord and obeying what he guides me to do. He is in charge of calling to these kids; I am simply a tool, a laborer. I may be planting, nurturing, or reaping but only God knows what is in the hearts of those in this group.

I encourage you to be a part of the village today. We are all his beloved children. How is he calling you to labor for him and his kingdom today?

Lord,
Thank you for the reminder of who is in charge. Help me listen and guide my words as I do your work. If nothing else, I pray the people I see today walk away from me feeling loved. I offer my labor to you. Amen.

Oct 6 - *Psalm 8:3-4 "When I look at your heavens, the work of your fingers, the moon and the stars that you have established; what are human beings that you are mindful of them, mortals that you care for them?"*

I enjoy an annual tradition to star gaze with my Dad and my kids. For the last several years we have met up with a group of amateur astronomers in the mountains where there are dark skies, away from city lights.

In the middle of Colorado wilderness we could not miss the work of God's fingers on this small planet. My four year old son asked "what is over there?" I responded "trees, dirt, animals." He asked "what is after that?" My response was "more trees, dirt and animals."

We saw the splendor of his creation here on the many walks we took around the area where we camped. We saw the splendor of his work when we gazed through the many telescopes that were there to see galaxies, nebulae, planets, and stars that are never ending. When I see these things I am humbled.

This awesome most powerful creator of the heavens and earth loves each and every human being he has created. He loves and cares about you and me. He wants our love back.

Wow! Our God is an awesome God!

Lord,
Thank you for the creation of the telescope and the ability to see things beyond our small world. The splendor of the heavens reminds me of your awesome power and the tender flower in the field reminds me of your gentle care for each of us. Thank you for these reminders Lord. Amen.

Oct 7 - *Mark 10:14-15 "But when Jesus saw this, he was indignant and said to them, 'Let the little children come to me; do not stop them; for it is to such as these that the kingdom of God belongs. Truly I tell you, whoever does not receive the kingdom of God as a little child will never enter it.'"*

It is such a blessing to be in the presence of little children. The energy and joy they bring to their day is uncontainable. They live every moment to the fullest and they are aware of so much that we as adults do not see.

This is how I imagine us in the kingdom of God. We are made new and fresh through his redeeming love and when we search in true belief with all our energy, we will find him. If we come searching with flashlights and GPS, using external means and tools as we adults are prone to do, we will miss him.

His kingdom is not of this world which we submerge ourselves in. We need to set aside our technology, set aside our perceptions and suppositions. Remember what it is to be innocent and new, like a little child.

When we search for his kingdom in this way, our blessings overflow.

Lord,
As I spend time with children today, please open my eyes to see as they see. Draw me into your kingdom in joy and energy that knows no bounds. Give me the courage and words to share your kingdom and love with others. Amen.

Oct 8 - *Psalm 19:14 "Let the words of my mouth and the meditation of my heart be acceptable to you, O Lord, my rock and my redeemer."*

When I dragged myself out of bed this morning there was joy in my heart.

As much as I love to sleep, I love my quiet time even more.

There is a song phrase going through my head about God making beautiful things out of dust and as I sat and tried to focus the song kept beating. I pictured ashes sitting on foundations where homes used to be. I saw the smoke in the air from the forest fires earlier this year. There was so much destruction happening on so many levels.

As I struggled to hear the Lord speaking I finally prayed this verse and a wave washed over me. God is here and he loves to be with us. He renews us. He creates new and beautiful things from the ashes and dust.

Sometimes when I get a song stuck in my head the redundancy gets to me. I may leave this one. It is a good meditation in my heart.

Lord,

Thank you for breaking through the chaos in my head to quiet my soul. You know the destruction that occurs and you bring new creation through it. Help all those struggling to see the new creation being made in the midst of the destruction. Bring us all to a new and deeper level of trust in you as we experience the flow of losing the old so the new can come. Please guide my mouth and heart in the words and meditations today so they remain acceptable to you and so I can serve you in your love and light. Amen.

Oct 9 - *Ezekiel 36:26-27 "A new heart I will give you, and a new spirit I will put within you; and I will remove from your body the heart of stone and give you a heart of flesh. I will put my spirit within you, and make you follow my statutes and be careful to observe my ordinances."*

The Bible is filled with stories of Israel being disobedient, turning from their sins, and coming back to the Lord.
In this passage, the Israelites have not turned back to the Lord. He brings renewal and blessings to them despite their wandering ways in order to bring honor to his name.
God desires nothing more than our devotion. He longs for us to listen and follow him; to honor and praise him with all we do and say. We are no different than the Israelites of long ago. We are often wayward and deceived people. We are self-oriented and self-serving most of the time.
I long for the day when I wake up each morning acknowledging the presence of the Lord, and continue each moment of the day honoring and living for him. I long for the day when this nation I live in will turn to him for guidance in all we do and seek to serve him in every way.
I know this is coming ...someday.

Lord,
We need you but we do not seek you. We seek you only to turn the other way when we do not want to follow. Forgive our sins and give us new hearts and spirits for you. Open our hearts and spirits to be led only by you, all for your glory. Amen.

Oct 10 - *Hebrews 3:6 "Christ, however, was faithful over God's house as a son, and we are his house if we hold firm the confidence and the pride that belong to hope."*

The reference to us being his house caused a little research on my part today.

I know the common belief that his spirit lives in us and we are his temple but this verse felt different. The verse made me think of nobility and I know very little about that.

Most little girls like to dress up and play princess and mine is no exception. She often tells me she is a princess, my son is the prince, I am the queen, and my husband is the king. I tease her and remind her that the princess is not in charge so she needs to remember to listen and obey the queen.

Not too long ago, Prince William of England married Kate bringing her into the house of Windsor. I think about her being molded and formed into royalty as it is expected.

We too have been brought into a house of royalty. We are being molded and formed into royalty as it should truly be. We are his house because he is our ruler; we are his heirs and subjects.

Go into your day feeling blessed to be a part of the house of Christ. Live as heirs of his kingdom and serve him well.

Lord,

Thank you for making us a part of your royal kingdom. We are blessed to be in the house of Christ and I pray that we live bringing honor and glory to your holy kingdom, the one true kingdom that reigns forever. You are my king; I bow to you and you alone. Amen.

Oct 11 - *John 11:40 "Jesus said to her, 'Did I not tell you that if you believed, you would see the glory of God.'"*

God has a plan.

In this story of Lazarus, Jesus intentionally waits to go and visit even though he knows his friend is ill. In verse 4 he says the illness is for God's glory, so he could be glorified through it. When he comes to Bethany, Martha and Mary are weeping for the loss of their brother. When he saw their tears and the tears of their friends he was deeply moved.

I love this verse reminding me again that God sees our tears and sadness. He does not discount our feelings; our feelings move him. Jesus thanks God for hearing his prayer and says it aloud so that the people around him would learn and believe that he was sent by God.

Jesus' entire ministry was bent on teaching us about God. He was sent to renew our relationship with the Divine. He showed us how to love, how to pray, and how to live in faith. How often do I come to God asking, maybe even hoping, but not believing or looking for the glory?

Somehow, if we open our hearts to the deep love of Christ, we will see the hand of God in everything.

Oh, that I would believe so I could see.

Lord,
There is always a tiny part of me that holds doubt. I know that you can do anything; I want to believe it with all my heart. Erase the doubt I have and allow me to believe and see that you are deeply and lovingly involved. Bring me to a deeper level of trust in you. Thank you for your word to guide and teach me. Thank you for your love. Amen.

Oct 12 - *Exodus 16:28 "The Lord said to Moses, 'How long will you refuse to keep my commandments and instructions?'"*

This battle began at creation and has never stopped.
Starting with Adam and Eve eating fruit from the tree of knowledge, it has been downhill from there. God saves his people from Egyptian slavery only to have them build an idol of gold. He gives them commandments, guides them day and night, and protects them from attacks of other people. They cry out that they are starving so he provides manna, bread from heaven. He clearly states how to gather it, but do his chosen people listen and follow direction? No.
How am I like the Israelites? I know the commands of God. They are written on my heart. Yet, I do not live in love. Instead of having self-control, I fight for control. Instead of sharing love and grace, I spew frustration and anger. I am no different than the Israelites.
The good news is this: God is gracious and forgiving. He sent the ultimate sacrifice so that we can be redeemed. He gave us the gift of being able to walk with him always, as a new creation in him. His mercy is unending.

Lord,
I read this story of the desert and I am humbled. You gently remind me that we all disobey your commands, myself included. Thank you for your love and grace through Jesus the Christ. It is through this gift that I have hope. It is because of this, I can start again; loving you with all that I am and loving my neighbor. Praise God. Amen.

Oct 13 - *John 6:67-69 "So Jesus asked the twelve, 'Do you also wish to go away?' Simon Peter answered him 'Lord, to whom can we go? You have the words of eternal life. We have come to believe and know that you are the Holy One of God.'"*

Sometimes the teachings of Jesus are hard to swallow. He challenges us to the very depths of our souls. When things get hard, some turn away. There are so many options for "worship" out there. At every corner there are whispers of distraction pulling and tugging at us.

Living as Jesus taught and being accountable to the Holy One is not easy. Jesus knew this and spoke about it in several of his parables. He also promised on many occasions that he would not leave us, he would be with us. He encourages us to abide in him and he will abide in us. His Spirit is in-dwelling and I find no greater hope and joy than that.

No matter where I am, no matter what I have done, no matter how I feel, I know that God is with me. I do not wish to go away; I have received all I need from the Holy One of God.

Lord,
Thank you for all your teachings and blessings. Transform my day and my soul with your word and teaching. Let me be a source of living water to others so I may draw others close to you glorifying you in every way. Amen.

Oct 14 - *2 Timothy 2:21 "All who cleanse themselves of the things I have mentioned will become special utensils, dedicated and useful to the owner of the house, ready for every good work."*

In my kitchen I have drawers with cooking utensils as well as a jar on the counter with other cooking utensils.

I use the ones in the jar most often and the ones in the drawer are more specialized for certain tasks. I have flatware and some fine silver for special occasions. All of these utensils serve a specific purpose. I cannot use the tongs for serving soup and my ladle will not scoop up a slice of meat very well.

We are like utensils in God's kitchen. We are all created for a specific purpose in his kingdom. Some of us are used in everyday ways and some of us are much more specialized. All of us are valuable for the smooth running of the kingdom.

Do you know your purpose? Are you a slotted spoon or a ladle? Search and pray with God to find your use in his kingdom today. Allow yourself to be useful and ready for God to put into action.

Lord,
How often do I offer to be a serrated knife for you when I am really a butter knife? Both tools are useful but serve such different purposes. Please help me see and know what you call me to be and guide my steps in the tasks you have for me to the glory of your kingdom. Amen.

Oct 15 - *Acts 4:31 "When they had prayed, the place in which they were gathered together was shaken; and they were all filled with the Holy Spirit and spoke the word of God with boldness."*

It seems to me that there is a lot of shaking up going on lately. When I pray to God for something in earnest, he tends to rock my world; my place is shaken. I see the Spirit moving all around this world.

With my eyes wide open, I am amazed that I could ever miss the boldness in which he moves. It is this Spirit that drew me into his word again. It is this Spirit that moves me to rise each morning and write these simple words from my study of the Word.

There is trepidation in the shaking up. As I ponder the options, here are the two it boils down to for me: move in boldness with the Spirit of the Lord or be left behind and miss out on all the abundant blessings he has for me. When we walk in the Spirit, we are called to do things that can be challenging or difficult. I tend to take a step back and question the Lord as Moses did when God called him to save the Israelites from Egypt.

He shakes us up but he never leaves us to figure it out on our own. He has given us the Spirit to go forth in boldness.

Pray, trust, and go forth.

Lord,
Thank you for your Spirit. I implore you to guide every step I take in boldness for you. Keep my word and soul in stride with you every step of the way. Let your word be a light unto my path so I may lead others in your light as well. Amen.

Oct 16 - *Ezekiel 18:31-32 "Cast away from you all the transgressions that you have committed against me, and get yourselves a new heart and a new spirit! Why will you die, O house of Israel? For I have no pleasure in the death of anyone, says the Lord God. Turn, then and live."*

Yesterday my daughter and her friends decided they were going to live outside from now on.

She had gathered a few of her things in bags to carry and mentioned something about needing food. They set up "camp" on the sidewalk in front of one of the houses. When the time came for her to put away all her things and come home she was not happy. She seemed to think she, at the age of six, could really just live on her own in the "wilderness."

As I read this passage of Ezekiel, I realize how much I am like my daughter in my walk with God. I think I have it all figured out and I am ready for the wilderness. It is humble pie for me when I come in from my play of independence.

When I choose not to abide in God, I am destined for failure. I cannot survive on my own so I choose to live in the shelter of my Lord and Savior. I choose to cast away my sins and embrace the love and grace he offers in a new heart and spirit.

I choose to turn and live.

Lord,
Forgive my rebellions and thank you for the reminder that I need you every moment of every day. It is a wild world out there with so many obstacles. I know I can only maneuver it with your help. Please take my hand and my heart; never let go. I walk with you and choose life with you. Amen.

Oct 17 - *1 John 4:21 "The commandment we have from him is this: those who love God must love their brothers and sisters also."*

Our hearts and souls are made for love.
We seek love from the moment we are born until the moment we leave this earth whether we recognize that search or not. I thought about songs that have been written throughout time that speak about love and I suspect that there is no subject that has been written about more.
This call to find love, to share love, is put into our souls by God. He is love and he created us in his image. This world is fractured and broken and so our love is not perfect either but his command is to love.
Do something kind for your neighbor; give your kids or friend a hug. Make or buy a little gift for someone you know, spend some time visiting a lonely person. Pray for your friends and family; pray for your antagonists and enemies. I have found as I work on this specific discipline it is much easier to love them even if I do not really like them.
Take some time to soak in the love of God this morning and then find a way to spread that love to someone else.
All we need is love...

Lord,
You fill us up whenever we come ready to be filled. Help us prepare our hearts for you so we can fully receive the love you have for us each day. Open our hands and hearts to receive and then again to share the blessing of love you give for all. Amen.

Oct 18 - *Ephesians 1:17 "I pray that the God of our Lord Jesus Christ, the Father of glory, may give you a spirit of wisdom and revelation as you come to know him"*

Each morning I sit in quiet stillness (more or less) reading the word and pondering its meaning to me. Then I sit down at my computer and write.

You get to read the fruits of my "labor" for whatever it is worth. When I started this journey to search and know the Lord more deeply I did not know where it would lead. I only know this: as I continue on this path, this prayer from Paul will be in my heart. I do not want to know him as I know the history of the United States. I can read a text book about the country where I live and it gives me knowledge.

The study to know God is a living study. He gives me a spirit of wisdom and revelation. He gives that spirit to each of us so that as we move closer to him, he is revealed to us, we are revealed in him, and we gain wisdom in the Lord. There is much to know about our Lord, a lifetime or more of learning is at hand.

I ask the spirit of wisdom and revelation to be with each of us as we continue on this path of coming to know our Lord.

Lord,
You abide in me. As I search to know you, to walk closer with you, I am encouraged to know you are there every step of the way. I ask for wisdom as I study, I ask for revelations as I come to know you more. Touch each of us in this way so that we may be changed through knowing you. Amen.

Oct 19 - *1 Peter 4:7-8 "The end of all things is near; therefore be serious and discipline yourselves for the sake of your prayers. Above all, maintain constant love for one another, for love covers a multitude of sins."*

The message throughout the Bible, the message God sends to us in so many ways, never changes. It is the message of Love. When I pray, Love is there.
Times when I have been angry or hurt, prayer has healed and restored beyond my imagination. Situations I thought were beyond hope were made whole through prayer. God's love is manifested through prayer.
Is there someone or something you are finding difficult?
I encourage you to take them to God in prayer. As you lift those struggles in prayer each day, the love of God transforms things.
There have been times I prayed for God to change someone else. I prayed fervently for that. When I finally came to him asking him to change my view to match his, the results were astounding. When we can see our world through his eyes of love, there is much beauty.
When we love one another it is easy to pray for one another. When we pray for one another it is easier to love one another. Let us pray and love.

Lord,
Pour your love into every crevice of my soul. Bring to my heart the struggles I need to lift in prayer and love. Open my eyes to the healing you grant through love and prayer. Above all, help me show my love for you in all I do and say. Amen.

Oct 20 - *Philippians 4:4-5 "Rejoice in the Lord always; again I will say, Rejoice. Let your gentleness be known to everyone. The Lord is near."*

God is good.

There are so many things in this world that can distract us or lead us away from abiding in God and this morning I was reminded how those distractions usually end up. In the past when I have discounted the power of God, or chosen not to let him lead my steps, I have invariably suffered pain, loss, and humiliation. Looking for love and fulfillment in man has been a dismal failure. Human love will never fill my heart or make me complete in the way I need to be. It has taken me *way* too long to discover this and the sad part is that I still search for fulfillment in man. It is human nature to seek fulfillment.

I believe God put that desire in our hearts so that we would search for him and find that we are complete in him. How many times will I fail to remember that only he can give me my heart's desire?

"The Lord is near." He is with us waiting to be called on to fill our heart's desire and to bring wholeness back to us. It is in his fulfillment that I am able to go forth, showing gentleness to others. He is so gentle with me; I cannot help but rejoice in him.

Lord,

I praise your name and rejoice in your love! You are near; your love and peace are here to restore and sustain me. Fill me up Lord. I want to share the gift of gentleness in this world today. I do everything in glory to you. Amen.

Oct 21 - *Psalm 33:20 "Our soul waits for the Lord; he is our help and shield."*

Waiting is not one of my favorite things to do.
I go through my days with a mindset that time is of the essence.
I like to make the most of the time I have; I like to be efficient.
Since I began my devotional time I have begun to see the benefit in waiting. When I sit in quietness, waiting for the Lord, I am still. There is a time of calm and quiet before the hustle and bustle of my day.
I do not always wait well. There are days my mind races forth and it takes much prayer and many attempts before I find the peace and calm of waiting. When I wait, he is there. He has never let me down; he has always been my help and my shield. I have not always seen him because I did not look for him. When I rush forth and do not wait I often make a mess of things. I pray for things and do not see what I hope for; it is tempting to stick my own "help" into those situations.
I thank God for the reminder that I must wait for the Lord, he is my help, and he is my shield. If I wait, he will help and protect me as I go forth with him.

Lord,
I wait for you, but not well. I trust in you but do not wait. You do not crunch yourself into my limited time window. As I sit this morning and wait with you, I see all the times you have been my help and shield despite me. Thank you for your grace and love. Help me grow in waiting and trusting in your help and shield. You are ever faithful. Amen.

Oct 22 - *Ephesians 1:20 "God put this power to work in Christ when he raised him from the dead and seated him at his right hand in the heavenly places,"*

We live in a world of power.

With the push of a button we have access to the world through our televisions and our computers. With the invention of batteries we can even take our tools for connection with us. There are laptop computers and smart phones that fit in our purses and pockets; the world truly is at our fingertips. Some of us get so used to having access to these things that, when they are gone, we are lost without them.

We come to rely on them too much. We are certain to plug in our cell phones and computers so they do not run out of power. How often do we remember to plug ourselves in for a recharge from the Divine power source? We cannot truly live by simply fueling our bodies and minds. We need to receive power for our spirits as well.

I encourage you to take time each day to plug in to the Lord. Recharge your spirit and soul with his power of truth and love. There will never be a power outage in God's world regardless of the shortages we experience in our world.

Lord,

Thank you for electricity and batteries. These inventions make our lives so much more convenient than they used to be. Use these common everyday tools to remind us to plug in to you for spiritual strength and renewal; nothing is more important. Thank you for always being there, providing for and renewing us when we ask in your name. Amen.

Oct 23 - *2 Corinthians 12:9 "but he said to me, 'My grace is sufficient for you, for power is made perfect in weakness.' So, I will boast all the more gladly of my weaknesses, so that the power of Christ may dwell in me."*

At face value these words seem odd. Why would we boast in our weaknesses?

Maybe it is just me (I don't think so) but I am always striving to do better, to be better. My goal is always to live as Christ lived. I am humbly reminded that I am not, nor can I ever be, perfect. God did not create humans to be perfect; he created us with free will. Even in Genesis he acknowledges the imperfection in humans.

As I prayed over this verse it became clear to me once more that because of my weaknesses I need God. Because of my weakness and sin, I make regular communion time with the Divine. I am brought to my knees in his presence to receive forgiveness and grace.

He tells us that his grace is sufficient for us. I am able to see his strength and power because I am weak and powerless without him. I can boast because it is only through his grace that I am made strong. I will stumble and fall.

The blessing is that he is ready to pour his amazing grace on me whenever I come for forgiveness. I am weak but he is strong. Yes, Jesus loves me!

Lord,
Thank you for your love and grace. I will never be strong without your strength in me. Without you I cannot truly live. Help me embrace my weakness so that I can fully embrace your strength and power. Amen.

Oct 24 - *Matthew 5:44-45 "But I say to you, Love your enemies and pray for those who persecute you, so that you may be children of your Father in heaven, for he makes his sun rise on the evil and on the good, and sends rain on the righteous and on the unrighteous."*

I live near a high school and there are times when I see a group of teenagers gathered around each other. It is easy for me to "see" they are up to no good. I watch the news and see stories of people protesting because someone believes something different than they do.

Most people live and let live but these verses ask for more. Who is your enemy? Is it a neighbor or family member? Is it a religious sect you disagree with? Is it someone who does not live according to your standards?

During any political campaign the politicians and media are my enemies. God tells each of us to Love our enemies and pray for them. We need to pray for them and to see them as God does. Every person is God's beloved; he loves every single person he created. As his disciples we are called to love as he loves.

When we love in the love of Christ, we are drawn closer to God. When we pray for those we see as enemies, we begin to see them as children of God, just like us.

Join me in prayer and love today.

Lord,
Soften our hearts, guide our prayers, and open our eyes to see our enemies as you see them. We are all your creation and we are all loved by you. Help us love as you taught us to. Amen.

Oct 25 - *Luke 11:34-35 "Your eye is the lamp of your body. If your eye is healthy, your whole body is full of light; but if it is not healthy, your body is full of darkness. Therefore consider whether the light in you is not darkness."*

There is a saying that the eye is the window to the soul. This passage almost says the eye is the window *for* the soul. How do we see things? Remember the fun houses with crazy mirrors that make things seem different and a little bit wrong? They make a short person look tall or a thin person look really wide. It can be fun and silly to see things that way. As we experience life and all its joy and sorrow, our view changes with the impact of those experiences. Life can bring light and it can bring darkness. The darkness is subtle and little by little it changes and skews our view; we do not realize that we are seeing the world with crazy, warped mirrors as our windows.

It is easy to believe that our light is true but in the verses today we are asked to reconsider. Do we truly see as God intends us to? Are the eyes of our soul polished and clean? Take time with me today to ask our Lord to show us any darkness that lurks and skews our view.

Lord,
I come to you in humble adoration. Your word brings healing, hope, and love. Thank you. I ask for cleansing light to shine through all who read this today, removing any darkness that lurks, even where we are unaware. Give us healthy eyes so we can see in truth and so our whole bodies shine full of your light. Amen.

Oct 26 - *Jonah 1:3 "But Jonah set out to flee to Tarshish from the presence of the Lord. He went down to Joppa and found a ship going to Tarshish; so he paid his fare and went on board, to go with them to Tarshish, away from the presence of the Lord."*

What in the world was Jonah thinking?
If he was thinking clearly he would know there is no place to run from the Lord. He was born and raised a Hebrew, worshiping the "God of Heaven" according to verse 9 of this story. Of course as we read on, a storm causes all sorts of trouble for the sailors and after doing all they can to save the ship, per Jonah's request, they throw him overboard.
Jonah ends up saved from drowning by being swallowed by a great fish. Even in the belly of that fish, Jonah knows God is there. He prays to the Lord from the belly of the fish with no doubt that he would be heard. As the story continues Jonah continues to battle wills with God and, of course, loses.
In my life, it is often in retrospect that I can see the will of God is a better choice than mine. How often have I tried to run away or argue with the Lord about what I should do? In the end, after near drowning, more arguing, and a bit of humble pie, I come to my senses again and realize God is Lord of all, even me.

Lord,
Please forgive my disobedience and arrogance. Thank you for the reminder of Jonah and the strife he subjected himself to out of disobedience. Help me follow you in truth and humility this day and tomorrow too. Amen.

Oct 27 - *Daniel 6:10 "Although Daniel knew that the document had been signed, he continued to go to his house, which had windows in its upper room open toward Jerusalem, and to get down on his knees three times a day to pray to his God and praise him, just as he had done previously."*

Recently I was talking with my daughter about "religion." It has come to her attention that not everyone believes the same things or prays to the same God. I explained that in our country, everyone is allowed to worship any god they want. I told her there are countries where people cannot openly worship our God without getting into trouble. We talked about servants of God that bring the message to those places where it is not allowed and how the message is spread in spite of danger.

We are blessed to have freedom of religion. We often forget, with freedom comes responsibility. It is easy for us to take our freedom for granted and become lackadaisical in our worship and prayer. Since we can do it anytime we want, we do not appreciate the blessing of those things.

I have been challenged by this story to be more intentional about my prayer and time with God.

Lord,
As I resolve to come to you more often and more regularly, let my heart be right for true prayer and praise to you. I know as I spend more time with you, I am changed and renewed. Guide me in this; I ask this only to honor you. Amen.

Oct 28 - *Psalm 18:1-2 "I love you, O Lord, my strength. The Lord is my rock, my fortress, and my deliverer, my God, my rock in whom I take refuge, my shield and the horn of my salvation, my stronghold."*

On days where life is bombarding me these verses soothe my soul.

I was awake at 2:30 this morning with the many things I need to do today and tomorrow running through my mind. Then the dog next door was barking and my spouse was snoring…

There are days that the kids never stop with noise and requests, whining and fighting. Times like these I think about escaping from it all. There are deeper waters that run in me too; the muck buried underneath them gets stirred up by a trivial little annoyance and then I need help.

Not a day goes by anymore that I do not call on the name of the Lord to calm me or to guide me. I stop for a moment to sit in his peaceful presence and feel the strength of my Lord fill me once more. He protects me from the barrage of negativity in this world and when I falter, he is my salvation. I come to him in repentance and humility and he forgives and cleanses me from all unrighteousness.

I cling to him; I live in him and I praise him.

Lord,
Your strength is my joy and your love is my guide. I cannot imagine living without you. It is with you as my shield and my strength that I go forth into my day prepared for anything. You will deliver me and save me. Amen.

Oct 29 - *Colossians 1:16 "for in him all things in heaven and on earth were created, things visible and invisible, whether thrones or dominions or rulers or powers – all things have been created through him and for him."*

Someone I was talking with recently referred to my God as the Christian God.

I found that title interesting because it is, in part, true. The God I worship is the God of Christians and Jews, but he does not stop there.

The God I worship transcends religion or sects. He is Creator of all we can see and all we do not see. He is Orchestrator of all that is, all that has been, and all that will be. All his creation sits in the orchestra pit waiting for his direction and guidance. With his power and wisdom, he uses his creation to make beautiful music. He does not only use the percussion section or only the violins. He uses each section and each instrument in their own unique way to blend together in a symphony like no other.

We may not all see or acknowledge our creator but that does not make him less of the Creator. He is and will always be the One through which and for which all things were created.

Lord,
Your creation is beyond my imagination. The music you hear from each of us when put together is beautiful. Bring us all together as one group, all in unity that we may follow you the Creator, and make a symphony like no other. May our music bless and glorify your holy name. Amen.

Oct 30 - *Isaiah 53:6 "All we like sheep have gone astray; we have all turned to our own way, and the Lord has laid on him the iniquity of us all."*

I was sitting quietly this morning, thanking God for the changes he has made in my heart when this scripture reference came, boldly, to me. I have never looked at this verse in the way I see it today.

First, as I continue to strive toward a life in God, I am reminded that every one of us has strayed and gone to our own way. As long as my soul resides on earth, this will not change.

The second part of the verse brings me the reminder of grace. The Lord has laid my iniquity, all my sin, on Jesus. The changes in my heart, the transformation in my life, is only possible because Jesus takes my sin and makes me new in the eyes of the Almighty. It is this precious gift that allows me to dare to approach the throne of God at all.

It is because Jesus walks with me and has already made me clean that I can present myself to God as an offering in thanks and adoration.

Lord,
I am speechless. You bring your word to me each day, teaching me and guiding me. I come to you searching and, in your infinite grace, you provide. More than providing, you pour your teachings and your grace into me until I am filled once again with your love and light. Thank you. Amen.

Oct 31 - *Galatians 5:7-8 "You were running well; who prevented you from obeying the truth? Such persuasion does not come from the one who calls you."*

A song that I do not really know runs through my mind this morning.

My husband received one of those singing birthday cards last year and a part of that song was what I woke up with this morning. The song phrase was about being an all-star and getting your game on. I have to believe there was a message in that because I have not heard that song in a VERY long time.

As I read the passage in Galatians I could see the message more clearly. God calls each one of us, through grace he redeems us. We are "all-stars" for his sake. We are called to go forth in truth, living in his word and in his love. When we deviate from the path, he calls us back – we need to "get our game on."

Okay, maybe it is a stretch, but the verses are clear. Do not be prevented from obeying the truth. There are many lures to lead us away from the life God calls us to and when we fall away, he faithfully calls us back. Keep focused on the goal, so we may continue to run well.

Remember who made us all-stars and let's get our game on!

Lord,

You speak in many ways, who am I to question your methods? Help each of us continue to run well, keep us from veering off the path you have shown us. The truth is written in our hearts, help us remember and follow your guidance. If I am an all-star, it is only because of your grace and mercy. Let me shine for your kingdom, always. Amen.

Nov 1 - *Psalm 68:4 "Sing to God, sing praises to his name; lift up a song to him who rides upon the clouds – his name is the Lord – be exultant before him."*

Yesterday afternoon was a time filled with music for me.
One of the groups I ring handbells with participated in a fund raiser and we, along with several other musical groups, provided a concert of vocal and instrumental music for a grateful audience of donors.
There is nothing that lifts me closer to the Divine than music.
My soul cannot keep still and I find myself transported to a different place of beauty. The feeling is hard to describe but what I can say is that when I sing or ring to the Lord, I feel him lifting me up.
All peoples of all nations have music and through music there is understanding beyond words. How does music move you?
What kind of music do you prefer and what message does it have for you?
Whether you have a voice of gold or a voice of tin cans does not matter to the Lord. Whether you shake a tambourine or bang a pot with a wooden spoon, it can still be a joyful noise. Listen to the sounds of the world around you today and allow the music that flows among those sounds fill your heart with joy.
Lift your heart and your voice in song to the Lord, the creator of music, the creator of all.

Lord,
Thank you for the music you place in our souls. Open our ears so that we can hear it clearly and open our hearts to sing songs of praise back to you in every moment of this day. You have blessed us, let us be a blessing to you. Amen.

Nov 2 - *Acts 8:22-23 "Repent therefore of this wickedness of yours, and pray to the Lord that, if possible, the intent of your heart may be forgiven you. For I see that you are in the gall of bitterness and the chains of wickedness."*

Simon Magus had been a magician.
As the apostles came to his town preaching the good news he was one of many who believed. He saw the power the apostles had when they laid hands on people and he wanted that power too. These verses are the response of Philip to Simon when he offered money to receive the Spirit.
God has given each of us gifts to honor his name and further his kingdom. Some of us sing, others teach, pray, or help people in his name. There are many ways to serve.
I am reminded in my own journey to ask myself this question: Is the intent of your heart true? Is the reason I do whatever I am doing to bring me praise or is it to bring glory to God? Even if we start out with right intentions, it is easy to let our selfishness creep in and take over until we are no longer seeking to glorify God but are now looking to see our own name lifted up.
I pray that is not so.

Lord,
Search my heart for deceit or wickedness. Let my gifts and service be given only to glorify you and no one else. Keep the intent of my heart pure and true so that, in forgiveness, I go forth serving and glorifying your holy name in everything I do. Amen.

Nov 3 - *2 Samuel 22:17, 20 "He reached from on high, he took me, he drew me out of mighty waters... He brought me out into a broad place; he delivered me, because he delighted in me."*

It is almost beyond my comprehension that the Lord of all, Creator of the Universe delights in me.

Who am I that God would consider a moment of his time for me? Yet when I consider my life and all he has done for me, it is beyond any doubt; what he says is true – he does delight in me. There have been many times that I have felt like I was drowning in the mighty waters, overwhelmed; powerless. When I called on his mighty strength, when I called out in my weakness, he heard me. It is only when I realize that my strength is nothing that I allow God to rescue me from the ocean of deception. I am not strong, except in the Lord.

My life is a testimony to his power. I live and am redeemed through the love and mercy of God Almighty and because of the infinite love and grace of our Lord Jesus, he delights in me. I wish I could share this blessing with every person I see or meet. Hear these words today: he reaches from on high; he draws you out of mighty waters.

He delivers you because he delights in you. Call on his name, he will come.

Lord,
I lift your name in praise this morning. I cannot find words to share the love I have found in you. Tears of gratitude stream down my face, I cannot speak. You are amazing, thank you for redeeming me and thank you for delighting in me. Amen.

Nov 4 - *Proverbs 4:20-21 "My child, be attentive to my words; incline your ear to my sayings. Do not let them escape from your sight; keep them within your heart."*

I need to write these verses on a sticky note and post them to my bathroom mirror.

There are times I am going along in my day and just when I need it most, the words of the Lord sneak into my mind and bring me strength, comfort, or healing. His words help me fight the thoughts that threaten to drag me down, they guide my own heart and the hearts of my children.

Words are powerful; they can build up and they can tear down. Do the words I use with my children build up or tear down? I hate to admit that, at times, my words tear down. My emotions get the best of me and I say things without thinking through them first.

I am not one to fly off the handle, as they say, but I need to be more attentive to his words and I need to be more attentive to my words.

As I learn to keep more of his words in my heart and do not allow them to escape from my sight I hope I have better words for my children.

Lord,
Help me keep my tongue in check. Your words bring instruction, correction, help and healing. Help me use my words for the same purposes. Protect my heart from painful words said to me and keep me from using words to inflict pain on anyone else. I ask you to write these words on my heart so that I always remember them and live by them. Amen.

Nov 5 - *Psalm 119:66-67 "Teach me good judgment and knowledge, for I believe in your commandments. Before I was humbled I went astray, but now I keep your word."*

I would love to say I have learned good judgment and have knowledge but I would be deceiving myself. I can say I am learning good judgment and am gaining knowledge all through the grace and Spirit of God.

How do we know when someone has good judgment? They make wise choices and live their lives according to God's word and guidance. Being able to discern, having good judgment is a gift from God, nothing we own within our own selves. It grows in us as we grow in the Lord.

The same is true with knowledge. How can we learn or gain knowledge in the Lord if we do not spend time with the Lord? How many years did I waste dipping my toes in the water before I finally jumped in with both feet?

This Psalm is a prayer and meditation about following the law of God. It is about learning and doing as we are taught and finding the blessings of obedience.

I am reminded that through Christ the law I must learn is to love God and love my neighbor. I go into today striving to live in obedience to this law of Christ.

Lord,
You have written your word on our hearts, your word promises this to be true. Help us listen to that voice, those words, and your teachings that we know as we work and play on this day that you have made. Keep us from going astray, guide us in truth and love so we do all things in glory to your Holy name. I ask all these things through our Savior and teacher, Jesus Christ. Amen.

Nov 6 - *2 Kings 4:6-7 "When the vessels were full, she said to her son, 'Bring me another vessel.' But he said to her, 'There are no more.' Then the oil stopped flowing. She came and told the man of God, and he said, 'Go sell the oil and pay your debts, and you and your children can live on the rest.'"*

I would put the whole story in my devotion but then I would run out of room on my page, it would be too long for some to read and there would be no reason for you to pull the Bible off of your shelf and read it for yourself.

The reason I started writing devotions was to encourage others to get into the word on a daily basis so I encourage you to get into the word and read this story. There are many stories in the Bible as well as in today's world where God is faithful to us and provides what we need.

This widow asks for help and does not question what she is told to do. She listens and obeys and she is rewarded for her faithfulness. I know if it were me my temptation would be to think, I only have a little oil left, why do I need to gather vessels for that?

Jesus' words "Oh you of little faith" come echoing into my heart. He is faithful forever.

If we ask in faith he provides whatever we need.

Lord,

Help my unbelief. I come to you so many times knowing you can provide but not knowing that you will. When I doubt, remind me of this story and encourage me to follow in complete trust; you never lead me astray. Thank you for your faithfulness and for caring for all of us. I sing songs of praise and thanksgiving to you this day. Amen.

Nov 7 - *Mark 6:38 "And he said to them, 'How many loaves have you? Go and see.' When they had found out, they said, 'Five, and two fish.'"*

Potluck meals are great.
You get to try new foods and there are always the standbys that you can count on. Everyone comes and there is great company to go along with a great meal. Have you ever been to a potluck where there was not enough food? I know I have been to many where there was worry about having enough food but it never seems to run short.
I wonder about this story sometimes. How can 5 loaves of bread and two fish feed 5 thousand people? I imagine the disciples were thinking the very same thing. There would never be enough! I don't know how it worked, I wasn't there, but I would guess the disciples did not know either and they were there.
I learn from this story that we are asked to give what little we have and then trust the Lord to use it as he will. One gift of food from one little person seems useless. Yet, that gift compounded by the love of the Lord fed thousands of people. What can we give that the Lord can compound?
Let go and allow God to work with your gifts to magnify his kingdom.

Lord,
Thank you for this story. Thank you for the reminder that I am not called to feed five thousand, I am asked to give what I have for you to feed the five thousand. Please take my meager offering and use it to further your kingdom in ways beyond my imagination. All glory and honor to you. Amen.

Nov 8 - *Jonah 4:1-2 "But this was very displeasing to Jonah, and he became angry. He prayed to the Lord and said '...for I knew that you are a gracious God and merciful, slow to anger, and abounding in steadfast love, and ready to relent from punishing.'"*

The injustice of it all...

These rampant sinners in Nineveh didn't deserve the mercy of God in Jonah's mind. He didn't want to give them a warning and he certainly didn't want to see God's grace given to them if they decided to repent.

When I read Jonah's story it is easy to see from my bird's eye view how selfish Jonah is being. He disobeys God and through the mercy of God he does not drown but is rescued in the belly of a fish. When Jonah repents and prays to the Lord, God allows Jonah to be delivered to dry land and try again. Even after just receiving all this grace Jonah cannot bear the thought that others would receive grace as well.

How often do we listen to a story on the news or read a story in the paper and cry for justice. As we learn to accept and embrace the grace and forgiveness of God, let us also learn that his grace is for everyone.

Join me in praying for all people to turn from our selfish ways and follow him, seeking his grace and steadfast love.

Lord,

Thank you for not sending me to Nineveh, I fear I may have run away just as Jonah did. Forgive me for the times I have run from what you called me to do. Encourage my heart to trust you and know that you are God of all people. Amen.

Nov 9 - *Ephesians 6:13 "Therefore take up the whole armor of God, so that you may be able to withstand on that evil day, and having done everything, to stand firm."*

I do not have the personality of a warrior.

The passages that speak about God being my fortress and my protection speak much more easily to my heart. I have always shied away from conflict and continue to do my best to keep peace. There are times, though, that we are called up to the front lines.

The battle Paul writes about is not a physical fight with other humans, per se. We need the armor of God to protect us from spiritual warfare. As we prepare for battle we do not know when or where it will be but we must be ready. Paul encourages spiritual discipline with this passage. The gospel of peace, belt of truth, sword of the Spirit; these defenses are strengthened and available through discipline.

Just as our soldiers learn and practice to use the defenses they are given for battle we also need diligence in practice to keep our defenses at the ready.

I stay in the fortress and protection of my Lord God for as long as I can but when he calls me to battle, I go out for him knowing he has given me the weapons and defenses I need to overcome the enemy.

Lord,

I do not like war; you have given me a spirit of peace. Help me learn what I need to in order to serve you in peace and in battles. You are my protection and my comfort. Help me trust that you lead me where I need to go. Amen.

Nov 10 - *Luke 17:33 "Those who try to make their life secure will lose it, but those who lose their life will keep it."*

It all comes down to perspective.

Do you look at the world from the outside in or from the inside out? We are creatures of security. We like to make sure we have what we need and desire and only then do we turn to think about others. The problem is we do not know what we truly need and our desires are misaligned. We get wrapped up in our own lives and lose sight of the bigger picture.

The squirrel is busy gathering nuts for himself and has no gumption to share with a squirrel that has less, but we are not squirrels. This passage in Luke is powerful and I would encourage you to read verses 20-37. There is so much to meditate on ...

As you go through today look to give instead of gather. Find ways to share rather than hoard. As you hear the voice of generosity calling, don't look back at your storehouses first. Trust in the Lord to continue to provide for you as he always has. Release control. Security for these things is truly in the hands of our God. When we do that, we have gained true life, life with God.

Lord,

I pray that these words jump from my computer screen right into the depths of my soul. Help my peace and trust in you remind me that I am not in control and that you, the all-knowing God of the Universe, are the one holding all the cards. Keep my eyes focused on you so I can see the needs in this world and be the help you would have me be. Amen.

Nov 11 - *Proverbs 27:19 "Just as water reflects the face, so one human heart reflects another."*

We have all seen pictures of still waters reflecting a beautiful scene so clearly it is a mirrored image. The water can only reflect whatever it "sees."

This verse caused me to think about what my heart sees and reflects. When I am around a negative person or someone having a hard day it can easily drag me down. I see it in my kids and in other people too. We are drawn into what others feel. If someone is filled with joy, that can pick me up and raise me into feeling joyful too. We are all connected and if our hearts "look" at each other we reflect each other's hearts.

If my heart is looking at God's heart, does it reflect that?

I believe it does. We are made to reflect him. When we do not focus on him, we reflect what we are focused on. If we remain focused on him, we reflect him in our own hearts. Sometimes as I homeschool my kids and teach Sunday school I am on the edge of anxiety. I want it to go well; I want it to be a great success. If I can remain focused on the true purpose and the true goal it will go well.

I pray for each of us today; I pray we remain focused on the Lord so that we can be a true reflection of him in this world.

Lord,
Forgive my anxiety; I know you have it all under control. Guide me and my team, guide all who are preparing to teach others in your word. Help us stay focused on you, so we can be a true reflection of you to others. Amen.

Nov 12 - *2 Thessalonians 2:16-17 "Now may our Lord Jesus Christ himself and God our Father, who loved us and through grace gave us eternal comfort and good hope, comfort your hearts and strengthen them in every good work and word."*

It is hard to see this nation so divided.
As I watched the most recent election unfold I was thinking about the last several elections and how close the voting has been in each of them. Our nation is divided.
Today there are many people rejoicing in the belief that the right choice prevailed and there are almost as many sitting in shock and disbelief at that same outcome. Regardless of which side of the fence you sit on these verses call us to see the good work of God, not of man.
God gives us comfort and hope because, through the gift of Jesus, he is our Father. Let's release the grip we hold on our beliefs in the political arena and hold hands with each other in the love of our one Father. Hold hope in your hearts through him, take comfort in your hearts through him and be strengthened in those gifts so that we can go forward doing good works to his glory. His word is truth and it says that God is good.
Trust and hope in him and his grace.

Lord,
Your hand is in everything whether we can see it or not. Help us trust in your power and guidance. Give us hearts filled with your comfort and hope so we can use our hands to serve you in word and deed. Unite us together in our love for you so that we might all work together for your kingdom. Amen.

Nov 13 - *Deuteronomy 6:7-8 "Recite them to your children and talk about them when you are at home and when you are away, when you lie down and when you rise. Bind them as a sign on your hand, fix them as an emblem on your forehead,"*

What are the things that we pound into our heads and the heads of our kids?

There are so many important things that we try to instill in them as our parents did in us. Don't talk to strangers, look both ways before crossing the street, and eat your vegetables are all things I was taught as a child to keep me safe and healthy. What if I had been given Scriptures over and over again to keep me safe and healthy?

I went to church as a child and learned songs and Bible verses growing up. Either I never heard it or the value and the importance of keeping these things written in my heart was not explained to me. What would our nation be like today if we all loved our neighbor as we love ourselves?

As I teach my daughter math, reading, writing, and science, I hope I teach that these things are important. I hope I teach that loving God and loving others as he loves us are most important.

Lord,
As you guide us let us guide our children. As parent, aunt and uncle, friend and neighbor, we have an awesome opportunity to share the love we have for you with them. Let the words bound in our hearts speak our love for you so we may be a living example to the children and others, drawing them all to your Divine Love. Amen.

Nov 14 - *1 John 4:19-20 "We love because he first loved us. Those who say, 'I love God,' and hate their brothers or sisters, are liars; for those who do not love a brother or sister whom they have seen, cannot love God whom they have not seen."*

I started my morning thinking about having no other gods before the one true God.

The first commandment reminds us that God rescues us from slavery, pulls us out of oppression, and in gratitude we are called to worship and follow him. Then this passage came clearly to my heart. The Bible tells us, too, that God is Love.

There is nothing that makes me feel closer to God and his love than when I am worshiping him and intentionally spending time with him. When I step into the daily tasks of my life, how do I keep that love flowing?

Yesterday my daughter and I helped move some food into a room for organizing our food bank at church. I told her what that food was for to help her realize there are people who struggle in our midst. If I can teach my children and myself to take care of our brothers and sisters in this world, then I know the love of God will flow amongst us.

It is in how we love each other that we show our love of God.

Lord,
Help me reach out to my brothers and sisters in love. I do not want to judge them because they are different; I want to embrace them because you created us all. Remove the barriers I put up and replace them with divine love. Let your love flow from me to the world around me. Amen.

Nov 15 - *1 John 4:9-11 "God's love was revealed among us in this way: God sent his only Son into the world so that we might live through him. In this is love, not that we loved God but that he loved us and sent his Son to be the atoning sacrifice for our sins. Beloved since God loved us so much, we also ought to love one another."*

We all have love in our hearts. This love we have within us is a glimpse of the love God has for us.

When I think about how my heart deeply aches for my kids I know God's heart aches for every single person he has created as mine does, only magnified because he **is** Love.

God sent the Christ, to be our atoning sacrifice on the small chance that we might actually turn around and love him back. Release old hurts and pain, release "control", release anger and frustration. Lay them down at the feet our Redeemer.

Allow those empty arms to be filled with the pure, healing love of God. When we do this, we can turn around and share that love with others.

Go share your love and you may receive even more love back!

Lord,
You came and showed us how to love; you gave and continue to give us so much love through your redemption in Christ. Christ is risen and through that act of love, we are able to love others. Free us from the burdens that keep us from loving and fill us with love so deep, so powerful that we are only able to love others; we have no other path we can take. Compel us to follow, to embrace your love, and to love one another in Christ. Amen.

Nov 16 - *Ephesians 2:8-9 "For by grace you have been saved through faith, and this is not your own doing; it is the gift of God – not the result of works, so that no one may boast."*

Bragging is something people are really good at.
If they don't like to brag about themselves then they surely brag about someone they know and love; a child, a spouse, or some other family member. We like to feel good about ourselves and maybe that is where this comes from. We like to feel privileged and special.
As I revisit these verses I have known since childhood, they take on new meaning. I am only now coming into any true knowledge of grace and acceptance that I cannot ever be good enough on my own doing.
Still with these things gained I know I must work for the Lord. Each day of mine should be fully dedicated to serving the King of my heart. As I work for him this verse needs to resonate in my soul. I work for him in gratitude only. The work I give to the Lord does not get graded in heaven or set aside in a pile to be counted at the end of my life to see how much I did.
God's grace and redemption is a gift to us and we can freely accept it but we cannot earn it. Just as our love is given to one another freely so it is with God. His love and grace are waiting for the taking, have you accepted it?

Lord,
Thank you for your love and thank you for your grace. We can dance and sing because of these gifts! We have been saved, Hallelujah! Amen.

Nov 17 - *Romans 8:28 "We know that all things work together for good for those who love God, who are called according to his purpose."*

Change is inevitable in this world.

The changing of the seasons, a change in leadership to our country and change in our personal lives. I have watched a drama unfold over the last few days that has me praying more than usual.

A lady I have recently befriended through homeschooling channels just found out she has an aggressive breast cancer to battle. I know many people who have had similar battles and I have always hoped and prayed for their healing. We have all seen people battle disease and win and we have all seen people battle disease and lose. I wonder if, in the end, they felt they lost.

This life on earth is a blink of an eye in the vision of eternity. We make grand plans for ourselves and our families and they do not always come to pass due to circumstances beyond our control. In the half of a blink that I have lived so far I have seen true evidence of this verse unfold.

Out of darkness comes light, out of pain comes healing, and out of struggle comes growth. Whatever your path is, keep your eyes focused on God and good will prevail... I know it, he promises it.

Lord,
You are the master planner. Help me trust in you with everything that I am. Take my life and use it according to your purpose so that I may be a part of the greater good in this world and the next. I give it all for your glory. Amen.

Nov 18 - *Psalm 138:1 "I give you thanks, O Lord, with my whole heart; before the gods I sing your praise;"*

It is a great start to the day when I wake up singing praises in my heart.

I woke up singing and went downstairs in my warm home to start a fresh pot of coffee. As I sipped my coffee and read scripture at my kitchen table I became very aware of the many blessings I have been given. I am surrounded by abundance.

My children do not really know what it means to want and not receive. I don't mean they get everything they ask for, but they do not lack for anything. How many people in this city wonder where they will find food or money for their next meal?

There is a movement in this city, in this country to help those in need. There are food banks and shelters; there is monetary assistance for those who cannot make ends meet. There are clothes drives and coat drives as the weather begins to get colder. All these things and more are the work of God caring for his beloved.

Let's join in the movement to care for our brothers and sisters and while we work to share the love of God, let's sing songs of praise and thanksgiving for we are truly blessed by him!

Lord,
You bless us beyond "things" and we cannot begin to see it all.
Open our eyes to the true blessings you have bestowed on us and
hear our songs of thanksgiving. Give us hearts of generosity so
all may be blessed as we are. I sing praises to you with my
whole heart. Amen.

Nov 19 - *Exodus 14:13 "But Moses said to the people, 'Do not be afraid, stand firm, and see the deliverance that the Lord will accomplish for you today...'"*

The Israelites were being chased by Pharaoh's army and quickly coming to the Red Sea with no place to go.

All through their journey to the Promised Land they complained to Moses about being released into the unknown. Many times they wished they could just go back to Egypt. It seems kind of crazy to think that someone released and free would wish to go back into slavery or captivity but they did; and often I do too. There are times that I pray to the Lord in fear of the unknown. I feel him drawing me away from captivity into a new freedom; out of my comfort zone.

There is a part of each of us that prefers to stay where we are. A part of us does not want to stretch beyond where we are into the great unknown. The Israelites were taking a big risk trusting Moses to lead them out of Egypt and into the desert; that was a big step of faith in him and in their Lord.

He calls us to step out in faith today. We are freed from slavery and we need to trust in him to lead us forward on the journey of faith. It feels like a big risk, but we can trust him to deliver us.

Lord,
Help me remember the Israelites when I begin to dig my heels in. Give me courage to trust in you with all my heart, soul, and might, knowing you deliver me from captivity into freedom. Thank you for your faithfulness. Amen.

Nov 20 – *Galatians 5:22-23 "By contrast, the fruit of the Spirit is love, joy, peace, patience, kindness, generosity, faithfulness, gentleness and self- control. There is no law against such things."*

Thanksgiving is a day of gathering and celebrating the bounty we all have.

We gather with friends and family or sit in quiet reflection on our own but Thanksgiving Day has been set aside in our nation since its birth.

As we look at the table overflowing with food let us take a moment to remember tables that have very little or no food. Let us take a moment to remember food lines to receive a free turkey dinner and the people who need those free meals. Regardless of whether we are in need, or if we are singing songs of praise for the bounty we have, we need to remember the deeper bounty that we have all been offered for the taking.

When we receive God's Spirit, when we accept him into our lives, he gives us living fruit. These fruits are gifts we receive and gifts we are to share with others. As we prepare our meals let us also prepare to share love, joy, peace, patience, kindness, generosity, faithfulness, gentleness and self-control. In these gifts we are truly and deeply blessed.

Through the sharing of these gifts we can all raise our hands and hearts in thanksgiving to God.

Lord,
Thank you for all you have given us, we are truly and deeply blessed. Help us share the bounty in our homes as well as the bounty in our hearts. Move us in your Spirit. Amen.

Nov 21 - *2 Timothy 1:7 "for God did not give us a spirit of cowardice, but rather a spirit of power and of love and of self-discipline."*

Do I hide behind the mask of shyness?
As I review my days in search of cowardice I wonder how much I am shy and how much I am a coward. I know I am an introvert so there is some truth in my lack of outgoingness. I also know there are times I do not step forward with my thoughts and feelings because I do not want to risk anything. It is those times I feel I am being a coward.
The Lord guides us when we allow him to. It is my spirit that is weak and cowardly but he has given us all a spirit beyond that human one. The Holy Spirit that resides in us when we accept him is the spirit of power and love and discipline. This Spirit guides our own into self-discipline and call us forth to be a person of power and love in the Lord, Jesus Christ.
There have been times when I have stepped out of my comfort zone and spoken my thoughts as I felt I should and the times I did that in love; it has always been a good thing.
Whether you are a very forthcoming person or a bit shy like me, let us all allow the spirit of power, love, and self-discipline guide our words and deeds so we may glorify God in all we do.

Lord,
Forgive my cowardice and my lack of trust. When you nudge me, help me recognize it and listen to you. Open my heart to allow your spirit to guide mine. I want to live the life you call me to; I want to walk the path you have for me. Amen.

Nov 22 - *Matthew 5:17 "Do not think that I have come to abolish the law or the prophets; I have come not to abolish but to fulfill."*

The laws can be frustrating and sometimes seem unnecessary. Have you ever been sitting at a red light knowing you could turn right but the sign says you may not turn on red?

As a child I know there were "laws" my parents had that I just could not make sense of and it made them hard to follow. I cannot imagine trying to keep over 600 laws for my religion. I can see how easy it would be to get so caught up in following the laws that I would forget to live.

This statement of Jesus' seems odd. He picked grain and healed people on the Sabbath. He preached words that stung the leaders of the church. What it really comes down to is this: If we love God with everything we are and have, and we love our neighbors as ourselves, we are following the teachings of Jesus and we are fulfilling the law.

The next time I am sitting at one of those intersections where the law just doesn't make sense to me, I will try to remember this: I cannot see the reasons for the law but I cannot see everything. Trust and obey, love God and love my neighbor.

Lord,
Thank you for sending Jesus to save us and to fulfill the law. Help me live as he calls us to; in love. May all I do and say reflect the love you have given to me onto those around me so that we are all shining in your love. Amen.

Nov 23 - *Psalm 78:52-53 "Then he led out his people like sheep, and guided them in the wilderness like a flock. He led them in safety, so that they were not afraid; but the sea overwhelmed their enemies."*

It is interesting to watch little kids as they learn to spread their wings and separate from their parents to a certain degree.
At first they are fearful but they learn to trust that their parents will be there. They gain trust and then only occasionally do they run back to touch home base and reassure themselves of that protection and safety.
Sheep are even more trusting with their shepherd. They put complete trust in their shepherd. They know the call he makes and come when they hear him calling. They call to him when they come into any kind of trouble and keep calling, knowing he will come to their rescue.
God is our shepherd and as he did so long ago he keeps us in the safety of his love, guiding our every step if we listen. He leads us in safety and whenever danger comes his power overwhelms that enemy like the sea washing over the Egyptian armies long ago.
Trust in the Lord to guide you, listen for his voice, and follow as an obedient child, like a sheep to his shepherd; he will keep you safe.

Lord,
Thank you for your protection and your guidance. Help us hear you and trust in your voice so we are not led astray. Wipe away our enemy of darkness so we can shine in your glory and step forth faithfully into your kingdom. Amen.

Nov 24 - *Ephesians 4:2-3 "with all humility and gentleness, with patience, bearing with one another in love, making every effort to maintain the unity of the Spirit in the bond of peace."*

When my family gathers for celebrations it is always quite a sight.

Normally there are about fifteen of us all together. The kids run around playing, the men sit in the family room talking and watching sports, and my sisters and I, along with our grown girls, are usually in the kitchen talking and preparing the food. I love these times and I love the conversations we share during clean up as well.

I know we all come from different places in our lives and we do not agree about everything but I appreciate that we can come together, share our thoughts and feelings, and walk away still feeling the love and peace of the Spirit between us. We have learned to be humble and gentle, patient and loving. It wasn't always that way to be sure.

I love my family with all my heart and even though we do not all share the same thoughts and beliefs; the love is deep and true. I know this is unity, and it can only come from the Spirit he gave us.

Lord,
Thank you for the deep love and peace that runs through the hearts of my family, I am so very blessed. Help each of us reach out as you call us to, in humility, gentleness, patience, and love. Guide us in your Spirit of unity so that we may spread your peace and love to everyone. Amen.

Nov 25 - *Psalm 25:1 "To you, O Lord, I lift up my soul."*

As we quickly move into the holiday season people are feeling a wide range of emotions.
Joy and love, happiness and excitement, loneliness, brokenness, stress and pain, peace and calm; all these feelings fill our hearts and the hearts of people all around us.
This morning I pray for each of you that you would lift up your soul to the Lord. If you are joyful and happy, lift your soul to him. If you are sad or lonely lift your soul to him. In your stress and hurt lift your soul to the Lord. In your peace and calm, lift your soul to our Lord.
Whatever you are feeling, whatever your circumstances, wherever you are, lift your soul to the Lord. He will meet you in any place and any time.
As I sit here writing with the "thousand" items I need to get done running in the background of my mind, I keep repeating this verse to my heart. This season of decorating and baking, singing and ringing bells, teaching and playing, brings a busy time that threatens to overwhelm me. I will make this verse my mantra for this season, and maybe beyond that.
He gives me whatever I need whenever I lift my soul to him.
Just knowing and believing in that brings much relief to me.

Lord,
I lift my soul to you and ask that you would give me strength so that I continue to lift my soul to you. You meet me wherever I am and you know what I need most. Be with those who are struggling so much right now and help them lift their souls to you to receive your blessings too. Amen.

Nov 26 - *Hebrews 12:7 "Endure trials for the sake of discipline. God is treating you as children; for what child is there whom a parent does not discipline?"*

We have all seen them; children who we think lack discipline. They run rampant over whatever is in their path. I have seen kids talk back to their parents, and kids that totally disregard any warning their parents give. Sometimes I think these are my kids although I have been reassured many times by my friends that my children are very good.

I think we all have a child within us that occasionally runs rampant and disregards the voice of warning we receive. Just as my young daughter does, I think I know better than that parental voice that tries to guide me in discipline.

I get so frustrated with my kids when they choose to disobey. It is beyond my understanding that they think they know more than I do. As I turn the mirror around I realize they do not think they know more than I, they simply choose to learn by experiencing the trial rather than listening to the voice of reason.

I see this clearly, because I do it too.

Lord,
Forgive my deaf ears and hard heart. Open my eyes to see myself more clearly in my children so they may teach me to be a better child and through you I may teach them to be better children. Thank you for trials and discipline. Amen.

Nov 27 - *2 Corinthians 5:1 "For we know that if the earthly tent we live in is destroyed, we have a building from God, a house not made with hands, eternal in the heavens."*

Beauty is in the eye of the beholder.
In this country, people strive to stay "beautiful" all of their lives. There are wrinkle creams, hair dye and tanning lotions... the list goes on and on. A couple of years ago, on a whim, I colored my hair. I suspected that I would be stuck coloring my hair until I was willing to pay a lot of money for someone else to get me out of this mess, and I was right.
We strive to be beautiful on the outside, decorating our earthy tent yet, the list of names in my prayer journal grows and grows. There are some that become praise for healing but there are never ending prayers for people battling something internally. This "internal" battle of our bodies is still the earthy tent.
On the day that I pass from this earth into heaven I know without a doubt that I will be blown away by the beauty of our heavenly bodies. I simply need to look at the beauty of his creation here for a small glimpse of it.

Lord,
You created us in your image. Help us see beyond the skin deep into our souls. We are eternal souls designed to reside with you; these earthy shells left behind. Help us love each other so one day we can all rejoice in the beauty of heaven. Amen.

Nov 28 - *Psalm 25:2 "O my God, in you I trust; do not let me be put to shame; do not let my enemies exult over me."*

As I look at my life it is hard to imagine a tangible enemy. There are bad guys and bad things happen but there is no one hanging over my head waiting to take my freedom or my life simply because I exist.

I cannot imagine the feelings that some people around the world have, fleeing from their homes, taking only what they can carry on their backs. Other people suffer taunting and abuse from captors as they are imprisoned either physically or mentally. We all have our enemies, some more tangible than others. Selfishness, fear, worry, hatred, hopelessness; these are a few of the less tangible enemies that I struggle with and I know I am not alone in this.

When I keep my trust in God and allow him to guide my heart these things have no control over me. They seem to fade away and I am left with only the deep and true love of God filling my heart.

I trust in him and he will keep me from shame. He guides my steps in righteousness and my enemies will not exult, Praise God!

Lord,
You protect us like a mother hen, wrapping your wings around us to keep us warm and safe. When we step out into the world you are still there. Help us trust in you at all times and in all things so that we glorify you and do not shame ourselves. When we walk with you our enemies are powerless; you are all powerful! Hallelujah and Amen.

Nov 29 - *Matthew 6:22-23 "The eye is the lamp of the body. So, if your eye is healthy, your whole body will be full of light; but if your eye is unhealthy, your whole body will be full of darkness. If then the light in you is darkness, how great is the darkness!"*

Have you ever heard that the eye is the window to the soul? If you look carefully into someone else's eyes you can see so much about them. We don't often make eye contact in this society and I suspect it is because we like to hide our souls from others.

As I sat in my front room "chewing" on this scripture passage the light from the sun was streaming in the window. Our souls are like homes; a place to be protected from the elements outside with windows to allow light in and for us to look out. Do you live in a light filled home or in the utter darkness of a cave?

Is your soul being filled with true light or sitting in darkness only remembering what light looks like?

Spiritual blindness can be healed. The Prince of Light eradicates darkness in your soul if you ask him to. He comes in and deep cleans until the windows sparkle and no speck of dust blocks the bright light shining in.

Do not wander in darkness anymore. Do not live life in utter darkness or even in shadows. Allow the light of God to cleanse and heal you; be filled with his light and love today.

Lord,
Please banish darkness from my soul. Bring your warm and loving light in and place it where the darkness hides. Make me a true child of your Light, allowing my soul to be full of light and nothing else. Let me shine for you! Amen.

Nov 30 - *Psalm 42:1 "As a deer longs for flowing streams, so my soul longs for you, O God."*

Tomorrow the kids and my husband head to the western slope of Colorado and I get four days of alone time.

With all the busy days I have had lately and the busy days yet to come I cannot express the longing I have held in my heart for these four days of solitude. As I read this verse a picture forms in my mind.

A deer must always be watchful and wary of danger. They are ready to run at the slightest hint of trouble in order to stay safe. It is a calm, relaxed moment when they can take time for a long drink in a flowing stream.

Lately it has been even harder to be still and listen for the voice of God. I am not distressed over this because I know God speaks in many different ways and will get through to me somehow. However, like the deer in this verse, I long for a quiet peaceful time of sitting in the presence of the Lord.

I long for distraction and chaos to stop pulling at me so I can relax and enjoy the calm sweet presence of peace in the Lord. I can almost taste it now...

Lord,
Thank you for being here even in the busy times; even in the chaos and distractions. Help me make time to sit and relax in your presence, help me relish the solitude when I have it. I ask you for refreshment for my soul, peace for my spirit. Amen.

Dec 1 - *1 Corinthians 4:20 "For the kingdom of God depends not on talk but on power."*

Ah, the clichés that come to mind as I read this verse. Talk is cheap, put your money where your mouth is... clichés become what they are because there is truth in them.

We can say we love the Lord until we are blue in the face (there is another one) but unless we live it out, our words are empty. We must put our energy, our power, into action to back up our words and when we move into action the kingdom of God becomes alive.

His kingdom is not a far off palace in the sky or a destination that we will someday go to. It is very easy to see it that way. Someday, when I die, I will go to the Lord and reside with him but that is a whole different reality. His kingdom is here and now. He lives in the hearts of his disciples and through his followers his kingdom is manifest today.

This only happens if we move beyond our words and our speeches and step into action. We need to show his love and mercy. We need to live in his peace and righteousness. We need to serve all of his children.

It is in these actions that others are drawn into the kingdom of God.

Lord,
Soften my heart and open my hands to release the power I have and receive your power instead. It is only through your power that I can serve your kingdom. Stop my chatter and move me into action. As you lead, I will follow. Amen.

Dec 2 - *1 Peter 3:3-4 "Do not adorn yourselves outwardly by braiding your hair, and by wearing gold ornaments or fine clothing; rather, let your adornment be the inner self with the lasting beauty of a gentle and quiet spirit, which is very precious in God's sight"*

My little girl loves to dress up.
She likes to play dress up with her princess dresses but even more she likes to wear fancy dresses that sparkle and twirl. We are quickly coming upon the time of year where there are many holiday parties and church services that we can dress up and adorn ourselves with beautiful clothes for.
Stores are filled with fancy dresses and suits to make us look beautiful and handsome for whatever our event may be. We are inundated with ideas that our hair should not be allowed to show gray, our wrinkles should be hidden or erased, all so we can present ourselves as "beautiful."
Today's verse reminds us that true beauty, ageless beauty, comes from within. Our spirit shines through whatever we put on the outside of our bodies.
Take time this season to seek the Spirit of God. This Spirit brings us to a place where we can be gentle and quiet. Then as we move into our days, we are able to shine that inner beauty of gentleness and quiet out into the world.

Lord,
As we dress for our days or our parties, whatever we have to do, remind us to "dress" our hearts for you. Lay your Spirit of gentleness and quiet in our hearts so as we go and go and go, we do it with that precious underlying beauty that only you can give. Use us to be agents of peace and quiet; of gentleness this day. Amen.

Dec 3 - *1 Thessalonians 5:16 "Rejoice always"*

I think little kids have rejoicing down pat.

I can easily picture my kids dancing and singing songs, making music and laughter, because they do it a lot. My daughter likes to sing her reading lessons to me and is planning to have a dance for her birthday.

She would have a party every day if she could. Part of it is just her personality and her desire to be with people but I know there is a rejoicing in her heart as well.

It is not always easy for us to find rejoicing in our hearts. Sometimes we carry a very heavy load that weighs us down and that makes it so hard to rejoice.

I was thinking back to the time when my Mom was still alive and battling her cancer so hard. How can I rejoice in that?

Now that the deep sorrow is less, I can rejoice that I was able to spend precious time with her. We were not caught up in daily tasks but we were able to just spend time together for the simple joy of it.

I rejoice that I helped care for her as she used to care for me. I rejoice that the relationship with my Dad is so much deeper; we treasure him even more with my Mom being gone.

If we search deep and long, we can rejoice amidst whatever life is handing us right now. Rejoice in the Lord always, again I say rejoice!

Lord,
Thank you for opening my eyes to see the possibilities. Place a song in my heart and a dance in my step so that regardless of what I am doing, I am also rejoicing. I lift my voice, my life to you in hopes that I will be glad and rejoice always. Amen.

Dec 4 - *Romans 8:6 "To set the mind on the flesh is death, but to set the mind on the Spirit is life and peace."*

I get so focused on this life, here on earth.
We live here in this flesh for 80 years, give or take, but we have an eternity in spirit. I am not suggesting that we should ignore the time we have here or the people who surround us. We are given the task of learning to love one another while we are here. The problems start when we get caught up in the world and its ways; the flesh.
I have come to realize (to some small degree) what things draw my mind to the flesh. My children are a mirror for me to gaze in and when I do, I learn from them. They love each other, they share and are kind. Then in the blink of an eye they are fighting and bickering over something as simple as a space on the couch or a toy that neither one has played with in weeks.
When I am focused on the world I want to bicker and fight over the smallest things too. When I let go of the worldly, selfish desires of my heart I immediately feel the peace and presence of the Spirit residing in me.
I step in faith looking to the day I remain in the mind of the Spirit forever.

Lord,
Thank you for your Spirit and thank you for your grace. Help me move step by step away from the mind of the flesh and into the mind of the Spirit. I pray this for everyone. Amen.

Dec 5 - *2 Timothy 3:7 "who are always being instructed and can never arrive at a knowledge of the truth."*

I remember sitting in many a math class feeling just this way. I cannot tell you how many years I struggled through math managing to pass the class but never feeling like I gained any knowledge or understanding of it.

To this day I do not believe I can do geometry or algebra beyond a remedial level. How can this be? I studied it, I was instructed in it over and over, yet I never really got it.

My spiritual journey was similar to this for many years. I went to church and Sunday school growing up. I read my Bible verses and grew up in a Christian home but the truth never *really* sunk in. I learned and studied but did not really gain knowledge in the truth; I was blind.

It is only by the true grace of God that he keeps trying and never stops calling to his sheep and it is by his grace that I finally heard his voice, allowed him to lead me, and began gaining knowledge in the truth.

When I look back at the path my journey has taken, the grace that covers it is overwhelming to me. I cannot grasp the depth of it but I know it is real. This much I know and understand.

Lord,
Thank you for opening my eyes and helping me to finally see in truth. We all walk around blind, thinking we can see only to find we are deceived and blindly stumbling in darkness. Through your divine grace, help us see and allow us to learn and live in you. Amen.

Dec 6 - *Psalm 138:3 "On the day I called, you answered me, you increased my strength of soul."*

In case you are in doubt, God is good.

I am currently participating in a Bible study and part of today's lesson was about receiving what we ask for. After I closed my study and started my meditation, this is the verse I was led to.

I have come to realize that things I wish for most of all, deep peace and contentment, are not given in lifetime chunks. Growth and change occur more in the battlegrounds of life.

As I look back on the petitions I have brought to the Lord I see he has answered me. I have come asking for the spiritual equivalent of sweets or dessert without eating my vegetables first. I have asked to be a full grown flower blossoming in beauty without planting my roots deeply in the ground.

In his infinite grace, God hears my requests and grants them in his divine knowledge, giving me what I need to move one step closer to my hearts deepest desire. Each gift he has given has, in fact, strengthened my soul.

Today, with this truth, my soul sings songs of thanksgiving and praise.

Lord,

You tell us to ask and we shall receive. So often we feel ignored by you only to realize later you are right there all the time, answering and giving us what we truly need. We are short sighted; thank you for seeing through what we think we need and giving us what you know we need. Prepare our hearts as we prepare once again to celebrate your greatest gift of all. Amen.

Dec 7 - *Psalm 25:9 "He leads the humble in what is right, and teaches the humble his way."*

Did you ever wonder why God chose Mary and Joseph to be the parents of the Christ child?

These two were simple, quiet folks just doing the best they could. They were humble. As I started my morning with my mind already trying to organize my day, I had moved past my quiet time before I started.

My day has so many "important" tasks to be accomplished! I have a doctor appointment, school, and a field trip along with the normal daily cleaning and cooking. When I stop and sit still, I realize that when I am wrapped up in my busy schedule, I am not feeling humble.

I come to sit in the presence of the Lord, humbly asking for him to lead me and teach me. My schedule will wait. This time in the morning needs to be my first priority. We are not kings or noblemen. We are not celebrities or politicians. Most of us are just simple, everyday people doing the best we can.

Let's be humble and open our hearts to the voice of God. He speaks to those who listen, like Mary and Joseph. Let him speak to you; he leads you in what is right, he teaches you his way.

Lord,
It is in the acceptance of my lowliness that I realize I need you. Keep my heart humble and keep my ears open to hear your guidance. Remind me of the beginning days when the Christ child began his life on earth in a stable...humble beginnings for the King of salvation. Amen.

Dec 8 - *John 1:9 "The true light, which enlightens everyone, was coming into the world."*

I have a story about light.

I recently bought several cheap book lights for a music gig I had. We were ringing handbells outside at night so I knew we would need more light and we didn't have it.

The lights worked; sort of. Some of them flickered on and off, others didn't work at all. A few worked well and others died out quickly. Did I say they were cheap? The cost of the batteries is at least 4 times as much as it would be to buy new lights!

Since then, we have purchased better and more expensive lights to help us read music. As I read this passage the book lights came to mind. Every light we have is needed to help us see, but they all fade away eventually. We replace bulbs and lights because the old ones no longer serve our needs. Even the sun, the moon, and the stars are not eternal.

All sources of light will eventually die but one. The true light, which enlightens everyone has come, is coming and will come again. He is eternal and his light never fades.

Come and seek the one true light with me.

Lord,
We live in darkness or dim light most of the time and we just squint to make do with what we have. As we move into a time of preparation and celebration, prepare our hearts to receive all the light of your glory. My heart leaps at the vision of the skies filled with angels, shining in the eternal light. Fill us with this light so we may shine for this world, glorifying your holy name. Amen.

Dec 9 - *2 Corinthians 3:15-16 "Indeed, to this very day whenever Moses is read, a veil lies over their minds; but when one turns to the Lord, the veil is removed."*

I have a bit of a problem when it comes to hearing on the phone. I actually went and had my hearing tested because I thought there might be something wrong with my hearing; it was fine. I think it is my listening that lacks.

Being a visual person, I rely on facial expression and physical presence as a big part of communication. In the story of Moses, he hid his face with a veil so people would not be frightened by the glory shining in him from talking with God. Paul says the people's minds were hardened; a veil hid the meaning of the scripture from them.

How many years would I open my Bible, skim a passage thinking I was reading it, and then go off to live my life. True meaning was not coming through. There was a veil over my mind.

Just as I must block out distractions while on the phone, so must I be intentional to truly hear the Lord. When I turn to the Lord the veil is removed.

"Let those with ears hear" resonates clearly today.

Lord,
Open my ears and quiet the noise in the background that distracts me from hearing your truth. Your Spirit is my guide but unless I listen, I cannot follow. Help me hear what you are saying clearly so that I do not feel lost or confused. Remove the veil, the block from understanding, so I can go forth a changed and blessed person. Help me share these blessings with those I see and talk with each day. Amen.

Dec 10 - *Colossians 3:18-19 "Wives, be subject to your husbands, as is fitting in the Lord. Husbands, love your wives and never treat them harshly."*

I was led to these verses at 2:00 in the morning. I knew I was in for trouble.

At first glance, it is a control issue. Maybe I see it this way because I have control issues; I am not alone in struggling with verse 18. I sat and meditated and I came to realize this is about relationship, not about control.

The buck has to stop somewhere, in any relationship. Whether it is a spousal relationship, a work relationship, or a friendship, there is always the last word.

The best boss I ever had made me feel like a teammate rather than a subject under their control. The building of that relationship and honoring it was so important. As I learn to let go, I am able to embrace and celebrate the gifts and strengths of others. As I learn to build relationships with others, so I learn to build my relationship with God.

Sometimes I am called to bend to the needs and wishes of others. I am also called to bend to the guidance of the Lord. As I prepare to worship the new born King, I must prepare my heart to come on bended knee.

Lord,

Thank you for bringing me through this passage unscathed. I tend to shy away from it; yet, in your grace you guided me and taught me. Help me see the gifts that others bring, enhancing my life. As I let go, reassure me that I am only letting you in where you belong. When all is said and done, I bend to you Lord. You are my Lord and my King. Amen.

Dec 11 - *Ephesians 5:8 "For once you were darkness, but now in the Lord you are light. Live as children of light-"*

Each day is getting a little bit shorter. We are quickly coming upon the shortest day of the year.
The earth goes through cycles, so do we. We have seasons filled with light and seasons where we are stumbling in darkness.
During this season of Advent, we are called to prepare ourselves to receive the Christ child. I have written about God's light many times. Do I have anything new to say?
The message has been announced for thousands of years. It is my turn to teach Sunday school and we are learning about John the Baptist who came to prepare the way. It was his task to announce the blessed gift of salvation that God was sending.
Jesus came "to give light to those who sit in darkness... to guide our feet into the way of peace." (Luke 1:79) This is the light Paul is talking about here.
Take a moment with me this morning and picture the Christ child, lying in the manger with radiance beaming from his holy face. As we come closer to the celebration of his birth, let us search our hearts for darkness that lurks and allow the Spirit to renew and refine us.
When we come to the holy night of Christmas, may we be a reflection of his radiant light throughout the world.

Lord,
Through your Holy Spirit, we have been given the gift of Light and Love. Help us shine your light and announce it to the world around us until no one lives in darkness anymore. Amen.

Dec 12 - *Isaiah 58:11 "The Lord will guide you continually, and satisfy your needs in parched places, and make your bones strong; and you shall be like a watered garden, like a spring of water, whose waters never fail."*

There is talk about water where I live.
We saw snow on November 10th and not again until the trace amount last night. People are talking about a drought.
We see the lack of water in our world but do we see the lack of living water in our souls? We get so busy looking outward; do we take time to look inward? Our souls cry out for the living water to quench our thirst much more than grass and trees cry out for their water.
On this bitter cold morning, this verse is a breath of spring to my heart. It brings hope to my soul. It soothes, bringing God's love and peace once again.
He has never failed me and I know he will continue to guide me and satisfy my needs. His word and guidance make me strong in faith; in my bones. I am refreshed like a watered garden. I almost hear the rushing of water; his living water flowing through me in a never ending spring.
In the midst of this cold and wintery day, I have spring! Oh, joy and praise to my God!

Lord,
Thank you for the incredible blessings that you have given me today. Help me bring your refreshing, living water to others so that they may also receive the renewing spring of your living water in them. In the midst of drought, you bring abundance. You give us everything we could ever need. Lord God, you are so gracious! Thank you! Amen.

Dec 13 - *Psalm 37:23-24 "Our steps are made firm by the Lord, when he delights in our way; though we stumble, we shall not fall headlong, for the Lord holds us by the hand."*

My little boy loves to run.

He has so much energy and zest for life, it seems he has to get where he is going in a hurry. When he gets in too big a hurry he stumbles and falls. Then he comes running to me for comfort and kisses.

When I read this passage I almost laughed. How long will it take for me to learn not to run too fast? I have learned to hold the hand of the Lord most of the time and he has kept me from falling more times than I can count. Yet, the temptation to run is still there.

As we move forward closer to the stable on Christmas night, I am tempted to run as fast as I can to see the newborn king. Am I ready? Am I prepared to receive the king?

These verses remind me to stay the course. Keep my steps firmly guided by the Lord on my journey to Bethlehem. God is delighted that I want to go; I am headed in that direction but I need to hold his hand lest I get ahead of myself.

Will you join the journey to see the small babe wrapped in cloth and lying in a manger? Hold my hand; hold his hand and we can walk there together.

Lord,
I want to delight you. Thank you for the reminder that I need to hold your hand every step of the way. It is you that keeps me from falling and I thank you and praise you for this blessed assurance. Prepare my heart as I journey with you to the stable in Bethlehem once again. Amen.

Dec 14 - *Luke 1:41-42 "When Elizabeth heard Mary's greeting, the child leaped in her womb. And Elizabeth was filled with the Holy Spirit and exclaimed with a loud cry, 'Blessed are you among women, and blessed is the fruit of your womb.'"*

What I wouldn't give to sit and have a cup of coffee with these ladies. Can you imagine the stories they could tell?
Elizabeth was beyond child bearing age when an angel came and told her and her husband they were going to have a baby. Mary, who was a virgin, was visited by the same angel! He tells her that she will bear the Son of God.
If you are a woman you know once they received their angelic visits they never stopped wondering and questioning how this could and would be. When Mary comes to visit Elizabeth, John leaps in Elizabeth's womb! He already knows to proclaim this child.
Sometimes it seems like forever since the baby started growing inside the womb and as the birth grows closer, most parents wonder if they are ready. I can only imagine the wonder and anticipation Elizabeth and Mary had compared to those of us with babies announced by doctors.
Now we all wait in anticipation. We wait for angels to sing. We wait for a cry in the wilderness. We wait for the Lord.

Lord,
Waiting is hard for us. You call us to wait and so we try. Thank you for your words that tell us the story. We do not wait without knowing what; we only wait not knowing when. O come, O come Emmanuel. Amen.

Dec 15 - *Isaiah 60:3 "Nations shall come to your light, and kings to the brightness of your dawn."*

I love this time of year.
I love lighted trees and music and the spirit of love that spreads. Gifts are given to loved ones in the spirit of love. Santa Claus, an icon in so many parts of the world, visits homes leaving presents for girls and boys, all in the spirit of love.
Presents are flown to the far reaches of the world to bring love to children everywhere.
Long ago a star shone and Magi, men of importance and knowledge, came. They came to the light, seeing the star in the sky, and knowing this was something worth seeing. They brought gifts and so as we shop and wrap, let us also bring something to honor this gift of heaven.
We were created in his light and we are called to follow his light. Whether our path is easy cruising, stumbling along in a barren desert, or in a forest so thick with trees we struggle to see the sky, we can come to his light.
Look deep in your soul; it is our soul that finds true light. He sent Jesus so that his redeeming light could shine for the entire world to see. He brings the brightness of his dawn for all nations; he brings it for you and me.

Lord,
Sometimes your light seems to be so far away and then I remember to search with my heart and not my eyes. Help me set aside differences and division and open my arms to embrace in love and light. Use me to share your light with others so that all nations, all people will come. Amen.

Dec 16 - *Matthew 5:8 "Blessed are the pure in heart, for they will see God."*

I began my quiet time asking for cleansing.
I need cleansing in my body to rid it of toxins, so I asked for cleansing of my mind and my soul, even those things I have forgotten or do not recognize. I know this prayer is likely to stir up muck but I want to be rid of it.
When I came to seek his word I was led to this verse. I thought I must have heard wrong. I had a different passage in mind. As I sat in meditation it didn't take long to see how this verse tied in with my prayer. It is moments like this one where the presence of God is glaringly apparent to me; I can claim without hesitation, God is Emmanuel.
He came to us as a babe so that we could learn the true nature of the Almighty and he never left. I see glimpses of him just like I did in my quiet time. When I look back at my path his presence and guidance are obvious.
The impurities in me will not cease to exist in this lifetime so I know I will not see God in all truth and glory yet. I continue to seek purity and to seek God in the meantime.
Will you join me?

Lord,
I thank you with all that I am and all that I have been given. To realize once again that you are Emmanuel is humbling indeed. You come seeking us. You come to redeem and rescue us. I am humbled. I am yours. I offer my days, my nights, and my life to you. Help me see you more clearly each day until the day I stand at your throne in glory. Amen.

Dec 17 - *Hebrews 4:1 "Therefore, while the promise of entering his rest is still open, let us take care that none of you should seem to have failed to reach it."*

Oh, how I wanted to stay in bed.
I was trying to compromise with God as I lay there telling him all the things I had to do today and asking why I couldn't just have my meditation right there.
I saw a picture in my mind: a lady weighed down with gifts, her hands were full with no room for anything else. The Lord offered a morsel of food to her but she couldn't figure out how to take it with all those bags. Then she realized she needed to set down all those things and accept the free gift given to her by the Lord.
That got my fanny out of bed! How ungrateful can I be? Each day I come before the Lord and he meets me where I am. He gives me food from his word and he does not stop there. If we are willing to set aside our burdens he will fill us with his love, peace, rest... he will fill us with what we truly need.
Take a few minutes and join me in setting down all those things we carry that weigh us down. Release those things and open your hands as I open mine so we can receive life and love, grace and mercy, wonder and awe.

Lord,
Thank you for your faithfulness. I am so ashamed that I put all those things at a higher priority than you and I am so grateful for the nudge to remind me what is truly important. Help us all feel and see those nudges that keep us on the path to entering in your rest. Amen.

Dec 18 - *Philippians 4:6-7 "Do not worry about anything, but in everything by prayer and supplication with thanksgiving let your requests be made known to God. And the peace of God, which surpasses all understanding, will guard your hearts and your mind in Christ Jesus."*

Violence and tragedy hit us and we are wounded. Acts of war against innocent people happen and we cannot understand it. When horror becomes real to us, how do we move past it? I barely allow myself to even think about it lest it overwhelm me. I came to God this morning with verse seven on my heart. Verse six tells us how we begin to move forward. Whatever we feel, wherever we are, he calls us to bring our requests to him in thanksgiving. I bring my anger and hurt, my lack of understanding, to him. I even bring it to him in thanksgiving because I am thankful that he receives what I have. He already knows our hearts and when we bring all that to him we begin to receive his peace that surpasses all understanding. This peace guards our hearts and our minds in Christ. I long for his peace to heal. I urge you to bring it all to the Lord. Thank him for receiving it and give it all to him. "Let there be peace on earth and let it begin with me..."

Lord,
Thank you for listening to us, whatever we have to say. Heal the broken hearts that weep in mourning this day. Let your peace and love prevail in us and in the world. Amen.

Dec 19 - *Psalm 112:4 "They rise in the darkness as a light for the upright; they are gracious, merciful, and righteous."*

With all that is in the news it is easy to see the darkness. If we are not careful the darkness can overtake us just as it attempts to overtake the world. This battle between darkness and light has been going on since the beginning of time. We all play a role in it; we all take part.

In the color spectrum there are shades between each color, bleeding from one to another. In this darkness there is no gray. It is like standing in a shadow or standing in the sun. There is a distinct line and you are either in darkness or you are in light. When there seems to be darkness all around it is hard to keep searching for the light.

Search, and keep searching, for the light is true and it is here. In the midst of darkness people who bring love and healing, care and prayers, nurture and rebuilding, are agents of light. We can be God's light in this dark world.

Allow God to fill your heart with his love. When you are glowing with love, go and be gracious, merciful, and righteous. Be an agent of his divine love and light!

Lord,
Give us what we need to seek your light. Do not let the darkness take over even one more of your children. Help us be the light and love that brings people to you and draws people away from darkness. You sent your Son to bring light to the world. Help us spread that light and love everywhere to your glory. Amen.

Dec 20 - *Habakkuk 1:5 "Look at the nations, and see! Be astonished! Be astounded! For a work is being done in your days that you would not believe if you were told."*

Habakkuk the prophet was frustrated with all the injustice, violence, and evil in his world. He wondered why God didn't step in and so he went to the Lord to voice his questions. There are only 3 chapters in this little book but so much to contemplate. As my children dance and leap around the Christmas tree, they show such excitement for this season of joy. I want to reach deep into my soul and find that same joy; joy that makes me leap and dance for Jesus.

I need to look beyond the injustice, violence, and evil in this world. All those years ago, God had not forgotten his people and today he is still amazing us.

There are stories, every day, of unbelievable mercy, love, care ... God is with us. Emmanuel.

Lord,
As I move my home into the season of Christmas, move my heart to be there too. It is such a busy time of year that I tend to forget the reason I am busy. My music, church, baking, teaching my kids, all I do is in honor of you, in celebration of your love and your unbelievable gift. Thank you for Christmas, God. Thank you that I can celebrate the birth of Jesus freely and openly, shouting and singing at the top of my lungs. Fill the hearts of those who cannot so they can exude your love and joy in actions. Amen.

Dec 21 - *Matthew 1:21 "She will bear a son, and you are to name him Jesus, for he will save his people from their sins."*

We don't know much about Joseph.
He had established himself and was ready to take a wife. Mary, a young maiden, would be his wife and they were making preparations. Joseph finds out she is with child so he decides to "dismiss her quietly" according to verse 19. God sends an angel to speak to Joseph in a dream.
History is written because Joseph listened to the message in the dream and followed the instruction. How would our lives be different if we were as open to listening and following?
Scripture says he was a righteous man. He followed the laws given but he followed more than just the law. His faith in God went deeper than going through steps simply because it was the law. He was open to listening and following through guidance not written in a book of rules.
I am on a path in which I cannot see much beyond where I am. Where am I being led? I would not be a bit surprised if Joseph was asking those very questions as he took Mary as his wife. God is faithful.
Just as he guided Joseph and Mary, he guides us. Do we hear him? Do we listen and follow in trust, as Joseph did?

Lord,
When you ask us to do something out of the ordinary we often balk. Give us courage to follow you even when we cannot see the path. Just as you guided Joseph and Mary, guide us too. Open our hearts to the everlasting love you sent in the form of a babe, lying in manger. Amen.

Dec 22 - *1 Corinthians 10:3-4 "and all ate the same spiritual food, and all drank the same spiritual drink..."*

I have done a lot of baking in the last few days. There are cookies and sweets just begging to be eaten.

My family, my daughter especially, has a sweet tooth. Not a day goes by without requests for a sweet and now it is even worse. I do my best to give healthy foods and make sweets minimal. I have eaten too many cookies in the last few days and my body makes sure to remind me.

When I eat well, I feel well and when I eat poorly... If my body is like this how much more is my spirit? It is yummy to eat spiritual sweets but those tidbits do not help my spirit grow healthy or strong. If I try to sustain my spirit on Sunday school and church with no "meat and vegetables" prayer and study, I will fare poorly.

I need good spiritual food every day at least as much as I need good healthy food for my stomach every day. What I take in and believe does change me. It is what I believe and "eat" that causes me to think and say certain things. It is those things that cause me to act and do as I do.

Join me in the search for a little more protein and roughage to offset all the sweets. The Lord feeds us; he feeds us well.

Lord,

Help me remember my body is a temple unto you. Let me live savoring the healthy sustenance you provide. Guide my heart in healthy eating habits so that I treat my body and my soul as they deserve to be treated. Guide me into health and growth and let it be for your glory always. Amen.

Dec 23 - *Luke 2:8 "In that region there were shepherds living in the fields, keeping watch over their flocks by night."*

Shepherds sat in a field watching the flocks of sheep, keeping them safe. The stars overhead would have been magnificent in such dark skies.
Did they notice a different star gleaming more brightly than the others? If they did I am sure it would have been dismissed. The nights would have been pretty quiet most of the time. Maybe they would have heard the bleat of a sheep or the scuffle of a nearby animal. This quiet night was about to be rocked.
An angel, shining in the glory of God, announced the birth of the Messiah! He told them where to find this sweet babe and then a "multitude of the heavenly hosts" joined him in singing praises.
I know when I sit in darkness any light can seem pretty bright. I cannot imagine how bright the glory of God shines but I bet the shepherds had to shield their eyes.
After the angels visited, the shepherds left their sheep to go see the Lamb. As they gazed upon that tiny newborn did any of them imagine the life he would lead?
As we gaze in, do our hearts remember the sacrifice this babe is making on our behalf?

Lord,
You came for us. You lived for us and you died for us. Speak to our hearts so we step ever closer to giving back to you. I want my songs of praise to tell others about you so they can find you and join in the songs of praise with me. Amen.

Dec 24 - *Luke 2:6-7 "While they were there, the time came for her to deliver her child. And she gave birth to her firstborn son and wrapped him in bands of cloth, and laid him in a manger, because there was no place for them in the inn."*

Are you all set for your "Hallmark" Christmas to unfold? There is the beautifully decked tree bursting with presents underneath. Scrumptious breakfast waits and entices the taste buds as the children help each other and share each other's gifts...

or...

the needles of the tree lay strewn among the hastily wrapped presents that are torn open in a rush of chaos. Breakfast is slightly burned because that family picture took too long. The kids are comparing what they got and who received better or more in the game of one-upmanship.

As Mary lay in the throes of child birth she wasn't feeling beautiful and pleasant. As Joseph watched and helped, I suspect he struggled to find the blessing in that moment.

Was there a shadow of doubt as they laid that sweet baby in a food trough? In the middle of chaos this precious gift was given. However you experience Christmas, allow this precious gift from God to remain in the center.

This gift of love shines a most beautiful light on everything.

Lord,
You came into this broken world to bring love and grace and you are still here, still giving to us. Let your love and grace seep into every crack and crevice of our Christmas so that despite anything else, we are filled with the true gift of Christmas. Amen.

Dec 25 - *1 Corinthians 13:13 "And now faith, hope, and love abide, these three; and the greatest of these is love."*

I sit in humble gratitude for the abundance of blessings I have. I am surrounded by family and friends. I am surrounded by joy, peace, support, and love. I have a warm home and I lack for nothing.

Without love how would I view my many blessings? This Divine Love that came to a manger in Bethlehem so many years ago changed our world forever. Love came to dwell among us, to live with us and to draw us into a gentle embrace that never ends.

There are struggles and hardships in many homes and places today. My heart lifts the love of God to those places, those homes, and those hearts. I simply hope in the love of God. I have faith that he spreads his love throughout every land, every time and every space.

I hear his call to me and to others to know his love. We are the bearers of this torch. We, who hold his love in our hearts, are called to share his love.

Empty the anger, sadness, envy, and selfishness from your heart and allow those spaces to be filled with Divine Love.

On this day of gifts, receive the greatest gift and then share it with others so we may all abide in Love.

Lord,

Without love I know I am nothing. Without love I cannot do anything. Remove the seeds of apathy and mistrust. Weed out selfishness and discontent so that I have more room for your love. Help me be a torch bearer of love shining your light and life, shining your love for all to see. Amen.

Dec 26 - *Matthew 2:12 "And having been warned in a dream not to return to Herod, they left for their own country by another road."*

The wise men are men of mystery.
I have read a lot about where these men came from and who they might have been but does it really matter?
We know they are foreigners who study stars. They have some wisdom; they ask Herod "where is the child who has been born king of the Jews?" Regardless of their beliefs, the desire to come and see this king draws them in. They open themselves to the divine presence of God.
Verse 11 says they knelt down and paid him homage. They presented precious gifts to a king who did not rule their nation. These foreigners heard our Lord, the God of all, speak to them in a dream and they listened.
Throughout the Bible God uses dreams to guide people. How does God speak to you? Are you open to hear the Divine?
We have come to the stable and seen the precious babe but what now? As the days of Christmas begin to fade away, let us remember the guidance of God never fades.
Seek him and when you find him, open your heart to hear what he will say to you.

Lord,
Help us not only hear but truly listen to you. You step into our lives and take our hands and hearts to lead us safely home, if only we would follow. Close our ears to the voices of deception so we can clearly hear your true voice. Thank you for guiding the wise men. Thank you for guiding us. Amen.

Dec 27 - *Galatians 6:2 "Bear one another's burdens, and in this way you will fulfill the law of Christ."*

There have been a few opportunities in the last weeks for me to hold a door for someone whose arms were full.

I see people helping elderly or disabled people across icy parking lots and supporting them as they walk. Cooking meals for someone who is ill or taking their kids so they can rest is a simple way to lift a burden.

There are so many ways to fulfill the law of Christ by bearing another's burdens. Praying for them is as powerful as any tangible assistance. The power of prayer not only changes the person I am praying for but it changes me.

Being in the presence of the Almighty is renewing and healing and when I move out of prayers for others I feel lifted as well.

Reach out and ease the burdens of others. Open the door for someone; help someone with their groceries. Give groceries to someone who does not have any. Most of all lift those you love and those you don't in prayer.

I pray for you and I ask that you pray for me. As we bear each other's burdens, we abide in Christ's law of love...

Love your neighbor as yourself.

Lord,
You call us to look for the least of these and serve them. Help us to see the burdens we can bear for others and encourage us to step forward in assistance. Teach our hearts to pray for our neighbors and friends and those we do not know as well so that the power of your love is spread to all through prayer. Amen.

Dec 28 - *Luke 24:49 "And see, I am sending upon you what my Father promised; so stay here in the city until you have been clothed with power from on high."*

Scripture tells us the Holy Spirit is our guide and our comforter. This is the power from on high that Jesus instructed his disciples to wait for.

This Spirit calls us into action for the Lord and warns us to stay true to the straight and true path of God. As we close out another year and get ready to start a new one it is common to review our past and set goals for the future.

I don't know what God has in store for me but I ponder it. The path he has led me on is nothing I would have ever guessed and so I am in a time of waiting, just as these disciples were instructed to wait.

How often have I made plans that are, in hindsight, laughable? I cannot count them! I cannot count the times I have prayed for a map or a blueprint so I could just follow that.

I am learning, very slowly, to wait on the Lord. I am learning, slipping and sliding, to hear and follow the guidance of the Spirit.

I trust that the power from on high will keep me from harm and guide my steps, my actions, and my words to bring glory to the kingdom of God.

Lord,
You know waiting is hard for me. I know you call me to wait. Please send word to me soon and open my eyes and my heart to see the works you do in me every day. I know you have plans for each of us; help us hear and follow those plans you have made. I seek to serve you Lord. Amen.

Dec 29 - *Psalm 37:40 "The Lord helps them and rescues them; he rescues them from the wicked, and saves them, because they take refuge in him."*

Life is filled with choices.
I try to narrow the choices for my kids without taking them away completely because they need to learn how to make wise decisions. I hear myself reminding them "make wise choices" when they are about to make a choice that is not so wise. The parallel of my relationship as a parent to my children and God as a parent to me as his child is not lost on me.
As I look back on my life it is crystal clear to me how many times God stepped in and rescued me from mayhem. The excitement of stepping out of bounds, of bending the rules a bit, always led to trouble. Inevitably I ended up broken and battered, seeking refuge in my heavenly parent.
God is faithful to those who seek him. What I am beginning to realize is that he is faithful to us in whatever moments we seek him, knowing we will stray again. I cannot imagine the freedom I will rejoice in when I shed this body and begin to shine in holy righteousness when I am joined with the Almighty.
Until then, I take refuge in him, and he continues to save me from myself.

Lord,
Please forgive me. I cannot promise never to do it again, that would be a lie. I promise to seek you, to abide in you, and to pray without ceasing with your help. Each day is one day closer to glory beyond words. Until then, help me be the person you created me to be. Amen.

Dec 30 - *1 Thessalonians 5:6 "So then let us not fall asleep as others do, but let us keep awake and be sober"*

Winter is a season of waiting. So many things are resting, sleeping and dormant during winter.

Animals burrow down and sleep deeply. The trees, grass, and flowers are all "dead" for the season. We were just waiting for the Christ child to be born and now we wait for the story to continue in the wise men's visit.

Waiting can be tiring in its own right. It is tempting to rest and close our eyes, to lay back and take a nap while we wait. This verse reminds us that we are to stay alert and ready.

Whether you are waiting for the story to continue, waiting on the Lord for direction, or waiting for the Lord to come again, we are to wait in a state of readiness.

There is time to sit and be still, but even then we are not idle. We listen with all our hearts and with deep intention. Know and trust that in the midst of winter, far beneath the frozen cold ground, life is still unfolding. The seeds that were planted by the wind or by hand are doing what they need to do, preparing to burst forth in the warmth of spring.

Wait with me. While we wait let us stay awake, let us pray for each other and let us remember that life is unfolding even now. Let's be ready to take hold when it bursts forth.

Lord,
Winter has just started but in you, life is eternal. There is no death, only a time of waiting. Help us stay awake, help us see you and do what you guide us to do each day while we wait. May our words and our deeds give glory to you. Amen.

Dec 31 - *Romans 7:22-23 "For I delight in the law of God in my inmost self, but I see in my members another law at war with the law of my mind, making me captive to the law of sin that dwells in my members."*

I started this morning in Chapter 40 of Ezekiel where the tables and vestibules for sacrifices are described.

There are tables for the burnt offering and tables for the sin and guilt offerings. I am certain I would be at that temple every day if I were completely honest with myself.

As it described the pegs that go all around the table for the flesh to lay on I could only picture Jesus, the one sacrificial lamb for all, lying on that table. He willingly sacrificed his life, a lamb led to slaughter, for my sins and guilt.

It is by this gift of life that I can continue to delight in the law of God without cowering in the corner or really getting blood on my hands. As I seek escape from the torment I realize that true freedom is at my fingertips. Nothing frees me but Christ and his Spirit.

As I step closer to releasing the old self and embracing the new, it is only in his Holy Grace that I can find the strength to do this. He is my Redeemer and my Sustainer.

Thanks be to God through Jesus Christ our Lord!

Lord,
You know our hearts and you desire a deep and true relationship with us. Thank you for sending your son to show us how to be in relationship with you. Thank you for destroying the barrier through Jesus' ultimate sacrifice. As we seek freedom, help us find it in you. Amen.

Printed in Great Britain
by Amazon

51080565R00215